Tru64™ UNIX Troubleshooting

Diagnosing and Correcting System Problems

Tru64™ UNIX Troubleshooting

Diagnosing and Correcting System Problems

Martin Moore

Steven Hancock

Digital Press
An imprint of Elsevier Science
Amsterdam • Boston • London • New York • Oxford • Paris • San Diego
San Francisco • Singapore • Sydney • Tokyo

Digital Press is an imprint of Elsevier Science.

∞ Recognizing the importance of preserving what has been written, Elsevier Science prints its books on acid-free paper whenever possible.

Library of Congress Cataloging-in-Publication Data
Moore, Martin L.
Tru64 UNIX troubleshooting : diagnosing and correcting system problems / Martin Moore, Steven Hancock.
p. cm.
Includes bibliographical references and index.
ISBN 1-55558-274-5 (pbk. : alk. paper)
1. UNIX (Computer file) 2. Operating Systems (Computers)
3. Software maintenance. 4. Debugging in computer science. I. Hancock, Steven M.
II. Title.
QA76.76.O63 M658 2003
005.4'32—dc21

2002034394

British Library Cataloguing-in-Publication Data
A catalogue record for this book is available from the British Library.

The publisher offers special discounts on bulk orders of this book.
For information, please contact:

Manager of Special Sales
Elsevier Science
200 Wheeler Road
Burlington, MA 01803
Tel: 781-313-4700
Fax: 781-313-4882

For information on all Digital Press publications available, contact our World Wide Web home page at: http://www.digitalpress.com or http://www.bh.com/digitalpress

10 9 8 7 6 5 4 3 2 1

Printed in the United States of America

We dedicate this book to every system administrator whose pager has started beeping at 3:30 on a Sunday morning. We hope that this book will help you get a little more sleep.

We also dedicate this book to our wives, Beth Moore and JoEllen Hancock. Thank you for putting up with the writing of another book, and with us in general.

Contents

Preface

The idea for this book arose shortly after the completion of the *Tru64 UNIX System Administrator's Guide* (Digital Press, 2001), of which we were two of the authors. We were quite happy with that book—and we certainly think you should go buy a copy if you don't already have one—but we also realized that there was a lot more that could be said on the subject of troubleshooting Tru64 UNIX problems. Although the earlier book does contain some troubleshooting information, its primary focus is on the performance of everyday system administration tasks. After taking a closer look at other UNIX books, we discovered that they all had a similar orientation; there simply weren't any that focused primarily on troubleshooting. As we discussed the idea, our common experience as UNIX system administrators and Tru64 UNIX support engineers convinced us that a troubleshooting book would be extremely useful. Our editors agreed, and the end result is this book.

Although this book is about troubleshooting Tru64 UNIX problems, we've tried to make the material as useful as possible for administrators of other operating systems as well. The common elements among the various flavors of UNIX should make much of the information in this book useful for other UNIX variants. Some parts, of course, are specific to Tru64 UNIX. In addition, the general troubleshooting principles and techniques in Chapter 2 can be applied to problems with any operating system—and even to non-computer-related problems.

The material in this book is based primarily on Tru64 UNIX version 5.1A, which at the time of this writing is the version of Hewlett-Packard's (HP) Tru64 UNIX product that is currently shipping. Version 5.1B was a few weeks from shipping at press time, and we have done our best to make the content applicable to that version as well.

During the preparation of this manuscript, HP acquired Compaq Computer Corporation. As a result, Tru64 UNIX, along with the Alpha processor on which it runs, changed owners for the second time. Compaq acquired the operating system in its merger with Digital Equipment Corporation in 1998. We've endeavored to reflect the new ownership throughout this book, but in case we've missed any, please substitute HP for any stray instances of Compaq.

Although both authors worked together on the entire book, our individual interests led to a natural division of the primary writing duties. We've tried to use a consistent style and "voice," but minor stylistic differences may still be noticeable. For the record, Steve was the primary author of chapters 1, 3, and 7-9, while Martin wrote most of chapters 2, 4-6, and 10-12.

Acknowledgments

Without the contributions of some special people during the past 12 months, this book would never have seen the light of day. Their support, both technical and moral, kept us going, especially in the final months of the project.

We offer our sincere thanks to Greg Yates, Ernie Heinrich, Sandy Levitt, Whitney Latta, Larry Scott, and Janet Aman for their advice and technical contributions to this book.

We cannot begin to express our gratitude to Theron Shreve and Pam Chester, our editors at Digital Press, for supporting this project. Thanks for offering encouragement when we needed it and for those "gentle reminders" as the deadline grew nearer.

Finally, we want to express our appreciation to our wives, Beth and JoEllen. Without their love and support, this project would never have succeeded.

Martin and Steve

1

Introduction

Problems are only opportunities in work clothes.

—Henry J. Kaiser

1.1 Tru64 UNIX History

The operating system that we discuss in this book has had a varied and interesting history. Recent history has seen some very interesting developments, culminating with the decision to merge key elements of Tru64 UNIX, such as the Advanced File System (AdvFS) and TruCluster, with the HP-UX kernel to create a powerful new enterprise UNIX. The merger of Compaq Computer Corporation (Compaq) with the Hewlett-Packard Company (HP) is sure to make the future of this product interesting as the two UNIX powerhouses combine resources to create exciting new synergies.

Tru64 UNIX began as an attempt to commercialize the Mach kernel, developed by researchers at Carnegie Mellon University, into the foundation for a new UNIX system. Nothing in the Mach kernel required the UNIX interface, but the researchers saw the benefit of taking a high-performance micro-kernel and providing POSIX operating system services around it. Although UNIX originally began as a small and easily portable system, by this time it had begun to move away from its roots and toward a more monolithic structure. Up to that point, many operating systems were constructed in a monolithic fashion, meaning that all the system's functions were provided from a single, large kernel program; as UNIX began to "grow up" in the late 1980s, it began to exhibit this trend.

A group known as the Open Software Foundation (OSF), making an attempt to reverse this trend, adopted the Mach kernel as its core. As a founding member of OSF, Digital Equipment Corporation (Digital) took much of the work done by the group and decided to commercialize it into a product running on a hot new processor they were developing at the time—the 64-bit Alpha processor. The operating system that Digital developed, based on the work done by the OSF, was named DEC OSF/1. The new operating system, designed from the ground up to be 64-bit, continued to evolve over time. More advanced features, such as symmetric multiprocessing (SMP), the Advanced File System (AdvFS), the Logical Storage Manager (LSM), and clustering, were added.

Around the same time, it became clear that Digital was the only member of the OSF to adopt the OSF/1 core for its UNIX operating system. The decision was made to change the product's name to Digital UNIX (at version 3.2C) in order to break away from OSF roots and emphasize its UNIX character. Before long, clusters of large "Turbolaser" 8000-series systems were shipping with this powerful and flexible operating system. Later, when Compaq acquired Digital, it decided to rename the product again to Tru64 UNIX (at version 4.0E) in order to better represent its 64-bit qualities and to eliminate the old Digital name.

The Tru64 development team began an incredible overhaul of the product in version 5.0. This major version and its successors introduced support for single system image (SSI) clustering and nonuniform memory architecture (NUMA) systems. Some of the important new features added to support SSI clustering were a new device-naming standard and a cluster file system. Tru64 UNIX was enhanced to support the global server (GS) series, supporting up to 64GB of physical memory and 32 processors. With the V5.1A release, the product gained the additional capability of local-area network (LAN) interconnect clustering in place of memory channel, providing much greater flexibility in designing and fielding new clusters. In the future, there will be additional support for the even more powerful "Marvel" Alpha platform. As of this writing, these systems seem sure to push the limits again for memory and processor support in the operating system.

1.2 Scope

This book is written for the average Tru64 UNIX system administrator who has a tough problem to solve and isn't sure how to troubleshoot it. We attempt to distill our years of experience in troubleshooting Tru64 UNIX problems into a disciplined approach. There are always tricks and techniques that can be used in any particular situation, and we will provide those whenever appropriate. The overriding goal of this book, however, is to instruct the reader in basic troubleshooting principles and techniques. From that foundation, specific practices follow naturally.

It is assumed that the reader is familiar with basic Tru64 UNIX system administration. Because of space constraints, this text is not meant as a comprehensive reference, and the reader is referred to the on-line reference pages or Tru64 UNIX documentation for in-depth coverage of a particular tool or option. The reader can also look for additional references in Appendix B of this book for more information on a particular topic.

This book discusses Tru64 UNIX version 5.1A, although in many cases the material is sufficiently general to be fully applicable to other versions. If a technique or feature applies only to a specific version of the operating system, that will be so noted.

1.3 Organization

This book is organized into 12 chapters, which cover the following topics:

1. *Introduction.* This includes a brief overview of the history of Tru64 UNIX and its current standing. We also describe the scope of the book and what we hope the reader will gain from it.
2. *Principles and Techniques.* This chapter is the foundation of the book. We present techniques for detecting problems and isolating their root causes. The material in this chapter is primarily of general applicability, not limited simply to Tru64 UNIX.
3. *Tools and Resources.* This chapter focuses on tools available for system reporting, error detection, and isolation in Tru64 UNIX, including parts of the operating system (e.g., Event Manager, Compaq Analyze, collect, and sys_check).
4. *User Accounts and Security.* This chapter discusses common problems with individual user accounts, such as login failures; password problems; enhanced security features; and shell environment problems.
5. *System Failures.* This chapter covers system failures such as system crashes, system hangs, and boot failures. Regarding system crashes, we do not provide a detailed course in crash dump analysis; this would be overly long, beyond most readers, and of little help except for those administrators who have purchased a Tru64 UNIX source license. We do provide a way for administrators to take a quick look at crash dumps and, in many cases, determine

whether the problem is a local issue (e.g., a hardware failure or full disk) or an operating system failure that needs to be referred to HP technical support.

6. *System Performance.* In this chapter, we focus on identifying and relieving system performance bottlenecks. We include general system-tuning information, but our intent is to focus on responding to performance problems rather than on tuning for maximum performance. The latter is a complex issue and beyond the scope of this book.

7. *Networking.* We focus on common problems with key Tru64 UNIX utilities, including the Network File System (NFS), Network Information Service (NIS), and Berkeley Internet Name Domain (BIND) services. We discuss ways to determine whether a network problem is caused by hardware, but troubleshooting specific network hardware components is outside the scope of this book.

8. *Storage.* Our focus here is on disk and tape issues: identifying hardware problems (but not troubleshooting specific hardware components), device-naming issues, and Logical Storage Manager (LSM) problems.

9. *File systems.* Here we cover common problems with the UFS and AdvFS filesystems. We also discuss problems with the Tru64 native backup utilities such as tar, vdump, and vrestore.

10. *System Configuration.* This chapter discusses problems that arise in various aspects of system configuration: installing or upgrading the operating system, installing patches, and configuring the kernel.

11. *System Administration.* This chapter includes problems in several areas of system administration, including licensing problems, printing problems, and job scheduling.

12. *Display Problems.* This chapter covers common problems with graphics consoles and X Windows displays. The discussion is limited to isolating and correcting such problems, and is not intended as a comprehensive treatment of computer graphics or X Windows.

2

Principles and Techniques

When you have eliminated the impossible, whatever remains, however improbable, must be the truth.

—Sherlock Holmes

2.1 The Troubleshooting Process

Every computer system, no matter how reliable, well-designed, or well-managed, will inevitably encounter problems. When a problem occurs, it is up to the system administrator to identify and correct the problem—and then, in most cases, to provide explanations to users or management. This chapter provides a basic set of troubleshooting principles and techniques that will apply to any problem situation. These principles and techniques lay a foundation for the Tru64 UNIX troubleshooting specifics in the remainder of the book.

For the most part, troubleshooting computer problems has never been a well-defined subject. College classes and training courses provide a great deal of information on the theory and operation of computers, but they tend to focus on what happens when the system works, not when it breaks. Some computer manuals provide troubleshooting information, but it's usually of a specific nature, focusing on the responses to specific errors. Such specific information is useful and necessary (in fact, it forms the basis for the latter chapters in this book), but it doesn't address the *process* of troubleshooting.

In our experience as technical support providers, we've found that troubleshooting ability seems to be independent of academic achievement, computer skills, or experience as a system administrator. One of the interesting things about training new support personnel is finding that some people just seem to get it. They have an intuitive knack for getting to the root of a problem and finding the proper solution. Other people don't have this knack and usually have to acquire their troubleshooting skills the hard way. The troubleshooting principles and techniques in this chapter are the result of our observation of such people (both with and without the knack), as well as the practices we've developed in our own work.

In general terms, the process of troubleshooting can be broken down into five components:

1. *Detection*—does a problem exist?
2. *Identification*—what is the problem?
3. *Analysis*—what caused the problem?
4. *Correction*—how can the problem be fixed?
5. *Prevention*—how can the problem be avoided?

Figure 2.1 depicts a somewhat idealized relationship among these components. In practice, not all problems encompass all five distinct steps. Some steps may overlap in troubleshooting a particular case; in other cases, some steps are unnecessary. However, it's useful to think of each component as an independent step when troubleshooting a problem. The following sections describe each component and explain how the five components relate to each other.

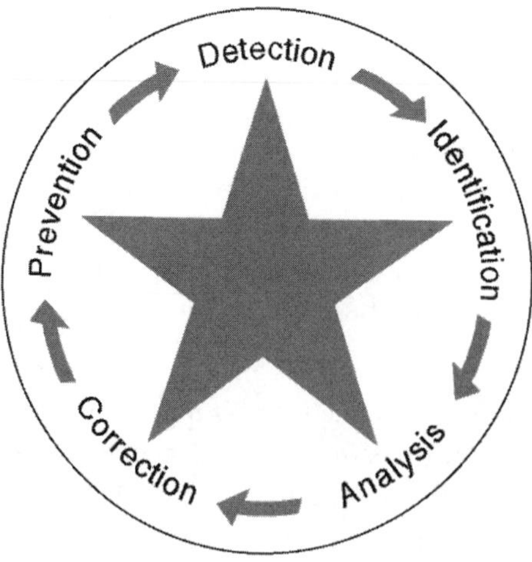

Figure 2.1 *The troubleshooting process.*

2.1.1 Detection

The first step in troubleshooting a problem is detecting that a problem has occurred. At first glance, it may seem unnecessary to list problem detection as a distinct component of the troubleshooting process. However, not all problems are equally obvious, and it is worth considering the various ways in which problems can be detected.

In the case of a major problem affecting an entire system (e.g., a system crash), it is immediately obvious to everyone using the system that a problem exists. In such cases, we can move on to the next step: identification of the problem. Other types of problems, however, are not so immediately obvious. It's important to detect and respond to such problems as soon as possible; early detection and resolution can prevent more severe problems from occurring. For example, if a disk is starting to experience occasional errors leading to bad-block replacements, replacing the disk will require only a little downtime. But if the problem isn't taken care of, the disk may continue to deteriorate and will probably crash at the worst possible time.

When a problem is first detected by a system administrator, troubleshooting can begin immediately. However, if a problem is first noticed by users working on the system, it must be reported to an administrator before it can be resolved. As such, it's necessary to have a way for users to report problems quickly and easily. The exact method used is dependent on local circumstances; it might be a help desk, a pager, an electronic mailbox, or a shout of "Help!" over the cubicle wall. Whatever method you choose, make sure that your users know how to use it. Users must be willing to report problems as soon as they occur. The best way to promote such willingness is to have an easy-to-use problem-reporting system and, most of all, to be responsive to problem reports.

A trickier issue is "invisible" problems. For example, RAID (redundant array of independent disks) storage systems are a popular method of providing storage redundancy at relatively low cost. Some RAID storage sets add an extra disk to a number of data disks, compute parity information across the data disks, and store the parity information on the extra disk. If any one disk fails, the RAID controller automatically regenerates the missing data from the remaining data chunks and the parity data. Because the data is still available, it appears that the storage set is fine, though perhaps a little slow. This is great for data availability—but not so great for problem detection.

Because there is no immediately obvious problem, no action will be taken to correct the problem unless there is some other means of detecting it. The RAIDset will continue to operate with one failed disk, but it will now be operating with no redundancy. If a second disk in the set fails, the storage set will go down and data will be lost. If the first failure had been detected promptly, the failed disk could have been replaced and the RAID-set restored to its normal level of redundancy before another disk failed. Detecting this kind of problem can be tricky; we'll discuss strategies for doing so later in this book.

Problems are characterized by their range of effect and by their severity. Range of effect defines who or what is affected by the problem: is the whole system or a critical function down, or is the problem limited to a subset (perhaps only one) of your users or applications? Severity defines the seriousness of the problem: is the system or function completely down, partially working, or just performing poorly? These two pieces of information are extremely important when reporting a problem. Not only are they necessary for problem identification, buy they help define the urgency of resolving the problem.

Let's consider a hypothetical problem. The system administrator of a student file server at a major university receives a report that some students are unable to log into their accounts on the server. Other students, however, are able to log in with no problem. In addition, some—but not all—students who were already logged in are now experiencing various problems.

This problem's range of effect is some (as yet undefined) subset of the system's users. Defining the exact extent of this subset of users will help to characterize the problem. For those affected, the problem is extremely severe; the system is completely unusable for them. We'll continue to follow this problem through the remaining components of the troubleshooting process. For now, we'll leave it and go on to discuss problem identification.

2.1.2 Identification

Once the existence of a problem has been detected, the next step is to determine exactly what the problem is. This might seem redundant; after all, doesn't the detection or report of a problem tell you what the problem is? To a certain extent, the detection and identification phases do overlap. In some cases, the problem report will contain all information needed to identify the problem. In other cases, though, more work must be done to determine exactly what the problem is—and identifying the problem is necessary in order to correct it. This, in fact, is the key difference between detection and identification. Detection is simply the awareness that a problem exists, whereas identification is the minimum characterization of a problem necessary to begin correcting it.

As an analogy, consider a visit to the doctor because you have a cough, a sore throat, and a fever. These symptoms cause you to detect that a problem exists, but they don't identify the problem. You might have a cold, the flu, a virus, or some obscure disease that you've never heard of before. The doctor will consider your symptoms in diagnosing your condition, but he may also check your vital signs, ask about your recent history, and perhaps do some other tests to identify the problem accurately. Only by identifying the actual problem can it be effectively treated. It might be possible to treat just the symptoms; while this might make you feel better, it probably won't cure the underlying condition. Similarly, when troubleshooting system problems, it may be useful to provide a workaround for a problem in order to quickly restore lost capability. However, this is just like treating only the symptoms of a medical problem. It may be helpful in the short term, but in the long term it's important to identify and correct the real underlying problem.

So how do you identify a problem? Identifying something—whether a problem, a car model, or an animal—is a process of comparing observed characteristics with a known model until a match is found. This definition divides the process of identification into two components: observation and comparison. Observing the characteristics of a problem begins with the initial problem report. At a minimum, the type of problem, its severity, and its range of effect must be noted. It may be that these pieces of information are sufficient to identify the problem. If not, it's necessary to continue gathering information about the problem. The gathering of information is not necessarily a passive process. Fully characterizing the problem often requires the troubleshooter to perform some actions and observe the results.

Once a problem is characterized, it must be matched with a known model in order to identify the problem. This may be an automatic process that you don't even have to think about. If the problem is of a type that you recognize, your mind matches the problem characteristics to a known model in your memory; your recognition of the problem provides the identification. On the other hand, if you're not already familiar with the problem, you'll probably need to consult other sources to find a matching set of problem characteristics. These sources may include coworkers, records of past problems you've encountered, Internet resources, and books such as this one. Every system administrator should maintain a list of resources for troubleshooting information. Appendixes A and B contain some valuable resources to add to your list.

Problem identification frequently is not a one-shot process. In many cases, the initial information won't be sufficient to identify the problem.

When this happens, identification becomes an iterative process. After consulting available resources, you determine that additional information is needed to characterize the problem completely. Using your troubleshooting resources and the techniques described in section 2.2, you gather additional information. This cycle is repeated until the problem has been completely identified. It's possible that the problem might be completely solved at this point. Sometimes the only way to identify a problem fully is to try various corrective actions and see which one fixes the problem.

Let's continue with the hypothetical problem from the previous section. Some of the student users of a university system are unable to log in, and some who have already logged in are now having various problems. The report of this problem made the system administrator aware of the problem, but it was not enough to identify the problem. In order to identify the problem fully and begin correcting it, more information is needed.

The first step is to characterize the range of effect. What is common among the users having problems, and what is different between those users and other users who are still working normally? After comparing a few users of both types, it becomes apparent that the problem is affecting only users with home directories on a particular disk. A quick check confirms that the directories on that disk are no longer accessible. Further checking reveals that the disk is off-line, and attempts to bring it on-line again are unsuccessful; the disk has failed. The problem has now been identified, and corrective action can begin.

2.1.3 Analysis

Once a problem has been identified, you can start working to correct it. If the problem is well understood and has a clear solution, there is probably no need to delve any further into what caused the problem. However, sometimes it's just as important to know why the problem occurred as it is to identify the problem. In such cases, it's frequently necessary to perform additional analysis in order to understand the root cause of the problem. This is particularly true when trying to resolve a recurring problem. It may be possible to fix the problem each time it occurs—especially if you're getting a lot of practice at it—but it's highly likely that there's something else going on that causes the problem to keep returning. In the long run, it's much better to find and address the underlying cause in order to prevent the problem from recurring.

Even if the problem isn't a recurring one, it may be desirable to perform additional analysis as a preventive measure to see whether any additional problems are lurking. In the university system example, the problem has been identified as a failed disk. That disk must be replaced and its files restored, regardless of whether any other problem exists. But it's worth doing some additional analysis to see whether there might be problems extending beyond a single disk. One possibility is to check the error log for disk errors. If there are numerous errors on the failed disk but few or no errors on other disks, then the problem can reasonably be assumed to be limited to the failed disk. However, if there are a number of errors on other disks, then it's time to look for a pattern. Are the disks all on the same bus or controller, or in the same storage cabinet? Any of these may indicate an underlying problem that, if not found, could lead to other disk problems in the near future. By rooting out and correcting the underlying problem now, those other problems can be prevented from ever happening.

In some cases, additional analysis is needed to refine the identification of a problem and determine the proper corrective action. For example, Tru64 UNIX panics if the root filesystem can't be mounted at system startup. When this occurs, the system console prints the panic message "vfs_mountroot: cannot mount root." This message is quite clear as to what the problem is: the root file system won't mount. This appears to be a specific, well-defined problem. However, there are no less than nine possible causes—each with a different solution—for this error:

1. The root file system is corrupted.
2. The /etc/fstab entry for the root file system is incorrect.
3. The root file system is AdvFS, but AdvFS isn't built into the kernel.
4. The root file system appears to be an LSM volume, but LSM isn't built into the kernel.
5. The /etc/fdmns link to the root file domain is pointing to the wrong device.
6. The root file system is an AdvFS domain with more than one volume.
7. The hardware configuration has changed, causing the device numbers to change.
8. The console firmware is outdated and incompatible with the current operating system version.
9. The root device has a nonzero logical unit number (a limitation in Tru64 UNIX versions earlier than V5.0.)

In such cases, additional analysis is needed to determine which of the several possibilities caused the problem. This, in turn, will determine the appropriate corrective action.

2.1.4 Correction

Once a problem has been identified, it must be corrected. Correction is the heart of the troubleshooting process, and it is the focus of most of the detailed information in this book. As a component of the troubleshooting process, correction includes any action taken to restore or replace lost functionality. This may include finding a workaround, as well as actually fixing the problem. There are times when a full solution may be too expensive, time-consuming, or risky to implement immediately; in such cases, a workaround can serve as a temporary measure until the real problem can be fixed.

With some problems—particularly minor problems—the most appropriate corrective action may be to do nothing. After identifying a problem and determining its solution, you might decide that implementing the solution is so disruptive or risky that it's better to use a workaround or, if no workaround is possible, to just live with the problem. For example, there may be a minor feature that you would like to use, but it's not available in the version of the operating system that you're currently running. Upgrading to a later version would provide that feature, but upgrading might not be a practical option. As such, the only choices are finding an alternative way of providing the desired functionality or doing without it.

Like problem identification, problem correction isn't always a one-shot process. Sometimes it's necessary to fix one part of a problem, then do additional analysis, and then continue with further corrective action. This is particularly true when there appear to be multiple problems present. It's possible that one of the problems may be causing the others; in such cases, fixing the first problem will probably resolve the others. As a rule, when you have multiple problems, fix the simplest problem first. This might resolve some or all of the other problems; even if it doesn't, it will at least remove one distraction and allow you to focus on the remaining problems.

There are also situations in which problem identification and correction go hand in hand. A problem may be narrowed down to two or three possible causes, each with a different solution, but there's no way to determine which of them is the correct one. When this happens, the only recourse is to try one of the possible solutions. If it fixes the problem, then the problem has been identified—and corrected at the same time. If the solution didn't work, then at least one of the possibilities has been eliminated. In cases where there are multiple possible solutions, try the quickest or least disruptive one first.

2.1.5 Prevention

It may seem a little strange to consider problem prevention as part of the troubleshooting process. After all, if a problem is prevented from occurring, there isn't much to troubleshoot. Nevertheless, prevention is part of the cycle shown in Figure 2.1. Problem prevention and detection are frequently related, as shown in the RAID system example in section 2.1.1. Early detection and correction of minor problems can prevent them from growing into major problems.

Problem correction is also related to prevention. After a problem has been solved, it may be possible to incorporate information learned from that situation into a method for preventing similar problems in the future. In the failed student disk example, the problem was corrected by replacing the failed disk and restoring from the latest backup tape. This caused considerable downtime and loss of a day's work, as the latest backup had been created the night before. Analysis of the problem showed a gradually increasing number of bad-block replacements on the failing disk. These errors indicated a worsening disk problem, but because they were automatically corrected by the disk controller, they were never noticed. If the administrators had been aware of the errors, a new disk could have been swapped in and the student directories moved to it, all with little or no down time. To prevent this kind of situation from happening again, the administrators set up a prevention scheme to monitor all of their disks and report even minor errors as soon as they occurred. With this early warning system in place, any disk that started to go bad could be replaced before it actually failed.

Prevention can also be thought of as proactive troubleshooting. The easiest problems to solve are the ones that are prevented from occurring at all. To paraphrase an old proverb: an ounce of prevention is worth a ton of troubleshooting. Preventive actions also have the advantage that they can be done at your convenience, instead of in response to a problem that occurs at a random—and usually inconvenient—moment.

Prevention includes not only avoiding problems, but also preparing for those times when problems do happen. No matter how reliable your system is or how proactive you are, some problems are inevitably going to happen. And no matter how much redundancy is present in your system, a severe enough incident can require you to restore your disks from backup—or even reconstruct your system from scratch. Catastrophes do happen; what would you do if a tornado hit your computer center? (This actually happened at one of the authors' previous jobs.) Disaster recovery is a topic beyond the scope of this book, but you should at least think about the questions listed below.

Are you prepared for the worst?

- Do you have current backups of all of your important file systems?
- Do you have copies of recent backups stored off-site?
- Do you ever test your backups by restoring a few randomly selected files?
- Do you have copies of the operating system and layered product media on hand in case you need to reinstall?
- Do you have a disaster recovery plan? Is it current? Is it in a safe place?
- Do you have your system configuration documented in case you have to rebuild from scratch? Is it up to date with your latest additions or changes? Is there a copy stored off-site?

2.1.6 Summary of the Troubleshooting Process

Troubleshooting is a process consisting of five major components:

1. *Detection*—becoming aware that a problem exists
2. *Identification*—characterizing the problem sufficiently to begin correcting it
3. *Analysis*—determining the underlying causes of the problem
4. *Correction*—restoring or replacing the affected function
5. *Prevention*—avoiding future problems

The arrows in Figure 2.1 connect the components of the troubleshooting process in a cycle: detection leads to identification, identification to analysis, and so on. Depending on the problem being solved, the troubleshooting process may or may not form such an orderly cycle. Some components may be unnecessary, some may happen simultaneously, or it may be necessary to go back and forth between some steps. The star in the middle of the figure is intended to show that each of the components may affect any of the others.

With some problems, it can be difficult to decide where to start or what to do next. Keeping the five process components in mind can help to determine the next steps in troubleshooting a problem. In the following section, we'll look at some of the techniques you can use to perform this process.

2.2 Troubleshooting Techniques

In the previous section, we discussed the steps that make up the troubleshooting process. Those steps define *what* you need to do, but they don't address *how* to actually do it. In this section, we'll introduce some techniques for your troubleshooting toolbox.

The following troubleshooting techniques are among the most useful that we've used or observed in our experience in technical support. It's important to remember that not all of these will be effective on every problem. You may find that a particular technique works very well in most cases, but doesn't help for a particular problem. When this happens, it's important to remain flexible and use another approach, rather than trying to force results from a technique that isn't working.

2.2.1 Reproducing the Problem

If the cause of a problem is not immediately apparent, one of the best ways to identify the problem is to reproduce it under controlled conditions. For problems that occur consistently, as in the failed login example, this is not difficult. Intermittent or transient problems, however, are much harder to troubleshoot. Such problems always seem to go away on their own before you really get started on troubleshooting them. But because the root cause of the problem was not identified and corrected, the problem may crop up again and again.

In order to reproduce a problem, it's necessary to recreate both the environment and the actions that led to it. If the problem is reproducible, you can then try varying some of these conditions; this will be discussed further in the following section. For intermittent problems, it's extremely important to record the environment and actions as accurately as possible. The common factors among multiple occurrences will determine the key elements that led to the problem. Intermittent problems can be very difficult to reproduce and solve, and the key element among occurrences may not be at all obvious.

In an ideal world, the cause of all problems would be immediately obvious; failing this, it would be nice if all problems were at least reproducible. However, this is not the case in the real world. Some problems, unfortunately, are not reproducible. These are among the most frustrating to experience, and they can be difficult or impossible to troubleshoot. Although some of the techniques in the following sections may aid in identifying and analyzing such problems, it must be recognized that with some problems, it may never be possible to identify or analyze them sufficiently to correct them. When this happens, there are really only three choices, none of them completely satisfying: live with the occasional recurrence of the problem, work around the problem, or resort to a "brute-force" approach, such as restoring from backup or even reinstalling the system. Although the brute-force approach usually eliminates the problem, the lack of a true understanding tends to lower confidence that the problem is really gone.

2.2.2 Isolating the Problem

In section 2.1.2, problem identification was defined as the minimum characterization of a problem necessary to begin correcting it. It was also noted that different problems can have similar or identical symptoms. In order to identify a problem correctly, it's necessary to determine which factors are common to all instances of the problem while eliminating those elements that aren't part of the problem. This allows you to drill down to the key elements that characterize the problem. The process of singling out these key characteristics is known as isolating the problem.

Isolating a reproducible problem is a straightforward process: vary one (but only one) condition at a time, and observe whether the problem still occurs. If this reveals an element whose presence or absence always determines whether the problem occurs, you've isolated the problem and are well on the way to identifying it. In the example of the failed student logins, many users were unable to log in, but this was not true of *all* users. It was also observed that members of the operations staff were able to log in. Therefore, the key element must be some characteristic that was true for the problem accounts, but not for the working accounts (or vice versa.)

The next step in isolating the problem was to list the conditions that could vary from one account to another. This list included the following items:

- Username (obviously each username is different, but is there some common factor among the problem accounts, such as location in the alphabet, length of username, etc.?)
- Home directory (again, each user has a different home directory, but are the problem accounts all on the same disk?)
- Group membership (same primary group, member of same secondary group?)
- Default shell
- Login environment (do all the problem accounts run a particular login script?)
- Password length
- Time of last login (is there some dividing point between the problem accounts and working accounts?)

Some of these possibilities (e.g., username length and password length) may seem a little far-fetched. It is true that they are unlikely, but even unlikely possibilities occasionally happen; the authors have seen both username length and password length turn out to be the key element in isolating a problem. The more likely possibilities should be checked first, but if none of them reveals a key element, it's worth looking at the unlikely possibilities.

The last item in the foregoing list illustrates another point to keep in mind: most problems have not always existed; they started occurring at some point in time. (If a problem *has* always existed, that's also useful information.) If something was previously working and is now broken, try to determine if any new circumstances were introduced around the same time. Did the system configuration change? Were other unusual events noticed? Even seemingly unrelated events may provide a clue to the nature of the problem.

In the example problem, it was quickly determined that there were two elements common to the problem accounts but not to the working accounts. All of the problem accounts belonged to undergraduate math majors, which meant they belonged to the same primary group. In addition, all of their home directories were in the same file system—not too surprising, since that file system was dedicated to use by undergraduate math majors. So how could you determine which one was actually the key?

In such cases, if one possibility seems more likely (based on your experience or intuition), then investigate that one first; if it doesn't yield any results, then investigate the other possibility. If both seem equally likely, then pick the one most easily investigated and try that first. (If there's still no way to choose among the possibilities, just pick one.) In the example problem, there were a number of ways in which the home directory location could be a key element; for example, the disk could be off-line or have no free space. It's not quite so easy to come up with a way in which primary group membership could be the problem. Looking at the more likely possibility first, it was quickly determined that the disk in question was off-line. The cause of the problem was identified, and the administrators could start working to correct it.

Just as some problems are not reproducible, not all problems can be isolated. Sometimes no common element can be identified. In other cases, there may be one or more common elements, but investigating them doesn't reveal the true cause of the problem. When this happens, it's necessary to resort to other troubleshooting techniques. However, failing to completely isolate the problem isn't necessarily a total failure. Even negative information is useful. If attempts to isolate the problem fail to determine exactly what the problem is, they may at least provide some good ideas as to what it is not.

2.2.3 Problem Decomposition

Problem decomposition is the breaking down of a large or complex problem into smaller, more manageable pieces. Decomposition is related to problem isolation; both techniques are ways of refining a problem down to a more tractable level. The difference between the two techniques is that problem isolation focuses on finding the key element of a single problem. Problem decomposition, in contrast, is used to break up a complex problem into smaller problems—each of which may then need to be isolated.

Decomposition is also a useful technique when there appear to be multiple problems happening at the same time. As noted in section 2.1.4, what appear to be multiple problems aren't always independent; in such cases, one problem is actually the cause of the others. Attempting to break the situation down into its components may reveal a cause-and-effect relationship among the multiple problems. When this happens, work on solving the root problem first; correcting this problem has a good chance of resolving the other problems as well. On the other hand, your efforts to decompose the problem may prove that there really are multiple, independent problems occurring, and you can work on solving these one at a time.

An example of this technique occurred in the case of a three-node cluster that experienced severe problems after some hardware components and firmware were upgraded. A combination of several unlikely events left the three members of the cluster with three different views of the attached storage, none of which matched the hardware database previously used by the cluster. As a result, the cluster was completely down. None of the members would boot, even to single-user mode.

This problem was too complex to attack all at once; it was necessary to break it down into more manageable pieces. The first step was to get one member booted successfully from the cluster's emergency repair disk. That member's hardware database was repaired, and the corrected database was copied to the cluster root file system. After adjusting some cluster parameters, the now-working member was rebooted to form a one-node cluster.

At this point, the cluster was sufficiently restored that it could be placed into limited production service, which reduced the urgency of solving the remaining problems. The corrective process was continued by copying the repaired hardware database to each of the other member boot partitions. Each member was booted to single-user mode in order to correct additional problems and then finally rebooted into the cluster until everything was back to normal.

The problems on this cluster were too serious and widespread to troubleshoot all at once. It was necessary to break the problem down to manageable pieces and resolve these one at a time. This step-by-step process allowed a complex and difficult problem to be solved in a systematic manner. It also allowed service to be restored to users before all parts of the problem were completely resolved.

2.2.4 Retrograde Analysis

Retrograde analysis is the logical deduction of causative events based on their observed effects. The term is borrowed from a particular class of chess problems in which a final position is provided and the object is to deduce the sequence of moves that led to that position. This technique is most useful when doing after-the-fact analysis of a problem—particularly a one-shot or intermittent problem—in order to understand it and prevent it from happening again. Ideally, all problems would leave clear and indisputable evidence of the events that caused them.

Unfortunately, problems are rarely so accommodating, and there is sometimes little or no evidence of what actually happened. In such cases, reasoning out what must have happened is the next best thing. In some cases, this will point to possible sources of evidence that were not previously apparent; with luck, you may find some information to confirm your theory of what happened. Sometimes, however, there will be no evidence to either prove or disprove the validity of retrograde analysis. Without such evidence, confidence will be less than 100 percent that the problem has been correctly analyzed. How much less depends on a variety of factors: how clear-cut the chain of reasoning is, the likelihood of other causes, and your experience with similar situations.

An example of using retrograde analysis occurred in the case of a system that kept crashing at random intervals. The system would display a panic message indicating an AdvFS problem and reboot, but it never produced a crash dump. Even though the system had crashed numerous times, there was no evidence of any problem in the system log files. The system administrator kept detailed records, but there was no discernible common factor among the crashes.

Because there was no direct evidence of a problem, retrograde analysis was used to deduce possible causes of the crashes. The AdvFS panic message provided a starting point. Recurring AdvFS panics are typically caused by one or both of the following:

- File system metadata corruption
- I/O failures while updating file system metadata

The verify(8) command was used to check the metadata on all of the AdvFS filesystems, but no errors were found. With metadata corruption ruled out, I/O problems appeared to be the likely cause. The typical sequence of events in an I/O-induced AdvFS panic is shown in Figure 2.2. Normally, however, this sequence of events should have left some indication of a problem in one of the system logs.

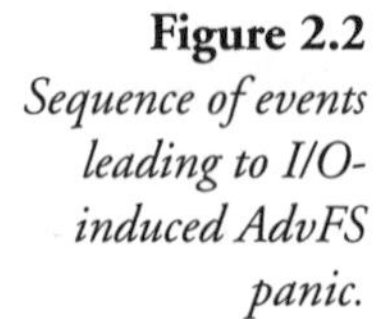

Figure 2.2 *Sequence of events leading to I/O-induced AdvFS panic.*

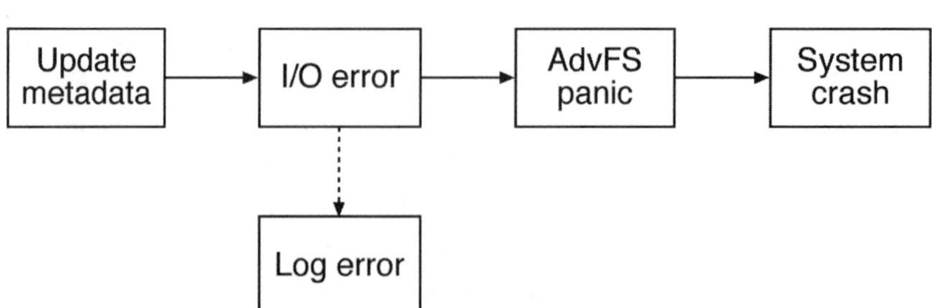

What circumstances could prevent I/O errors from being logged? Two possibilities surfaced:

- The system's error logging capabilities were not working.
- The I/O problem prevented information from being written to the log files.

The first possibility was quickly eliminated. Regular messages, such as system startup and shutdown events, were appearing normally in the logs. In addition, the logger(8) command was used to confirm that system logging was working. This left the possibility that the I/O problem was affecting the system log files. Deducing that this must have occurred led to a key insight: virtually all system logs are located in the /var file system. If an I/O problem affected /var, rendering it inoperable, the log files would necessarily contain no evidence of the problem. If the problem was transient, then the file system might return to normal operation by the time the system had rebooted, neatly concealing the fact that a problem had occurred.

At this point, retrograde analysis had produced a plausible explanation of the observed symptoms; however, there was no guarantee that it was in fact the true explanation. To verify this theory, error logging was redirected to a different file system located in a different storage array. This experiment produced some real evidence: on the next occurrence of the panic, the new binary error log recorded a hard I/O error on the disk containing /var, as well as on several other disks in the same array.

The questionable array controller did not have any errors stored in its memory, so a printer was attached to its console to capture its output. This yielded the final piece of the puzzle: the array controller was occasionally rebooting for no apparent reason. When this happened, all of the attached storage would go off-line until the controller finished rebooting. Replacing the faulty controller solved the problem for good.

In this case, the nature of the underlying problem prevented the system from recording any evidence of it. Retrograde analysis made it possible to work backward from the final result to deduce what must have occurred. This led to a plausible explanation that was verified by experiment, allowing the true cause of the problem to be identified and subsequently corrected.

2.2.5 Circumstantial Evidence

In legal terms, circumstantial evidence (as fans of courtroom dramas already know) is evidence that is not directly related to a fact in question. Instead, it is related to other circumstances from which the occurrence of the fact may be inferred. For our purposes, this simply means that when there is no direct evidence of a problem, it's a good idea to look around for any other evidence that might be useful. In particular, investigate any unusual occurrences in the same general area (e.g., storage), whether or not they happened around the same time. On the other hand, you should also check out anything that occurred near the time of the problem occurrence, whether or not it happened in the same general area. This is particularly effective when the affected system is part of a cluster; in such cases, checking the logs on the other cluster members frequently turns up valuable clues.

An example of this technique occurred in a situation where user logins would hang for a significant length of time, after which they would usually (though not always) fail. The system administrator quickly rebooted the system, hoping that the problem would go away. It did, but the administrator was left with the task of explaining to his manager why the problem had occurred and preventing it from happening again. No useful information was found in the system logs. However, the system was also an NFS server, and several of its clients recorded numerous "NFS server not responding" messages during the problem period. This information indicated a possible network problem on the server. Because the password database was distributed via NIS, a network problem could easily make logins slow or impossible.

With this clue in mind, the server's network interface was monitored closely. This monitoring revealed that the interface was experiencing periodic bursts of errors. Replacing the network interface card cured the errors, and no further login problems occurred. Without the clues found in the other systems' logs, there would have been no way to troubleshoot this problem, and it would undoubtedly have occurred again—much to the displeasure of the users, the system administrator, and the manager.

2.3 Troubleshooting Principles

No matter which techniques you use to troubleshoot a problem, there are some general principles that should serve as a framework for your actions. Keeping these principles in mind will make your troubleshooting activities smoother and more effective. A few of these principles have already been mentioned, but we'll repeat them here in order to have them all in one place.

2.3.1 Document Everything

One of the most frustrating experiences in troubleshooting is to successfully analyze and correct a complex problem, begin a follow-up analysis ... and suddenly realize that you don't remember exactly which commands you used to find and resolve the problem. Was it "hwmgr delete" or "hwmgr remove"? (Both are valid commands with slightly different effects.) This is just one of the reasons to document all of your actions and their results. In some cases, what seems to be a simple problem takes an unexpected turn; when this happens, it's helpful to keep notes as you go in order to know which avenues you've already investigated.

Documenting your actions applies not just to troubleshooting activities, but also to any changes made during normal system administration. If something goes wrong as a result of a configuration change—for example, a system fails to boot after you change some kernel parameters—it's extremely helpful to be able to see exactly what commands were executed. If keeping notes on paper isn't convenient, the script(1) command is very useful in these situations. This command records subsequent terminal input/output in a file. The resulting transcript files are not only useful for troubleshooting; they can also become part of a system's configuration records, and are an invaluable resource if you ever need to reconstruct or duplicate the configuration.

2.3.2 Preserve the Evidence

Documenting your actions preserves one kind of information: actions and their results. It's also important to preserve as much information as possible about the system's current state. For example, when a system hangs and becomes unresponsive, it's usually necessary to reboot the system. Unfortunately, rebooting clears the contents of memory, which destroys valuable information about the state of the system at the time that it hung. An alternative to just rebooting is to halt the system, force a crash dump, and then reboot the system. The crash dump preserves the contents of memory for later analysis.

Preserving evidence is not always necessary; some problems are straightforward and quickly resolved. In other cases, lack of time or other resources may render it impractical to preserve some evidence. For example, it might be necessary to recreate a corrupt file system and restore its contents from backup. Recreating the file system on the same disk partition will destroy the old, corrupted metadata. However, if a spare device is available on which to recreate the file system, the corrupt file system can be left intact for later analysis. Obviously, this depends on the availability of sufficient resources; if the file system occupies a 400GB RAIDset, it's not too likely that enough extra storage is sitting around unused.

2.3.3 Reduce Variables

When troubleshooting a problem, you may encounter multiple possibilities in trying to isolate or correct the problem. When this happens, try to change only one element at a time, then see what effect that has on the problem. This will help narrow the problem to a single possible cause. Similarly, when making changes to a system, it's best to do them one at a time, verifying that the system is operating correctly after each step. If a problem does arise, all that's needed is to back out of the last change, rather than trying to determine which of several changes caused the problem.

Unfortunately, changing only one variable at a time is not always practical. For example, if a system fails to boot after six kernel parameters have been changed, reverting to the previous configuration will no doubt correct the problem. However, this won't determine which of the six parameters was the real problem. Reverting one parameter at a time would isolate the real problem, but it might take several reboots to get there. Whether the additional information is worth the extra time and inconvenience is a tradeoff. In such cases, you'll have to make a choice based on circumstances such as the number of affected users, the criticality of the system, and the importance of knowing the exact cause of the problem.

2.3.4 Minimize Your Risk

Whenever you change a key system file—whether as part of troubleshooting or as normal system maintenance—be sure to save a backup copy of the original file. This will allow you to revert quickly to the original version in case of a problem. It can also be handy to distinguish your changes easily by comparing the old and new files with the diff(1) command.

This principle applies not only to files but to other components, such as entire file systems. For example, when performing an action that could affect a file system (e.g., upgrading to a new version of Tru64 UNIX) always make backups of any file systems that could possibly be damaged. The insurance value of backups is well worth the time it takes to create them. If something unexpected does happen, having current backups can make the difference between a temporary problem and an utter catastrophe.

One further extension of this principle is to delay irreversible actions as long as possible. For example, if a system is not accepting new logins but existing sessions are still working, don't log out of the system. Similarly, if a file system is damaged, it may be necessary to recreate and restore it, but this should be a last resort after exhausting all other possibilities to repair the file system. Sometimes a last resort is necessary, but make sure it really is the *last* resort.

2.3.5 Maximize Your Return

When troubleshooting a problem, choose your actions so as to get the most return for the least cost. In this case, cost includes both effort on your part and disruption of the system. In other words, try for a quick and easy fix whenever possible. If there is a choice among multiple possible solutions, try the quickest or least disruptive action first. If it works, the problem is quickly resolved; if it doesn't, not much is lost in the way of time or disruption.

For example, if you have an AdvFS file system with some metadata corruption, recreating the file system and restoring it from backup will undoubtedly resolve the problem. However, this is time-consuming and highly disruptive to users. Before resorting to this solution, it's worth trying the verify(8) command to fix the corruption; if that doesn't work, the more powerful fixfdmn(8) command can also be tried. Depending on the type and extent of the corruption, these commands may or may not repair the problem. Nevertheless, they should be attempted first because they may resolve the problem in a much faster and less disruptive fashion than rebuilding the file system.

This principle also applies when there appear to be multiple problems occurring. In such cases, one problem may be causing another, and fixing the first problem may resolve the others. In order to maximize your return, fix the simplest problem first. Even if it doesn't resolve the remaining problems, it will at least remove a distracting factor.

2.3.6 Verify System Integrity

Many seemingly mysterious problems are caused by incorrect ownership or permissions on system files. When other possibilities have been exhausted, it's a good idea to verify the integrity of the operating system software. The fverify(8) command will verify the ownership, permissions, and checksum of all files in a software subset; however, it's limited to one subset at a time and doesn't consider the effect of patches. A better method is the allverify tool available from HP technical support. More information on allverify is contained in Chapter 3.

2.3.7 Use Your Resources

Very few problems are totally new. It's highly likely that any problem you may encounter—or if not the exact same problem, one similar to it—has been seen before by someone. When you need advice on a particular problem, don't overlook the numerous resources available to provide assistance. These include written materials such as HP manuals, books such as this one, and articles on the Internet. It's also valuable to consult with other people; even if they don't have an immediate answer, it often helps to get a fresh viewpoint on a problem. In addition to your coworkers, there are a number of Web-based forums, newsgroups, and mailing lists available to connect you with Tru64 UNIX professionals around the world. A number of useful resources (both paper and electronic) are listed in Appendixes A and B.

2.4 Summary

Troubleshooting is an activity that every system administrator has to perform at some point. There are a number of resources that describe specific troubleshooting activities for various computers and operating systems, but there is a tremendous lack of information concerning the actual process of troubleshooting. In this chapter, we've attempted to address that lack by describing the troubleshooting techniques and principles that we've developed in the course of our technical support experience. It is our hope that these general-purpose techniques and principles will serve as a foundation for the specific Tru64 UNIX troubleshooting information to follow, and that they will better equip you to troubleshoot the problems that you encounter.

3

Tools and Resources

If your only tool is a hammer, you tend to see every problem as a nail.

—Abraham Maslow

When a problem crops up on a Tru64 UNIX system, the initial symptoms may or may not be sufficient to determine its root cause. Therefore, you will occasionally need to avail yourself of some of the system's tools to isolate the problem down to the failing component. Luckily, Tru64 UNIX provides an array of tools and facilities to aid the troubleshooting process. Your task is to choose the correct tool to use or log files to examine in order to find the information you need. Our task is to familiarize you with the tools available to make your troubleshooting tasks as easy as possible.

In this chapter, we discuss the major troubleshooting facilities and tools available for the Tru64 UNIX operating system. Specifically, we will cover the following four broad categories:

1. System-level error-reporting facilities
2. Process-level reporting facilities
3. System troubleshooting tools
4. Kernel debugging tools

These categories are discussed in the following sections.

3.1 System-Level Error-Reporting Facilities

In this section, we introduce some of the facilities and tools available on a Tru64 UNIX system for detecting and analyzing errors. Some of these are nearly identical to their counterparts in other versions of UNIX; others are unique to Tru64 UNIX. For example, readers familiar with another vendor's UNIX product will find the Tru64 UNIX syslog facility to be very similar to what they have seen before, whereas the binary error log facility would not be so familiar.

The three main facilities we will be discussing in this chapter are the following:

1. The system logger
2. The event manager
3. The binary error log

Extensive, in-depth coverage of these facilities is beyond the scope of this text; for detailed information, consult the Tru64 UNIX system documentation. Our goal is to make you aware of their existence as troubleshooting aids. It is important for a capable administrator to become as familiar with their use as possible. As with other tools of the trade, these facilities are the Tru64 UNIX system administrator's "bread and butter" when it comes to tracking down and correcting system problems. In addition, as with any software system, one or more of these facilities may fail to operate properly. Therefore, you may occasionally find that these reporting facilities will require troubleshooting themselves. In that case, you need a sound understanding of how they work in order to determine how they may be failing.

3.1.1 The System Logger

Most UNIX implementations provide a centralized facility for collecting and recording messages. This facility, commonly referred to as the syslog, is the primary logging mechanism used by many system processes and utilities. In addition, syslog's architecture allows nonsystem applications, including user and administrative scripts, to send messages to syslog for disposition. Because syslog is typically the destination for error messages from system processes, understanding how syslog works and how to interpret and manage the entries in syslog's configuration file is vital to effective system administration.

The syslog facility consists of the syslog daemon, /usr/sbin/syslogd, and the syslog configuration files: /etc/syslog.conf is the primary configuration file, and /etc/syslog.auth identifies the remote hosts that are allowed to forward syslog messages to the local syslog daemon. In Tru64 UNIX version 5, the /etc/syslog_evm.conf file is also used by syslogd to determine what information to forward to the event manager. We discuss the event manager in greater depth later in this chapter.

3.1.1.1 The Syslog Daemon

The syslog daemon, /usr/sbin/syslogd, is an executable system utility normally started at run level 3 during system startup and always running while the system is in multiuser mode. The syslog daemon reads messages sent to it from system processes, the kernel, and user applications. These messages can be informational only, warnings, or errors that need attention. The messages themselves are single lines, optionally containing a priority value indicating the severity of the message. These priorities are defined in the /usr/include/sys/syslog_pri.h header file. Messages are received by syslogd from three sources:

1. The device special file /dev/log, also called the domain socket
2. The device special file /dev/klog, which reads kernel messages
3. Other systems across the network via a socket specified in /etc/services

Most system processes and utilities—and optionally user applications—submit messages to syslog using the syslog(3) function call or the logger(1) command. These messages are relayed to syslog via the device special file /dev/log. Kernel messages are similarly sent to syslog through the device special file /dev/klog. Finally, syslog may receive messages from other systems via the network using a network socket specified in the /etc/services file, provided that the /etc/syslog.auth file allows it; see section 3.1.8 for more information about /etc/syslog.auth. The point in mentioning these syslog message sources is to identify these files when troubleshooting syslog problems. For example, if kernel messages are not being received and logged by syslog, ensure that the /dev/klog file exists:

```
# ls -l /dev/klog
crw-------    1 root     system     3,   0 Apr 24 22:00
 /dev/klog
```

If the file is missing or not correct (for example, it's not a character special device file), simply recreate the klog file:

```
# cd /dev
# ./MAKEDEV klog
```

Similarly, if syslog messages are not being received from other systems via the network, ensure that the /etc/services file exists and contains the following entry:

```
syslog     514/udp
```

Note that the /dev/log file is a socket that is created and maintained by syslogd itself. It exists only while syslogd is running. If the /dev/log file is absent, it's likely that the syslog daemon is not running. Simply restart syslogd and the /dev/log socket will be created:

```
# /usr/sbin/syslogd
```

Configuration Tip

Logging to a remote system, as well as the local log files, will help make sure the data is preserved if one or the other is unavailable. For example, a cleanup script gone amok might accidentally remove the system messages file and lose the local data needed to help troubleshoot a problem.

3.1.1.2 Starting and Stopping syslogd

The syslog daemon, syslogd, is normally started at boot time by the syslog startup script, /sbin/rc3.d/S09syslog, which is actually a symbolic link to /sbin/init.d/syslog. Syslogd is started early in the run level 3 boot process due to its importance in the error-logging process; however, any kernel messages logged before syslogd is started are stored in the kernel's preserved message buffer. The syslog daemon reads its configuration file when it starts up and rereads the configuration file when it receives a hangup signal (e.g., kill -HUP <pid>). The configuration file is simply a set of rules that instruct the syslog daemon what messages to log and where to log them.

When syslogd starts, it creates the file /var/run/syslog.pid. This file contains a single line with the process ID (PID) of the syslogd process. This file can be used to obtain syslogd's PID when it is necessary to stop or restart syslogd. For example, to terminate syslogd, you could use either of these commands:

```
# kill `cat /var/run/syslog.pid`
```

or

```
# /sbin/init.d/syslog stop
```

Running the syslog script with a "stop" will kill syslogd by using the "kill" command given above.

3.1.1.3 Disabling and Enabling syslogd Console Messages

A common destination for syslog messages is the system console. Depending on the amount of activity or the health of the system, the volume of messages printed on the console may be very low. Occasionally, however, the system administrator needs to diagnose one or more ongoing system problems from the console. If the syslog daemon is sending frequent messages to the console, it may be distracting and difficult to troubleshoot problems. Beginning with Tru64 UNIX version 4.0, the /usr/sbin/syslog command allows enabling and disabling syslog-generated console messages.

If you are working from the console and find syslog informational messages are hampering your effectiveness, simply issue the following command:

```
# /usr/sbin/syslog console_off
```

This disables syslog messages. Remember to re-enable syslog messages when the console work is completed so that the messages will once again be sent to the console:

```
# /usr/sbin/syslog console_on
```

If console messages are disabled and the system is rebooted, the default behavior of enabled syslog console messages is restored.

3.1.1.4 The syslog Configuration Files

The Tru64 UNIX version 5 syslog facility has three configuration files: /etc/syslog.conf, /etc/syslog_evm.log, and /etc/syslog.auth. These files are simply text files that the syslogd daemon reads at startup or after receiving a hang-up signal.

3.1.1.4.1 /etc/syslog.conf

This configuration file contains entries that specify the facility (see Table 3.1), which is the part of the system that produced the message, the message severity level (see Table 3.2), and the destination to which the syslogd daemon should send the message.

Table 3.1 *Available syslog Facilities*

Name(s)	Description
kern	Kernel messages
user	User-level messages
mail	Mail system messages
daemon	System daemon messages
auth	Security/authorization messages
syslog	Messages generated by syslogd itself
lpr	Printer subsystem messages
news	Network news subsystem messages
uucp	UUCP subsystem messages
cron	Clock daemon messages
megasafe	Polycenter AdvFS
local0	Reserved for local use
local1	Reserved for local use
local2	Reserved for local use
local3	Reserved for local use

Table 3.1 *Available syslog Facilities (continued)*

Name(s)	Description
local4	Reserved for local use
local5	Reserved for local use
local6	Reserved for local use
local7	Reserved for local use

Each line of the syslog configuration file contains a single entry. See Figure 3.1 for an example of an /etc/syslog.conf file.

Table 3.2 *Available syslog Priorities*

Name(s)	Number	Description
emerg	0	System is unusable
alert	1	Action must be taken immediately
crit	2	Critical conditions
err	3	Error conditions
warning	4	Warning conditions
notice	5	Normal but significant condition
info	6	Informational
debug	7	Debug

The syntax and format of the /etc/syslog.conf file must be followed exactly, as the syslog daemon will stop reading the syslog.conf file if an error or format violation is encountered. This means that a simple typographical error in the middle of the syslog.conf file will prevent syslogd from seeing any entries after the error. The most common error is using spaces to delimit the facility and severity levels from the destination. The only permitted delimiter is one or more tab characters. Spaces are not allowed in a syslog.conf entry.

Figure 3.1 *An example /etc/ syslog.conf.*

```
#
# syslogd config file
#
# facilities: kern user mail daemon auth syslog lpr binary
# priorities: emerg alert crit err warning notice info debug
kern.debug              /var/adm/syslog.dated/kern.log
user.debug              /var/adm/syslog.dated/user.log
mail.debug              /var/adm/syslog.dated/mail.log
daemon.debug            /var/adm/syslog.dated/daemon.log
auth.debug              /var/adm/syslog.dated/auth.log
syslog.debug            /var/adm/syslog.dated/syslog.log
lpr.debug               /var/adm/syslog.dated/lpr.log

msgbuf.err              /var/adm/crash/msgbuf.savecore

kern.debug              /var/adm/messages
kern.debug              /dev/console
*.emerg*
```

Troubleshooting Tip

If the syslog daemon is misbehaving, the configuration file may have a formatting error or may be simply unreadable. Try moving the existing configuration file out of the way (e.g., rename it) and copy in the system-provided file ".proto..syslog.conf"; then restart syslogd. This can quickly tell you whether the problem is in the old configuration file or not.

The first half of a syslog.conf entry specifies the source and severity of messages for which syslog should watch. The facility and its severity level must be separated by a period. For example:

```
kern.debug              /var/adm/syslog.dated/kern.log
```

More than one facility can be specified on a line by separating the multiple facilities with commas or semicolons:

```
mail,lpr.info /var/adm/syslog.dated/misc_info.log
```

```
auth.info;syslog.debug /var/adm/syslog.dated/syslog.log
```

Finally, an asterisk (*) may be specified in place of a facility, indicating that messages generated by all parts of the system are to be logged. All messages of the specified severity and greater will be logged:

```
*.emerg        *
```

A Tru64 UNIX–unique facility.severity pair is msgbuf.err. This facility.severity pair is crucial for recovering any messages that may be pending in the kernel syslog buffer in the event of a system crash. When a Tru64 UNIX system recovers from a system crash, any such messages recovered are placed in the file specified as the msgbuf.err destination in the syslog.conf file. When syslog starts, it looks for this file. If the file exists, syslog processes any messages contained within and then deletes the file. The default syslog.conf entry to provide this functionality is

```
msgbuf.err           /var/adm/crash/msgbuf.savecore
```

The second half of a syslog.conf entry specifies the destination where syslog will log the messages that match the facility.severity criteria defined by the first half of the syslog.conf entry. There are four possible destinations for messages:

1. *A file name that begins with a leading slash character (/).* The syslog daemon will append messages to this file. Note that this can be either an ordinary file or a device-special file such as /dev/console, which causes all messages sent to this destination to appear on the system console.
2. *A host name preceded by an "at" sign (@).* Appropriate messages are forwarded to the syslog daemon on the named host (if the named host's /etc/syslog.auth permits it). The named host must have a record in its /etc/syslog.auth if it is to receive these messages.
3. *A comma-separated list of users.* Appropriate messages are written to those users if they are logged in.
4. *An asterisk (*).* Appropriate messages are written to all users who are logged in.

Tru64 UNIX has the ability to create daily syslog log files. If you specify a path such as /var/adm/syslog.dated/mail.log as a destination, a new directory and associated log files are created each day. These file names have the form /var/adm/syslog.dated/<date>/<file>, where <date> is the day, month, and time and <file> is the log file name, such as mail.log. For example:

```
mail.debug                /var/adm/syslog.dated/mail.log
```

This is a nice feature because it produces a day-by-day account of the messages received. For example, an entry such as the mail.debug entry above will cause syslogd to log mail debug messages in the following file if syslogd was started or restarted on June 2nd at 6:54 P.M.:

```
/var/adm/syslog.dated/02-Jun-18:54/kern.log
```

Furthermore, the symbolic link "current" in the /var/adm/syslog.dated directory always points to the currently active syslog directory, making it easy to find the current set of syslog log files. Simply set the working directory to /var/adm/syslog.dated/current.

Configuration Tip

The daily log files from syslog.dated are generated every 24 hours, beginning from the time the syslog daemon was started. Because this could be any time of the day, data for a particular day may be split between two instances of the log files, making it difficult to put together data from a particular day's events. To avoid this problem, you can make the daemon reset its log files each day at midnight by adding a line similar to the following to the root crontab file:

```
0 0 * * * /sbin/kill -HUP `/sbin/cat /var/run/syslog.pid`
```

It's important to be aware that if a syslog destination is a normal file (i.e., it begins with a leading slash as in /etc/syslog.conf), syslog always appends data to that file and the file will grow indefinitely. Monitor such log files and trim them when necessary to avoid filling up the destination file system(s). The following is an example of trimming /var/adm/messages:

```
# cp /var/adm/messages /var/adm/messages.1
# cp /dev/null /var/adm/messages
```

Note that the existing messages file is copied to a backup, then the original messages file is emptied by copying the /dev/null file to it. This technique is used rather than simply deleting the original messages file, because if a syslog log file is removed, the log file will not be recreated until the next time syslogd is restarted.

As mentioned before, the facility.severity level pair(s) must be separated from the destination by one or more tab characters. Blank lines and lines beginning with a pound sign (#) are considered comments and are ignored. Finally, the /etc/syslog.conf file should not be world-writable. The appropriate permissions level on this file is 644, or readable by everyone and writable only by the owner (user bin).

As an example of some of syslog's configuration rules, consider the following syslog.conf entries:

```
kern.*      /dev/console
*.notice;mail.info      /var/adm/syslog/mail.log
kern.err      @saturn
*      /var/adm/messages
*.emerg      *
*.alert;auth.warning      root
```

These example configuration file entries log messages as follows:

1. Log all kernel messages to the system console.
2. Log all notice (or higher) level messages and all mail system messages except debug messages into the file /var/adm/syslog/mail.log.
3. Forward kernel messages of error severity or higher to the syslogd on host saturn.
4. Log all messages into the /var/adm/messages file.
5. Inform all logged-in users of any emergency messages and inform the root user, if logged-in, of any alert message or any warning message (or higher) from the authorization system.

3.1.1.4.2 /etc/syslog_evm.conf

The /etc/syslog_evm.conf file specifies which syslog messages to forward to the event manager (evm). Entries in this file have a format of facility.priority[+]. These facilities and priorities are roughly the same as for syslog.conf. The optional plus sign (+) indicates that if the priority is higher than listed it is also forwarded; otherwise, only the priority specified is forwarded.

Consider this fragment of an /etc/syslog_evm.conf file:

```
*.emerg
kern.info+
user.notice
```

All emergency messages are forwarded; kernel messages of informational priority and higher are forwarded; and user-generated messages with the priority of notice (but no other priorities) are forwarded.

3.1.1.4.3 /etc/syslog.auth

Finally, the local syslogd does not accept syslog messages from just any remote host. If a remote host is not listed in the /etc/syslog.auth configuration file and the file exists, syslog messages from that host are ignored. If the file does not exist, syslogd will accept messages from any host. It should be noted that the /etc/syslog.auth file is not created at installation time, so the default behavior is to allow all remote hosts to forward syslog messages. The format of this file is simply a list of fully qualified remote host names, one per line:

```
sunny.abc.com
cloudy.xyz.com
```

A local host with these entries would accept syslog messages from both sunny.abc.com and cloudy.xyz.com.

Configuration Tip

Make sure any system name used in the syslog.auth file is present in the hosts file in case of name resolver problems. If your DNS server became unavailable, for example, this would allow syslogd to still accept system log messages from other hosts.

3.1.1.5 Default syslog.conf

When the syslog daemon starts, it looks for /etc/syslog.conf by default. Alternatively, a configuration file may be specified on the syslogd command line when starting the facility. For example, to start syslog with the configuration contained in /var/adm/syslog.txt, use the following syntax:

```
# /usr/sbin/syslogd -f /var/adm/syslog.txt
```

If the syslog configuration file is absent, syslog defaults to these message rules:

```
*.err      /dev/console
*.panic    *
```

These defaults instruct syslog to send all error messages to the console and all kernel panic messages to all logged-in users. No files are written.

3.1.1.6 Sending Messages to syslog from Scripts

Since syslog is the primary logging mechanism for the operating system, it occasionally makes sense to use syslog for generating custom messages from system administration or user scripts. The standard mechanism to send messages to syslog from a script or the command line is the logger(1) command. The logger command provides a handy command line interface to the syslog() routine. The tool's syntax allows specification of both the facility and severity; in addition, it provides the ability to specify either the text of the message to be logged or a file that contains the message text. For example, the following command entered on the command line

```
# logger -p user.debug "Program error"
```

will cause syslog to log the following message:

```
# tail /var/adm/syslog.dated/current/user.log
Jul 13 22:23:05 mightydog root: Program error
```

This message will end up in the destination specified in /etc/syslog.conf for the "user.debug" facility.severity pair.

Before you call support

If the system is not logging the expected messages to the syslog facility:

1. Is the syslog daemon running?
2. Do the /dev/log and /dev/klog device special files exist? Do they have the correct major and minor numbers?
3. Is there a problem with the configuration file /etc/syslog.conf? Does the file exist? Is the file correctly formatted?
4. When using the logger(1) command, can you successfully send a test message?
5. Is syslog properly configured to log messages of the facility and severity for which you are looking?

3.1.2 The Event Manager

The event manager (evm) is a Tru64 UNIX facility intended to simplify and unify event reporting from a variety of channels into a single source. It works in cooperation with older mechanisms, such as syslogd and binlogd. In this section, we will provide a brief overview of what evm is and how to use it.

The components that make up the evm facility are as follows:

1. *Events*—indications that something interesting happened
2. *Event channel*—a facility used to post or retrieve event information
3. *Event poster*—a component that posts an event to the evm daemon
4. *Event subscriber*—an entity interested in particular indications

The event manager begins to work whenever something interesting (known as an event) happens. A component creates an evm event package that describes what happened and posts the event to the evm daemon. The daemon receives the event and enhances it based on its template event database, and then sends the event to any subscribing clients that have registered an interest in this type of event. The subscribing client receives the event and may perform some action because of it. Additionally, the system administrator may use the evmget(1) command to look at the event.

The evm facility also uses a number of command line utilities, which can be used to show, retrieve, sort, and post events. There is also a SysMan evm interface, but it is not covered here. The five evm command line utilities are as follows:

1. *evmshow*—converts binary events into human-readable format
2. *evmget*—retrieves events
3. *evmsort*—sorts a stream of events
4. *evmwatch*—subscribes to a set of events
5. *evmpost*—posts events

3.1.2.1 evmshow

Perhaps the most used evm command line utility is the evmshow command. You must use this command to view the stored events because they are in binary format. To display the contents of an old log file, use a command such as

```
# evmshow /var/evm/evmlog/evmlog.20010606
```

To insert a timestamp, rerun the command specifying that a timestamp be included:

```
# evmshow -t "@timestamp @@" /var/evm/evmlog/evmlog.20010606
```

For details about the evm command line utilities, see the appropriate reference pages or the evm documentation.

3.1.2.2 evmget

The evmget command is used to retrieve a stream of binary evm events. The evmget command makes a connection to a child process of the evm daemon, the get-server, and, based on the authorization checks by the get-server, processes events for which the user is authorized. The output is usually passed to the evmshow command:

```
# evmget -f "[priority > 300]" |
evmshow -t "@timestamp @@"
```

This command retrieves all events for which the user is authorized that have a priority greater than 300, and displays them with a timestamp via the evmshow command. The -f switch (filter) allows the selection of only the desired events.

3.1.2.3 evmsort

Because events are likely to be in no particular order when evmget retrieves them, some sorting needs to be done along the way. The evmsort command, as the name implies, does just that. The evmsort command reads binary events and can be used in a pipeline with evmget. Build on the previous example by adding a sort:

```
# evmget -f "priority > 300]" |evmsort |
evmshow -t "@timestamp @@"
```

Consult the evmsort reference page for information on fine-tuning a sort based on different fields.

3.1.2.4 evmwatch

The evmwatch utility allows real-time viewing of events. Again, the output will be processed through evmshow, and you may use a filter to select only certain events (e.g., those with a priority greater than 300):

```
# evmwatch -f "[priority > 300]" |
evmshow -t "@timestamp @@"
```

There is no need for an evmsort in the pipeline because these events will be displayed as they occur. A timestamp will be displayed with any events.

3.1.2.5 evmpost

Finally, the evmpost utility, as its name implies, posts events to the evm daemon. It takes input in the form of a file or stream of event sources, converts it into the binary evm format, and posts it to the evm daemon for distribution. A simple example of this is posting a system administrator event indicating that a particular operation completed successfully:

```
# evmpost -a "Disk dsk42 was successfully replaced"
```

3.1.3 The Binary Error Log

As noted previously, syslog exists on all modern implementations of UNIX; however, the binary error log facility is unique to Tru64 UNIX. This facility (often called the binlog from the name of the associated daemon, binlogd) generates the binary error log. The binlog is a mechanism similar in functionality to syslog that collects and logs messages from the kernel. The binlog daemon logs hardware and software errors and operational events, such as system startups and shutdowns.

Obviously, these messages are of great interest to a system administrator, and understanding how to examine and interpret the binary error log is one of the keys to troubleshooting system problems successfully. The binlog facility has two components: the binlog daemon, /usr/sbin/binlogd, and the binlog configuration file, /etc/binlog.conf. In addition, because the resulting binary error log is not in a human-readable format, there are three utilities provided by HP to view and manipulate this log. In order of their chronological appearance as products, they are uerf(8), DECevent, and Compaq Analyze.

3.1.3.1 The Binary Error Log Daemon

The binary error log daemon, binlogd, is an executable system utility normally started at boot time and always running while the system is in multiuser mode. The binlogd utility reads messages sent to it from the system kernel. These messages can be informational only, warnings, or errors that need attention. The messages themselves are single lines, optionally containing a priority value indicating the severity of the message. Messages are received by binlogd from two sources. The Tru64 UNIX kernel submits messages to binlog via the device special file /dev/kbinlog. Additionally, binlog may receive messages from other systems via the network by means of a socket specified in the /etc/services file. The only reason for mentioning these two sources for messages is to identify places to check when troubleshooting binlog problems.

For example, if kernel messages are not being received into the binary error log, ensure that the /dev/kbinlog file exists:

```
# ls -l /dev/kbinlog
crw------- 1 root   system 31,0 Apr 24 22:11 /dev/kbinlog
```

If the file is missing or not correct (e.g., it's not a character-special file), simply recreate the kbinlog file:

```
# cd /dev
# ./MAKEDEV kbinlog
```

Similarly, if other Tru64 UNIX systems are sending binary error log messages to a particular system but the messages are not being logged, ensure that the /etc/services file exists and contains the following entry:

```
binlogd     706/udp
```

Also ensure that the /etc/binlog.auth file is properly configured (see section 3.1.3.3.2).

3.1.3.2 Starting and Stopping binlogd

The binary error log daemon, binlogd, is usually started at boot time by the binlog startup script, /sbin/rc3.d/S10binlog, which is actually a symbolic link to /sbin/init.d/binlog. The binlog daemon is started fairly early in the boot process because of its importance in the error-logging process. When binlogd starts, it creates the file /var/run/binlogd.pid. This file contains a single line with the PID of the binlogd process. This file can be used to obtain binlogd's PID when it is necessary to stop or restart binlogd.

For example, you could use either of these commands to terminate binlogd:

```
# kill `cat /var/run/binlogd.pid`
```

or

```
# /sbin/init.d/binlog stop
```

Running the binlog script with a "stop" will kill binlogd by using the "kill" command given above.

3.1.3.3 The binlog Configuration Files

The binlog facility has two configuration files: /etc/binlog.conf and /etc/binlog.auth. These files are read when binlogd starts up and reread when it receives a hang-up signal. Like the syslog configuration files, these files are text files.

3.1.3.3.1 /etc/binlog.conf

The binlog.conf file contains entries that specify the event code (Table 3.3), which is the source of the message, the message priority level (severe, high, or low), and the destination to which the binlogd daemon should send the message.

Table 3.3 *Available binlog Events*

Number	Description	Category
100	CPU machine checks and exceptions	Hardware
101	Memory	Hardware
102	Disks	Hardware
103	Tapes	Hardware
104	Device controllers	Hardware
105	Adapters	Hardware
106	Buses	Hardware
107	Stray interrupts	Hardware
108	Console events	Hardware
109	Stack dumps	Hardware
110	Generalized machine state	Hardware
113	Double error halt	Hardware
115	Uncorrectable environmental	Hardware
120	Reporting of correctables disabled	Hardware
195	StorageWorks command console (SWCC)	Hardware
198	SWXCR RAID controller event	Hardware
199	SCSI CAM events	Hardware
201	CI port-to-port driver events	Software
202	System communications services events	Software
203	Logical storage manager note	Software
204	Logical storage manager warning	Software
205	Logical storage manager continuation	Software

Table 3.3 *Available binlog Events (continued)*

Number	Description	Category
206	AdvFS domain panic	Software
250	Generic ASCII informational messages	Informational
300	ASCII startup messages	Operational
301	ASCII shutdown messages	Operational
302	Panic messages	Operational
310	Timestamp	Operational
350	Diagnostic status messages	Operational
351	Repair and maintenance messages	Operational
400	Filterlog event	Filter log

Each line of the binlog.conf configuration file contains a single entry. See Figure 3.2 for an example of the default /etc/binlog.conf file.

Figure 3.2 *An example /etc binlog.conf*

```
#
# binlogd configuration file
#
#format of a line:   event_code.priority         destination
#
# where: event_code  - see codes in binlog.h and man page, * =
all events
#        priority    - severe, high, low, * = all priorities
#        destination - local file pathname or remote system
hostname
#

*.*                        /usr/adm/binary.errlog

dumpfile                   /usr/adm/crash/binlogdumpfile
crdlog                     /usr/adm/binary.crdlog
```

Troubleshooting Tip

The syntax and format of the /etc/binlog.conf file must be followed exactly because the binlog daemon, like the syslog daemon, is unforgiving of configuration file errors. Within the binlog.conf file, event code and priority pairs must be separated from the destination by spaces or tabs. Blank lines and lines beginning with a pound sign (#) are considered to be comments and are ignored.

The first half of a binlog.conf entry specifies the event code and priority of messages for which the binlog daemon should watch. The event code and priority level must be separated by a period. In addition, an asterisk may be specified in place of both an event code and a priority, indicating that all event codes and all priorities, respectively, are to be logged.

The second half of a binlog.conf entry specifies the destination to which the binlog daemon will log the messages that match the event–code.priority criteria defined by the first half of the binlog.conf entry. There are two possible destinations for binlog messages:

1. *A file name that begins with a leading slash (/).* The binlog daemon will append messages to this file. Note that this file should be an ordinary file, because the resulting messages are logged in a binary format.
2. *A host name preceded by an "at" sign (@).* Appropriate messages are forwarded to the binlog daemon on the named host (if the named host's /etc/binlog.auth permits it). Because the binlog is a Tru64 UNIX facility, binlog messages can be forwarded only to other Tru64 UNIX systems.

A special binlog.conf entry is necessary for recovering error messages that may be pending in the kernel binary event log buffer in the event of a system crash. When a Tru64 UNIX system recovers from a system crash, the savecore(8) command recovers such pending messages from a system dump and places them in file /usr/adm/crash/binlogdumpfile. When binlogd starts, it looks for this file and, if it exists, processes any messages it contains, then deletes the file. The default binlog.conf entry to provide this functionality is

```
dumpfile      /usr/adm/crash/binlogdumpfile
```

The primary binary error log destination specified by the *.* event-code.priority pair is always appended to by binlogd. This binary.errlog file should be monitored and trimmed when necessary to avoid running out of disk space. Another reason to trim the binary.errlog periodically is to keep the log to a manageable size in order to reduce the time needed to retrieve information from the file. To trim the binary.errlog and save current entries, do the following:

```
# kill -USR1 `cat /var/run/binlogd.pid`
```

This renames the current binary.errlog to /usr/var/adm/binlog.saved/binary.errlog.saved and then creates a new version of the binary.errlog file. There is a prewritten crontab(1) entry to do this routinely. If you choose to use it, log in as root, run `crontab -e`, and remove the comment character # from the entry:

```
#0 2 1 * * kill -USR1 `cat /var/run/binlogd.pid`
```

Note that the binary.errlog is a context dependent symbolic link (CDSL) and must not be deleted. For more information about CDSLs, see the hier(5) reference page.

Troubleshooting Tip

The /etc/binlog.conf file should not be world-writable. The appropriate permissions level on this file is 755 (i.e., readable and executable by everyone and writable only by the owner, who is user bin).

3.1.3.3.2 /etc/binlog.auth

The local binlogd does not accept binlog messages from just any remote host. If the /etc/binlog.auth file doesn't exist, is empty, or contains no valid remote host names, binlogd will not accept forwarded messages from any other host. If the file does exist, binlogd will accept messages only from the listed hosts. The format of this file is simply a list of fully qualified remote host names, one per line:

```
sunny.abc.com
cloudy.xyz.com
```

A local host with these entries would accept binlog messages from both sunny.abc.com and cloudy.xyz.com.

3.1.3.4 Default binlog.conf

When the binlog daemon is started, it looks for the /etc/binlog.conf by default. An alternate configuration file may be specified on the command line when starting binlog. The default /etc/binlog.conf file delivered with the operating system (Figure 3.2) is usually sufficient for most systems. In this configuration, all event classes and severity levels are logged to /var/adm/binary.errlog.

3.1.3.5 Examining the Binary Error Log

As mentioned previously, the log file generated by the binlog daemon is a binary file that is not directly human-readable. The format of the binary error log (binary.errlog) is such that the binlog daemon can quickly process and append events that it receives. An advantage of the binary error log's not being ASCII is that events can be extracted and sorted quickly by the HP-supplied tools. Three utilities are available for examining and manipulating the messages contained in the binary error log:

1. uerf(8), the UNIX Event Report Formatter
2. dia(8), the DECevent management utility
3. ca(8), the Compaq Analyze fault analysis utility

Each of these is discussed in greater detail in section 3.3.

3.2 Process-Level Reporting Facilities

Similar to their systemwide equivalents, several process-level error reporting facilities exist in Tru64 UNIX. These will be familiar to users coming from other modern UNIX operating systems. These facilities are generally utilized by programmers but can also be seen at the command line when using various utilities or tools. These process-level facilities include the following:

1. Standard error (stderr)
2. Errno

3.2.1 stderr

The standard error, or stderr, is the channel by which error messages are reported back to a process. For example, if you enter a command such as the following:

```
# cat bogus.file
cat: cannot open bogus.file
```

The resulting error message would not go to the normal standard output (stdout) but to another location—standard error. In this case, the standard error is the same as the standard output, so they go to the same place—the terminal. It is possible to redirect the errors from a utility to a different place from where the standard output goes, such as a log file. As an example of this concept, consider the following fictitious command entered at the Bourne shell command line:

```
# mydaemon > /dev/console 2> /var/adm/mydaemon.log
```

In this command, the standard output of the daemon is being sent to the console device, while the standard error (file decriptor 2) is directed into a log file.

3.2.2 errno

Usually, the first indication a user gets that something is wrong is an error returned after a system command or utility has been issued. When an error condition is encountered while executing a UNIX system call, the kernel returns a status back to the caller indicating whether the system call failed or succeeded. Successful execution of the system call generally returns a status of 0 to the caller, while an unsuccessful result usually returns a -1. A return status of -1 is an indication to the caller to check a global status variable called *errno* for further information about the failure.

As an example, consider the following fragment of code:

```
fd = open("/steve/test2", O_RDONLY, 0666);
```

In this case, an application or utility is using the *open(2)* system call to request that the UNIX kernel open a file to allow further operations such as a *read(2)* or *write(2)*. We won't go into the details of all the steps the kernel must go through, but the end result of the kernel's activity is to give a process-unique file descriptor number back to the application. If this number is a non-negative integer, it is assumed that the open() call succeeded and the returned number is a file descriptor. A status of -1 indicates that an error occurred. The above line of code does no error checking of the return status; therefore, the application might subsequently attempt to use an invalid file descriptor of -1.

A better way would be to check the return status from the open() call and print an error message to the standard error device as follows:

```
if((fd = open("/steve/test2", O_RDONLY, 0666)) < 0){
fprintf(stderr, "Could not open file /steve/test2.\n");
exit();
}
```

With this improvement, a user would know that an error occurred and would have some idea of what the problem was. We also have built into the application that we don't wish to continue unless we can successfully open the needed file. The problem now is that the error message doesn't tell the user anything about why the operating system couldn't open the file. There are a number of possible reasons why this could have happened—the file didn't exist, or the user didn't have permissions to open that particular file. This is where the errno facility comes into play. We'll make a third attempt to write this code fragment as follows:

```
if((fd = open("/steve/test2", O_RDONLY, 0666)) < 0){
fprintf(stderr, "Could not open file /steve/test2. Error
  number %d encountered.\n", errno);
exit();
}
```

This is by no means the best we can do to improve this code, but this may be typical of an error condition in a poorly written UNIX command or utility. Given this information, you might receive an error message from the application such as the following:

```
$ ./steve_test2
Could not open file /steve/test2. Error number 13
encountered.
```

This doesn't look very helpful, but if you know what to do, this information is enough to narrow down the nature of the problem. A list of possible error numbers is contained in the file /usr/include/errno.h. Look in this file for a better idea of the error:

```
$ grep 13 /usr/include/errno.h
#define EACCES          13          /* Permission denied */
```

Now you know that the problem was due to insufficient permission to access the file. Because the error message also indicates which system call was being used, you can check the reference page for the open() system call for more information to troubleshoot the problem.

```
$ man 2 open
ERRORS
  If the open() or creat() function fails, errno may be
  set to one of the following values:
[EACCES]
   Search permission is denied on a component of the path
   prefix, or the type of access specified by the oflag
   parameter is denied for the named file, or the file
   does not exist and write permission is denied for the
   parent directory, or O_TRUNC is specified and write
   permission is denied.
```

With this information, it was determined that the user did not have search permission on the file in question. Once this issue was corrected, the utility ran smoothly.

It is possible to get the errno from the shell prompt as well, rather than using a programmatic approach, such as the one shown above. For example, say the cat(1) command was used in an attempt to type out the contents of a nonexistent file:

```
# cat bogus.file
cat: cannot open bogus.file
# echo $?
2
```

In the Bourne shell, the result of the above echo command will be the errno of the immediately past failed system call. In this case, the value of 2 translates to ENOENT, which corresponds to "No such file or directory." Keep in mind that since there is only one variable, errno, it cannot hold a history of failed system calls. Therefore, if a command has more than one of these errors, the previous ones will not be saved. It is up to the tool creator to log these properly as shown above.

3.3 System Troubleshooting Tools

Some of the log files we've discussed so far would not be of much use without tools to read their contents and decode the output. This is certainly true of binary data logs, such as the binary error log file. In the next three sections, we will discuss the three tools available for decoding the Tru64 UNIX binary error log. Each has its own reason for being, because not all can be used for all classes of issues you may wish to examine in the log files for all system types. Following that, we will discuss some other tools available with Tru64 UNIX or from HP support: sys_check, allverify, and collect. Each tool is useful for solving different problems with Tru64 UNIX configuration or performance.

3.3.1 uerf

The uerf utility is a legacy part of the Tru64 UNIX operating system; it is a tool to translate the binary error log produced by the binlog daemon into human-readable output. When executed with no options, the uerf command simply reads the file specified as the destination for the *.* entry in the /etc/binlog.conf file (typically /var/adm/binary.errlog) and displays, each entry in chronological order, oldest events first. This default ordering is not tremendously useful because the most recent events are usually the ones of immediate interest, especially when investigating a problem. A commonly specified command line switch, -R, outputs the records in reverse chronological order, showing the most recent events first.

The binary.error log file is owned by root and belongs to the adm group, and the default permissions level is 640. If you want to use the uerf command to translate the default binary.errlog, you must belong to the adm group or be the root user. Optionally, you can change the ownership or permissions to allow others to access this file via the uerf command. For instance, to allow all users to read the file:

```
# ls -lL /var/adm/binary.errlog
-rw-r-----    1 root     adm      323016 Apr 24 22:41
/var/adm/binary.errlog
# chmod 644 /var/adm/binary.errlog
# ls -lL /var/adm/binary.errlog
-rw-r--r--    1 root     adm       23016 Apr 24 22:41
/var/adm/binary.errlog
```

[Note: the L switch was used above because the file is a context dependent symbolic link (CDSL). These symbolic links are used in Tru64 UNIX V5 and later to keep member-specific files (e.g., log files and configuration files) distinct among members in a cluster where the file system is shared. Using the L tells ls to follow the link instead of reporting on the link itself.] This change will persist across reboots as long as the file is not removed or renamed, in which case the binlogd will recreate the file with the original default permissions. There is probably no good reason to allow world access to the binary.errlog, but it can be done.

Because the binary.errlog contains all binlog events since the binary.errlog was started, sorting out useful information would seem at first glance difficult. However, by using several of uerf's command line parameters, you can view only certain types of events, events related just to particular devices, events in a specified time range, or event summaries categorized by quantity. Additionally, because uerf's output can be many pages, piping this output to a favorite pager, such as more(1) or pg(1), is recommended. Some commonly used uerf commands include the following:

1. Display the most recent system startup events, including the system configuration information:

   ```
   # uerf -R -r 300 | more
   ```

2. Show a summary report of all events in the binary.errlog:

   ```
   # uerf -S
   ```

3. Show all events between 8:00 A.M. on February 18, 2003 and 6:00 P.M. on February 20, 2003:

```
# uerf -t s:18-feb-2003,8:00 e:20-feb-2003,18:00
```

4. Show all events from a backup binary.errlog:

```
# uerf -R -f /var/adm/binary.errlog.old
```

5. Show all memory-related events, such as single-bit corrected read errors and double-bit uncorrectable errors, in reverse chronological order, with the most detailed output:

```
# uerf -R -M mem -o full
```

These, along with the many other uerf command line parameters detailed in the uerf reference page, can be combined (as in the last example above) to narrow the search query further. All specified parameters are combined together using a logical AND by uerf when determining matching events. Basically, the uerf command allows the system administrator to query the binary.errlog for the records of interest. For example, if you suspect a particular disk is beginning to fail, keep a watch on the binary error log for events from that disk. One possibility would be to run the following uerf command via cron(8) each night before midnight to e-mail you the disk-related events that have occurred since the previous midnight:

```
uerf -R -D -t s:00:00
```

Useful though it may be, the uerf command does not provide absolutely every useful piece of information that exists in the binary error log, although specifying the -o full command line switch does provide more detailed output. The uerf command's main advantage is that, to this point, it exists on all Tru64 UNIX systems. To address uerf's translation shortcomings, a more advanced tool was created to replace uerf: DECevent.

The uerf utility will not provide useful information for newer architecture Alpha systems and should not be counted on for accuracy. Compaq Analyze is the best tool for analyzing these newer formatted files.

3.3.2 DECevent

DECevent is an optional product available directly from HP technical support, on the Tru64 UNIX Associated Products CD-ROM, or downloadable from the HP DECevent Web page at http://www.support.compaq.com/svctools/decevent/.

According to the Web page, "DECevent is a rules-based hardware fault management diagnostic tool that provides error event translation. During translation, the binary portion of an event log is transformed into human-readable text. These events can then be displayed on the screen or printed." In essence, DECevent is simply a better uerf(8). DECevent, or dia(8) as the DECevent executable is called, has a command syntax similar to uerf's and reads the same binary.errlog as uerf. See the dia(8) reference page for the differences. The output from DECevent is more detailed than the equivalent uerf output. Although much of the DECevent output is unintelligible to the average person, it provides a level of detail that HP field engineers and technical support specialists need to identify and resolve problems quickly.

To diagnose problems on the Alpha EV6–based and later platforms, Compaq Analyze must be used. The exception to this rule is that DECevent will work on the AlphaServer GS60 and GS140 systems.

3.3.3 Compaq Analyze

Compaq Analyze (CA) is another optional product on the Associated Products CD. You can find out more about Compaq Analyze by visiting the CA Web page at http://www.support.compaq.com/svctools/webes/ca/ca.html.

To quote the Web page, Compaq Analyze is "a rules-based hardware fault management diagnostic tool that provides error event analysis and translation." Compaq Analyze is a replacement for both uerf and DECevent. CA does both bit-to-text (BTT) translation and multievent correlation analysis.

CA reads the same binary.errlog that uerf and DECevent read, but uses different command syntax and a different translation and analysis engine. The idea behind this new syntax is that once one is familiar with CA, it does not matter whether the platform is UNIX, OpenVMS, Windows NT, or some newly added operating system; the command is the same. There are currently three syntax flavors of CA on Tru64 UNIX: the old common syntax, a DECevent-like syntax, and the new common syntax. The default syntax is configurable, and this setting is systemwide. To set the default CA syntax for your system, use the command

```
ca syntax n|u|x
```

where n is for the new common syntax, x is the old common syntax. and u is for the UNIX-like DECevent syntax.

Whether you use uerf, dia, or CA, the concept is the same. The tool translates the binary error log into something that can be understood by a system administrator or support specialist. You should use the most recent tool that's compatible with your system type—that is, use ca on all new systems and dia on most pre-EV6 Alphas. Also, CA and dia have the added functionality of analysis. Table 3.4 lists some of the more useful CA commands and their dia equivalents and describes what they do.

Table 3.4 *Useful ca and dia Commands*

Desired Output	CA Command	DIA Command
Bit-to-text output in reverse order	`ca tra rev`	`dia -R`
Summary of events	`ca sum`	`dia -o summary`
Provide analysis of events	`ca ana`	`dia ana`
Specify alternate binary.errlog for bit-to-text formatting	`ca tra input <filename>`	`dia -f <filename>`

In addition to the CA command line interface, there is a GUI-based interface that you can access by Web browser. See the documentation for instructions on setting up your browser. Point your browser to port 7902 for the system that you wish to analyze, for example: http://sunny.abc.com:7902.

From this view, you can see both an analysis of events from the binary error log as well as a full view of the BTT translation. Compaq Analyze is part of a suite of service tools from the Web-Based Enterprise Services (WEBES) kit. This kit also includes the Compaq Crash Analysis Tool (CCAT) and the Revision and Control Management Tool (RCM).

Some of the WEBES tools communicate with a new daemon, desta (distributed enterprise service tools architecture), or the Director daemon. If CA is installed, desta monitors the system log files for new events to translate or analyze. It also responds to manual analysis. If CCAT is installed, desta automatically processes new crash dump files during the boot process. It also responds to manual crash dump analysis commands.

3.3.4 sys_check

The sys_check(8) tool was originally developed to gather essential system information for use by HP technical support in diagnosing problems with a Tru64 UNIX system. By default, the tool creates an HTML-formatted document containing a summary of the information found and hyperlinks to various types of system information. The tool can also gather more detailed logs, system configuration files, and even crash dumps, if they exist. To run sys_check and gather all the configuration and log files, use the following command:

```
# sys_check -escalate
```

This data is useful not only to HP support, but to a system administrator as well. It can be useful when diagnosing a problem with the system. The HTML document may also provide some parameter adjustment suggestions for improving system performance. As with any tuning suggestion, you should understand the implications of making the change beforehand. Any tuning change undertaken blindly has a potential for disaster and is highly discouraged. If you have any questions about tuning suggestions, we recommend calling HP technical support.

Troubleshooting Tip

sys_check data is gathered into a large compressed tar file. We suggest running this tool periodically and archiving the data so that historical comparisons can be made. This is often useful when you want to see the state of the system at some point in the past and compare it with the current state. For example, if a daemon began misbehaving at a certain time, you could go back to the sys_check data and look at the configuration file when the daemon was working properly and compare it to the current version of the file.

3.3.5 allverify

In the past, the only tool available with the Tru64 UNIX operating system that you could use to verify the integrity of a software subset was fverify(8). This tool is still available today, but it has some serious limitations. First, it will verify only a single software subset at a time; with possibly hundreds of subsets installed, it is difficult to check an entire system. Second, because fverify works only on a single subset, it cannot know whether a file is legitimately patched using the dupatch utility. This could lead to false indications that a file is corrupted or of unknown origin. Third, fverify checks ownership and mode for a given file based on the information in a subset's inventory, but it doesn't check whether these characteristics were changed by the subset's postinstall script. This could lead to a false indication that a file's mode or ownership information is incorrect. Finally, fverify does not correctly handle the CDSLs commonly used in Tru64 UNIX version 5.

The allverify tool is a TCL script available from HP technical support that addresses the limitations of fverify. You can use the allverify tool to determine whether all of the subsets currently loaded on your system are installed correctly, with a high degree of assurance that errors reported really are incorrect files on a system. The script allows files to be marked as "volatile," meaning that it won't report whether the file has changed from the originally installed version. This is useful for files, such as the password file, that are known to change frequently. A typical command to check your system without making changes and producing verbose output would look as follows:

```
# allverify -nv
```

When you get this tool from HP support, it comes with a reference page that explains all the available options and how they work.

3.3.6 Collect

It is important to understand what is considered normal activity on the system, so that abnormal behavior can be compared with it. In such cases, a baseline of previous performance levels is invaluable in putting a new performance problem in perspective. The collect(8) utility, if configured to run automatically, is a performance-monitoring tool that collects system performance information. In addition, there is a GUI, called collgui, that you can run against collected data to get a quick picture of historical system performance. The collect utility itself is available on patched V4.x systems and is standard on V5.0A systems and later. The collgui tool is in a separate kit and is not officially supported by HP; however, it is very useful in visually tracking performance trends. The collgui kit can be obtained from the following location:

```
ftp://ftp.digital.com/pub/DEC/collect
```

To turn on the autorun feature of collect so that it survives reboots and keeps a historical record of the system's performance, execute this command as root:

```
# rcmgr set COLLECT_AUTORUN 1
```

You might be concerned that collect will impact the system's performance. Because collect is a very lightweight tool and tunable as far as its collecting interval and the specific statistics that it monitors, it typically takes less than 1 percent of the system CPU. It can also be configured to suspend and resume operation based on the amount of free disk space, so you do not have to be overly concerned about storage space for the compressed data files. In addition, the collect utility is not just a tool that produces historical data. You can also use collect on a live system with a command such as the one shown below. This command will run at an interval of 2 seconds and will report only on the selected subsystem "disk."

```
# collect -i 2 -s d
Initializing (2.0 seconds) ... done.

#### RECORD    1 (990531569:0) (Tue May 22 06:39:29 2001) ####

# DISK Statistics
#DSK      NAME  B/T/L    R/S RKB/S  W/S WKB/S   AVS   AVW  ACTQ   WTQ  %BSY
   0      dsk0  0/0/0      0     0    0     0  0.00  0.00  0.00  0.00  0.00
   1   cdrom0  1/0/0      0     0    0     0  0.00  0.00  0.00  0.00  0.00
   2      dsk1  5/1/0      0     0    0     0  0.00  0.00  0.00  0.00  0.00
   3      dsk2  5/2/0      0     0    0     0  0.00  0.00  0.00  0.00  0.00
   4      dsk3  5/3/0      0     0    0     0  0.00  0.00  0.00  0.00  0.00
   5      dsk4  5/4/0      0     0    0     0  0.00  0.00  0.00  0.00  0.00
   6      dsk5  5/5/0      0     0    0     0  0.00  0.00  0.00  0.00  0.00

#### RECORD    2 (990531571:0) (Tue May 22 06:39:31 2001) ####

# DISK Statistics
#DSK      NAME  B/T/L    R/S RKB/S  W/S WKB/S   AVS   AVW  ACTQ   WTQ  %BSY
   0      dsk0  0/0/0      0     0    0     0  0.00  0.00  0.00  0.00  0.00
   1   cdrom0  1/0/0      0     0    0     0  0.00  0.00  0.00  0.00  0.00
   2      dsk1  5/1/0      0     0    0     0  0.00  0.00  0.00  0.00  0.00
   3      dsk2  5/2/0      0     0    0     0  0.00  0.00  0.00  0.00  0.00
```

```
4     dsk3  5/3/0     0     0     0     0  0.00  0.00  0.00  0.00  0.00
5     dsk4  5/4/0     0     0     0     0  0.00  0.00  0.00  0.00  0.00
6     dsk5  5/5/0     0     0     0     0  0.00  0.00  0.00  0.00  0.00
```

3.3.7 Auditing

Tru64 UNIX has a built-in tool that is very useful for troubleshooting programs that you can't debug because no source code is available. It is sometimes useful to look at the system calls (and their results) that a program is executing to help narrow down the reason a program is failing.

As an example, let's consider a problem where a program is generating an error message that doesn't seem to correspond with what the kernel is returning to the shell:

```
# df /.
Filesystem   512-blocks       Used   Available Capacity  Mounted on
/dev/rz3a        253374     252678           0    111%    /
# cp /vmunix /tmp/1.8
/: write failed, file system is full
cp: /tmp/1.8: No space left on device
# echo $?
1
```

This return value corresponds to errno 1, which is EPERM:

```
# grep EPERM /usr/include/errno.h
#define EPERM            1               /* Not owner */
```

However, based on the error message coming from the cp program, one would expect the error to be ENOSPC, which is errno 28:

```
# grep ENOSPC /usr/include/errno.h
#define ENOSPC           28               /* No space left on device */
```

So why don't these two results agree? With auditing enabled, this question can be easily answered. Examining the audit log would reveal the following:

```
# audit_tool `auditd -q` -e exec -e write:0:1 -e exit
audit_id:    0              ruid/euid:   0/0
```

```
pid:          517         ppid: 506                cttydev: (6,0)
event:        execve
char param:   /sbin/cp
char param:   cp /vmunix /mnt/mfs
inode id:     38712       inode dev:    (19,50)    [regular file]
object mode:  0755
result:       0
ip address:   16.140.128.93 (slug.zk3.dec.com)
timestamp:    Fri Aug  2 13:17:48.82 2002 EDT


audit_id:     0           ruid/euid:    0/0
pid:          517         ppid: 506                cttydev: (6,0)
procname:     /sbin/cp
event:        write
inode id:     3           inode dev:    (255,1)    [regular file]
object mode:  0755
descriptor:   /mnt/mfs/vmunix (4)
error:        No space left on device (28)
ip address:   16.140.128.93 (slug.zk3.dec.com)
timestamp:    Fri Aug  2 13:17:48.82 2002 EDT


audit_id:     0           ruid/euid:    0/0
pid:          517         ppid: 506                cttydev: (6,0)
procname:     /sbin/cp
event:        exit
result:       1
ip address:   16.140.128.93 (slug.zk3.dec.com)
timestamp:    Fri Aug  2 13:17:48.82 2002 EDT
```

From the audit log, we see that the error message obtained was indeed correct—but the error number returned to the shell was coming from the exit() call following the write() call. This example graphically illustrates the point made in section 3.2.2: the errno variable does not retain a history of errors; it retains only the error returned by the last failed system call.

3.4 Kernel Debugging Tools

There may occasionally be times when you'll need to get into the depths of your system's kernel in order to troubleshoot a tough problem. Fortunately,

Tru64 UNIX has some helpful tools available for analyzing the system at the kernel-data structure level. Naturally, to be successful at using these tools requires an internals-level knowledge and source code access that you may not have. If you don't, we recommend you acquire the necessary skills either by taking an internals class, reading an internals book, or consulting an expert.

Because we don't discuss system internals here, these tools may not be of much use to you even if you learn the syntax of the tool itself. One of the reasons you might need to use these tools is if your system experienced a panic and you want to try to analyze the resulting crash dump to determine what the problem was. Also, you may want to look at some kernel variables to determine whether kernel tuning may be necessary. We discuss these topics in Chapter 5, so please consult that chapter for more information on how to use these tools to perform those functions.

3.4.1 The dbx Debugger

The standard debugger that comes with Tru64 UNIX is called dbx. This has been the traditional debugger since the days of Ultrix, and it has changed little since then. It can be used for debugging user-level programs with an appropriate developer's license, or for debugging at the kernel level with no additional license required. Usually, in order to have useful data included in a program or kernel module for use when debugging, programs must be compiled with debugging information included by using the "-g" flag (same as the -g2 flag) to the C compiler. This option tells the compiler to include the maximum amount of symbol table information in the executable that can be used later for debugging. Without this information, the task of debugging an executable program is much more difficult and is akin to reading the program's disassembled raw instructions. Including this symbol table information comes at the cost of a larger executable.

The dbx debugger can be used to examine a program in one of two ways. First, you can use it to analyze a core file created from a program that received a signal that caused it to core dump. Many administrators find core files on their system and consider them a nuisance, because they appear only to take up space on the file systems and need to be cleaned up from time to time in order to conserve disk space. This is most likely true in the case of user directories where programmers develop and test their code. In that environment, it would be normal to find lots of core files from programs under active development.

A correctly functioning executable program should not produce a core file, so it should raise a red flag if you find core files in system directories. As most programmers know, a core file can be a useful diagnostic tool if you know what to do with it. If you find a core file in the root directory or another system directory, you should first try to determine the program that created the file:

```
# file /core
/core:  core dump, generated from 'lpd'
```

To examine a core file generated from the line printer daemon, you would use a command such as the following:

```
# dbx /usr/lbin/lpd /core
dbx version 3.11.10
Type 'help' for help.
Core file created by program "lpd"
warning: /usr/lbin/lpd has no symbol table -- very little
is supported without it

signal Segmentation fault at >*[__select, 0x3ff800d5758]
      beq     r19, 0x3ff800d5770
(dbx)
```

You can also use dbx to examine a running program. For example, to examine a system program named volnotify with a process identifier of 682, you would use a command such as the following:

```
# dbx -pid 682 /usr/sbin/volnotify
dbx version 3.11.10
Type 'help' for help.
warning: /usr/sbin/volnotify has no symbol table -- very
little is supported without it

stopped at>*[__poll, 0x3ff80112b28]     beq     r19,
0x3ff80112b40
(dbx)
```

Similar to the way you use dbx to analyze user programs, you can analyze either a running kernel or a crash dump. To use dbx to examine the kernel on a running system, you would use a command such as the following:

```
# dbx -k /vmunix /dev/kmem
```

Alternatively, to look at a crash dump with a file name of vmzcore.1 and with a kernel called vmunix.1, you would use this command:

```
# dbx -k vmunix.1 vmzcore.1
```

For example, if you wish to examine a kernel parameter named ubc_maxpercent, you can issue a command such as the following:

```
(dbx) print ubc_maxpercent
100
```

3.4.2 The Kernel Debugger

The kernel debugger, kdbx, is essentially the dbx debugger with a wrapper around it that provides some enhancements for looking at crash dumps and running systems. A typical kdbx command line to examine a running Tru64 UNIX system's kernel would be the following:

```
# kdbx -k /vmunix /dev/kmem
```

A similar command for examining a crash dump with a kernel name of vmunix.1 and a crash dump name of vmzcore.1 would be as follows:

```
# kdbx -k vmunix.1 vmzcore.1
```

For example, if you wish to examine the name cache entries, you can use the kdbx macro "namecache" as follows:

```
(kdbx) namecache
 namecache       nc_vp      nc_vpid  nc_nlen    nc_dvp          nc_name
=========== =========== ======= ======= ============ ====================
k0x00207f68  k0x0188c600 4756552      11   k0x01531400  resolv.conf
k0x00207fe0  k0x011f7200 4357353      10   k0x016a9e00  syslog.log
k0x00208058  k0x014cfa00     777       2   k0x0148a600  sh
k0x002080d0  k0x014cea00     954       3   k0x0185fc00  log
k0x00208148  k0x015dbc00 4747389      13   k0x011df400  stopping.html
```

3.5 Summary

This chapter provides an overview of the troubleshooting tools and facilities available to the Tru64 UNIX system administrator. It is vitally important to become familiar with these tools before problems occur, so you don't waste time when trying to work a real problem by still trying to understand how the tools work. With these tools and your available knowledge, in conjunction with the troubleshooting principles and techniques presented in the previous chapter, virtually any system problem can be solved.

4

User Accounts and Security

The problem is not that there are problems. The problem is expecting otherwise and thinking that having problems is a problem.

—*Theodore Rubin*

Problems affecting user accounts are among the most frequent to arise in system administration. The wide variety of such problems—and the fact that many of them are caused by a user's own actions—makes it necessary for an administrator to be familiar with their causes and solutions. In this chapter, we'll discuss the principal types of account problems and how to deal with them. This is not a comprehensive list of all possible user account problems; such a list would be impractically huge, if not impossible to produce. The problem areas covered here include the most common types of problems that an administrator might encounter. For other types of user account problems, the troubleshooting techniques presented in this and other chapters should at least provide a way to approach them.

Some types of user account problems, such as login and password problems, are greatly influenced by the system's security configuration. A system's security level (base security or enhanced security) often determines the correct method of troubleshooting a user account problem. Because these topics are so closely linked, we'll also discuss security-related problems in this chapter.

4.1 User Account Problems

The general term user account problems includes problems that prevent one or more users from accessing their accounts or using them effectively. These problem areas include the following:

- Login problems
- Password problems
- Shell problems

All three of these areas are discussed in the following sections, as are problems that a system administrator may encounter while performing account maintenance tasks.

There are a couple of general principles to keep in mind when troubleshooting user account problems. First, many of these problems can be caused by incorrect file ownership or permissions. For example, an administrator (in a misguided attempt to increase system security) might change the permissions on the root directory so that only the root user can access the directory. Such a change does indeed make the system more secure—so secure that only root can log in. This is because a login operation requires access to a number of system and user files. Access to a file in UNIX is determined not only by the permissions on the file itself; it also requires search (execute) access to all directories in the full path to the file. Because the root directory is in the path to every file on the system, restricting access to root effectively denies access to all other files and directories.

Incorrect file permissions can be an issue not only with the root directory, but with any important file or directory. For example, if user directories are located under /usr/users, incorrect permissions on any of the intermediate directories (/usr or /usr/users) will prevent access to a user's home directory, which will cause logins to that account to fail. In addition, a number of utilities (such as the login program) require the setuid permission bit to be set in order to perform certain privileged operations. Removing the setuid bit from utilities that need it is another mistake frequently made by administrators trying to increase system security.

Troubleshooting Tip

Incorrect ownership or permissions on system files can cause a variety of user account problems. Verify system files with the fverify(8) command or the allverify utility available from HP technical support.

These types of problems sometimes produce informative error messages that quickly reveal the problem, but in other cases the symptoms can be quite mysterious. In such cases, one of the first troubleshooting steps is to verify system software integrity with the fverify(8) or allverify(8) commands. (The allverify command is not part of the Tru64 UNIX distribution. It can be obtained from HP technical support.) However, these commands only check files that are listed in software subset inventories. Files or directories not listed in the inventories must be checked manually. These include locally defined directory structures and two key system files: the root directory and /etc/sia/matrix.conf. The root directory is created by the system installation process, while /etc/sia/matrix.conf is built from a prototype file. As such, neither is listed in any software subset inventory. The correct ownership and permissions for these two files are shown by the following:

```
drwxr-xr-x 30 root system 8192 Feb 12 09:50 /

-rw-r—r—    1 root bin    2185 Mar 8—08:07
/etc/sia/matrix.conf
```

The above example is from a system running Tru64 UNIX V5.1A. Prior to V5.0, /etc/sia/matrix.conf was a symbolic link that usually pointed to either bsd_matrix.conf or OSFC2_matrix.conf. On older systems, the ownership and permissions on the target file, rather than the symbolic link, are significant.

When troubleshooting user account problems, it's also important to pay close attention to the problem's range of effect. Does the problem affect one user, a group of users, or all users? As shown in Chapter 2, the range of effect is often a key piece of information in isolating the problem. Account problems affecting all users (possibly excluding root) are usually caused by permission issues or some other systemwide problem, whereas problems affecting only one user are most likely due to some problem with that particular account. Problems affecting some, but not all users are probably the most interesting. As shown in the example in Chapter 2, it's necessary to find the common element among the affected users in order to isolate the problem.

4.1.1 Login Problems

Most login problems are login failures. After a user enters a user name and password, the system denies access, usually with an error message. A distinctly different type of login problem is a login hang: after a user name or password is entered, the login session fails to respond at all. Because the troubleshooting methods are different for these two classes of login problems, we'll discuss them separately.

In this chapter, we discuss problems that occur when using nongraphical login methods: telnet, rlogin, or a serial terminal. Problems can also occur when logging in at a graphics console or via an X Windows connection. However, these problems are best attacked with the troubleshooting methods appropriate to graphical display problems, so they are covered in Chapter 12.

4.1.1.1 Login Failures

The most common type of login failure is entering an incorrect user name or password, either of which generates the familiar "login incorrect" message. When this error is encountered by a single user, it's usually just what it seems to be: the user has forgotten or mistyped the password. When a user consistently gets this error, verify that both user name and password are being entered properly. Novice UNIX users sometimes don't realize that user names and passwords are case sensitive, and the problem may be due to nothing more than the Caps Lock key being on. If the user is typing the user name and password correctly, the most likely explanation is that it's the wrong password. Try giving the user a new password, and then verify that the user can log in with the new one.

If the user still gets the "login incorrect" message with a new password, verify that the problem affects only that particular user. If it does, there may be a problem with the user's entry in the /etc/passwd file. The pwck(8) command will check the password file for consistency; in addition, beware of invisible characters, such as control characters, embedded in the password file entry. Examining the file with vi(1) or more(1) will display control characters (e.g. ^A for Control-A). Other utilities, such as cat(1) and grep(1), don't display such invisible characters.

Another possible cause of the "login incorrect" message is corruption in the hashed password database, which is discussed in greater detail in section 4.1.2.3. To check for this possibility, temporarily remove the hashed database by deleting or renaming two files in /etc: passwd.pag and passwd.dir. (If these files don't exist, you're not using the hashed database, so it can't be the problem.) If removing the two files enables the user to log in, it positively identifies the cause of the failure as hashed database corruption. To correct this, simply remake the hashed database with the following commands:

```
# cd /etc
# mkpasswd passwd
```

Even if hashed database corruption isn't the cause of the problem, you should remake the database if you removed it to perform this test, or system performance may suffer.

Under enhanced security, a login can fail with violation of any of numerous security parameters. These failures generate a variety of error messages, some of them more informative than others. We'll discuss these errors and how to fix them in section 4.2.3.

Troubleshooting Tip

Use the command "rcmgr get SECURITY" to determine the system security level. If this command returns "ENHANCED," the system is using enhanced security. If the command returns "BASE" or nothing, the system is using base security.

Login will also fail if the user's default shell can't be started. This is almost always due to one of two causes. The first possibility is that the shell program (e.g., /usr/bin/ksh) isn't executable because of incorrect permissions on the program file or any directory in its path. This problem generates the message "login: No shell: Permission denied." The second possibility is that the shell program is missing or corrupt, which results in the message "login: No shell: No such file or directory."

Interestingly, logins do not fail if the user's home directory is inaccessible, which most often occurs when the home directory is NFS mounted, although it can also be due to a permission problem or a disk going off-line, as in the example in Chapter 2. When this happens, the system will allow the login but will print the message "No directory!" and log the user in with the root directory as the current working directory. Because the home directory is inaccessible, the user's shell startup files are not executed. Some problems (e.g., overly restrictive permissions on the root directory) can cause both the shell program and home directory to be inaccessible. In this case, the system displays the "No directory!" message and terminates the login.

Software licensing is yet another area that can cause login failures. For nonroot users to log in, two licensing conditions must be met:

- There must be an active OSF-BASE, UNIX-WORKSTATION, or UNIX-SERVER license.
- There must be an active OSF-USR license with sufficient units to support the number of concurrent nonroot users.

If either of these conditions is not met, login will fail with the following message:

```
Too many users logged on already.
Try again later.
```

When this message appears, correct the licensing problem using the techniques described in Chapter 11.

Most of the preceding errors apply also to attempts to switch user ID with the su(1) command. There is an additional error that applies only to su—namely, attempts to switch user ID to root. The error message is "You do not have permission to su root." Unlike most other UNIX variants, Tru64 UNIX requires a user to belong to the system group in order to be able to su to root. When a user receives this error, one of the following is true:

- The user accidentally left off the user name argument from the su command (root is the default argument).
- The user should be in the system group, but isn't. To fix this, add the user to the system group, then have the user log out and log back in again.
- The user is trying to gain unauthorized privileges. The appropriate response to this situation is highly dependent on local policies.

One final login failure worth mentioning occurs only when root is trying to log in remotely (e.g., via telnet from another host). By default, Tru64 UNIX restricts root logins to the system console or the primary display on a system with a graphics console. Attempts to log in remotely as root fail with the error "root login refused on this terminal." Remote root logins are enabled by the file /etc/securettys; to allow root to log in via a network connection, add a line to the end of this file consisting of the string `ptys`. Similarly, if you have a terminal or modem connected to a serial port and you wish to enable logins from that port, add a line with the serial port's device name (e.g. "/dev/tty00"). The root account is obviously a prime target for remote attacks, so it is best to restrict root logins to the system console unless there is a real need for remote root logins.

Troubleshooting Tip

When connecting via telnet, a login failure usually terminates the connection immediately—before any error message can be displayed on the client end. This, unfortunately, loses valuable information and can make troubleshooting login failures via telnet a hit-or-miss proposition. On the other hand, rlogin connections don't close the connection until after the error message is received and displayed. As such, it's useful to try connecting via both telnet and rlogin in order to display any resulting error messages.

4.1.1.2 Login Hangs

When a user login hangs, it indicates that access to a needed resource (a file, directory, or program) within the login process is hanging. The first step in troubleshooting such problems is to determine which resource is the problem. If any of these resources is accessed via network, that's the best place to start looking. For example, if the network information service (NIS) is used to distribute password information, check for NIS problems. For a quick test, use the command "ypcat passwd | grep <username>," which displays the user's entry in the distributed password database. If this command also hangs, it strongly indicates a problem with NIS; see Chapter 7 for more information on troubleshooting problems with NIS or other network components.

Similarly, if users' home directories are accessed via NFS, test their accessibility outside the login process. Can you list the directory contents with ls(1) from the NFS client? If so, does "ls -l" also work? If either of these commands fails, repeat both checks on the NFS server itself. (It's important to try both, because "ls" with no arguments simply reads the directory structure, while "ls -l" actually does a check on each file within the directory.) If either command fails on the server, there's a problem with the directory or the device on which it resides. On the other hand, if the directory is accessible on the server but not from the client, then NFS is the culprit; once again, see Chapter 7 for information on troubleshooting NFS problems.

Logins can also hang if they're trying to access a particular resource, such as passwords, from the wrong source. Make sure that the /etc/svc.conf file is correctly set up for your system configuration. The /etc/svc.conf file on a system using NIS and BIND should contain the following lines:

```
aliases=local
auth=local
group=local,yp
hosts=local,bind,yp
netgroup=local,yp
networks=local,yp
passwd=local,yp
protocols=local,yp
rpc=local,yp
services=local,yp
```

For systems that don't use NIS, the "yp" fields should be absent. In addition, "bind" should never be present on any line other than "hosts." In all configurations, it's important that "local" be the first entry on the right side of each line; if it isn't, the system may try to use remote databases before using local databases, which can cause poor performance or login hangs.

If network access to resources is not an issue, make sure that local resources are accessible outside the login process. For example, can you open the password file with vipw(8)? Does "ls -l" work in the user's home directory? If attempts to access a file or directory result in an I/O error, there is most likely a real problem with the file or directory itself, the file system that contains it, or the underlying device. See chapters 8 and 9 for information on troubleshooting storage-related problems.

Another possibility is that an important file has been locked by another process. In such cases, you can use the fuser(8) command to list open files in key file systems—for example, /, /usr, /usr/users (if a separate file system)—and the file system that contains the user's home directory. On a busy system, this could produce a very large output, so the best bet is to redirect the output to a file and then use grep(1) or another tool to look for files that could be causing a problem. The fuser output will include the process ID of the process(es) using the file. With this information you can track down the processes involved and take appropriate action. For example, on a V5 system using enhanced security, you might see prpasswdd (the enhanced security daemon) with one or more of the authentication database files open. If prpasswdd has a problem, it can cause logins to hang or fail. This can usually be cleared up by restarting the daemon with the command "/sbin/init.d/prpasswd restart." (See section 4.2.1 for more details on prpasswdd.)

4.1.2 Password Problems

Apart from users forgetting their passwords—a problem that system administrators can't do much about—the main types of password-related problems are the following:

- Inability to change passwords
- Ineffectiveness (the password-change operation seems to work, but the password doesn't really change)
- Corruption of the hashed password database
- Missing or corrupted password file
- Lost or forgotten root password

We'll discuss each of these areas in turn in the following subsections.

4.1.2.1 Inability To Change Passwords

Under normal circumstances, nonprivileged users can change their own passwords, while the superuser can change any user's password. (Using enhanced security, it's also possible to deny users the ability to change their own passwords.) Some problems in this area affect both root and nonroot users, whereas others affect only nonroot users.

The most common cause of inability to change passwords is the existence of a lock on the password file. This situation produces the error message "password file busy—try again." In most cases, this is a temporary error caused by other users changing their passwords, default shell, or finger information. It can also be caused by a system administrator performing account maintenance, as described in section 4.1.4. If this error persists for more than a short time, use ps(1) to list the current processes on the system and check for commands likely to open the password file, such as passwd, chfn, and chsh. If this doesn't help, another possibility is to use the fuser(8) command as described in section 4.1.1.2.

Nonprivileged users will be unable to change local (non-NIS) passwords if the passwd(1) command has the wrong ownership or permissions. The correct values are shown in the following:

```
-rws--x--x 3 root   bin   33024 Aug-1-2001
/usr/bin/passwd
```

The same problem can occur when using dxchpwd(1X), the GUI for changing passwords under Enhanced security. The correct values for this program are as follows:

```
-rwsr-xr-x 1 root   bin   33024 Aug-1-2001
/usr/tcb/bin/dxchpwd
```

Under Enhanced security, a user's ability to change passwords may be restricted or even eliminated. One possible restriction is to specify a minimum time between password changes. This is to prevent users from defeating the password expiration feature by rapidly changing passwords enough times to fill up their password history and then returning to the original password. If a user attempts to change passwords before the minimum time has elapsed, the result is an informative error message:

```
Password not changed: minimum time between changes has
not elapsed
```

Enhanced security can also be configured to prevent users from choosing their own passwords. In this case, users must accept system-generated passwords, which can be configured for various options (pronounceable pseudowords, random letters, or random alphanumeric characters). Restrictions can also be placed on user-selected passwords. These restrictions include defining the minimum and maximum length as well as checking for "trivial" passwords: palindromes, login names, group names, and all words defined by the spell(1) program. An additional site-specific password policy (e.g., requiring passwords to include at least two numbers and three letters) can also be used. Attempting to select a password that violates any of these format restrictions will result in an error message that explains why the password isn't a valid choice. The "solution" in this case is to have the user choose a password that satisfies the local password requirements.

4.1.2.2 Ineffective Password Changes

Occasionally, users will attempt to change passwords and appear to succeed. However, the new password doesn't work. Experimentation shows that the user's old password is still in effect. This is almost always caused by a failure to update the hashed password database. This database consists of two files—/etc/passwd.pag and /etc/passwd.dir—that organize the information in /etc/passwd into a more efficient format for searching by system routines. Without the hashed password database, the system must perform a sequential search of the password file. This can lead to significant performance degradation on systems with a large number of users.

Utilities such as dxaccounts, vipw, passwd, and usermod normally recreate the hashed database to reflect the updated password file. (However, editing /etc/passwd with vi does not.) But if the modification time on /etc/passwd.pag is in the future, the hashed database appears to be current and is not updated. System routines will continue to use the old information in the database, making it appear that the change did not take. Also, if the hashed database is corrupted, it may not be updated properly, leading to similar symptoms.

If a password change appears to be ineffective, try removing the hashed database files (/etc/passwd.pag and /etc/passwd.dir) temporarily. Try the new password again; if it works, this verifies that the hashed database was the cause of the problem. You can then recreate the hashed database with the following commands:

```
# cd /etc
# mkpasswd passwd
```

After recreating the database, verify that the new password continues to work.

4.1.2.3 Password Database Corruption

As noted in the previous section, corruption of the hashed password database (or an incorrect timestamp on it) can cause password changes to appear to be ineffective. This is also true of other account maintenance tasks; if the hashed database is not updated properly, the change may not appear to have worked. The remedy for this type of problem is the one given in the previous section: recreate the hashed password database.

It's important to note that corruption of the hashed password database can have other, more far-reaching effects. Because the hashed database is used to translate user names to UIDs, corruption can cause files to appear to belong to the wrong user, or just to a numeric UID. In a worst-case scenario, root may not be properly identified as UID 0. This will cause root to lose its ability to perform privileged functions—among them, removing and recreating the hashed database. In such cases, it may be necessary to boot the system from an alternative disk or installation CD-ROM, mount the normal root file system on /mnt, and remove the hashed database files in the /mnt/etc directory.

4.1.2.4 Missing or Corrupted Password File

The previous section discussed corruption of the hashed password database. What about corruption of the password file itself? An incorrect password file entry can cause a wide variety of errors. Fortunately, Tru64 UNIX includes three utilities to verify the integrity of user account information. The pwck(8) and grpck(8) utilities check the password and group files, respectively, while authck(8) checks the enhanced security authentication database. For example, pwck checks each entry in the password file for the proper number of fields; verifies that the user name, UID, and GID are valid; and checks for the existence of the user's home directory and default shell. These utilities can be extremely helpful in tracking down user login problems. It's also a good idea to run them periodically as part of regular system maintenance.

If the password file is missing or the root entry is corrupt, the situation is more serious. When this happens, it is necessary to boot the system from another disk or an installation CD-ROM, mount the root file system on /mnt, and restore the password file from backups. If a good recent backup is not available, /etc/.new..passwd contains a bare-bones password file with a null password for the root account. This file can be copied to /mnt/etc/passwd, after which you can boot to single-user mode from the regular boot disk. At this point you can change the root password and, if necessary, recreate other user accounts.

4.1.2.5 Lost or Forgotten Root Password

If the root password is forgotten or lost, the only recourse is to break into the system and reset the root password. This requires access to the system console and the ability to halt and reboot the system to single-user mode. It is necessary to halt the system because only the superuser can gracefully shut down the system, and in this situation, the root account is inaccessible. If the system is in secure console mode, the process of breaking in becomes more difficult. Secure console mode requires the root password to be entered when the system enters single-user mode. Because the root password is unknown, you can't just boot to single-user mode and change the password. In this case, it's necessary to boot from another device, such as a Tru64 UNIX Installation CD-ROM, mount the normal root file system, disable secure console mode, and then boot (from the regular root disk) to single-user mode.

The procedure to reset the root password is as follows:

1. Halt the system, either by pressing the HALT button or, on some system types, typing the Control-P (^P) key combination from the console. This brings the system to the console prompt, which is usually something like ">>>."

2. If the system console is secured with a password, enter the console password:

   ```
   >>> LOGIN
   Please enter the password: <enter the console
   password>
   ```

3. If you know that the system is not in secure console mode, proceed to step 10. If you're not sure, go ahead and proceed to step 10 anyway; if you get a password prompt when the system reaches single-user mode, you'll know that the system is in secure console mode, and you can then return to step 4.

4. Insert a Tru64 UNIX Installation CD-ROM in the CD-ROM drive and boot the system from that device. Substitute the appropriate device name for DKA400 in the following command:

   ```
   >>> BOOT DKA400
   ```

5. When the installation software starts up, exit to a shell window. If you are using a serial terminal as the console, select option 3 (Exit

Installation). If you are using a graphics console, pull down the File menu and select Shell Window.

6. Mount your root file system. If the root file system type is UFS, enter the following command (substitute the appropriate device name for dsk1a):

```
# mount /dev/disk/dsk1a /mnt
```

7. If the root filesystem type is AdvFS, you may need to create a temporary domain subdirectory and link it to the appropriate device. (If the installation process has already created the directory and device name link shown below, just skip those steps.) Again, substitute the appropriate device name for dsk1a:

```
# cd /etc/fdmns
# mkdir root_domain
# cd root_domain
# ln -s /dev/disk/dsk1a
# mount root_domain#root /mnt
```

8. Edit the rc.config file on the root filesystem and change the value of the SECURE_CONSOLE setting to NO. If there is no SECURE_CONSOLE definition in /mnt/etc/rc.config, add the following line:

```
SECURE_CONSOLE="NO"
```

9. Unmount the root filesystem and halt the system to return control to the console:

```
# cd /
# umount /mnt
# halt
```

10. Boot the system to single-user mode:

```
>>> BOOT -FL S
```

11. When the system reaches single-user mode, mount the local file systems:

```
# /sbin/bcheckrc
```

12. Change the root password:

```
# passwd
New password: <enter the new password>
Retype new password: <enter the password again>
```

13. Resume booting the system to multiuser mode by typing the Control-D (^D) key combination.
14. Log in as root using the newly changed password to verify success.
15. If you changed the value of SECURE_CONSOLE in step 8, change it back to YES if you wish to continue using secure console mode.

4.1.3 Shell Problems

In this section, we'll discuss some problems with user shell environments. This is not a comprehensive guide for troubleshooting shell or script problems, which would be beyond the scope of this book; our intent is to cover common types of shell problems that affect a user's ability to log in and perform work. These include problems in the following areas:

- Shell login scripts
- Environment variables
- Process limits
- File and directory permissions

We'll discuss each of these in the following sections.

4.1.3.1 Shell Login Scripts

When a user logs in, the user's default shell (defined in /etc/passwd) automatically executes a number of startup scripts containing environment variables and commands. The first of these is a system-wide initialization file: /etc/profile for the Bourne and Korn shells, /etc/csh.login for the C shell. After the global login script, the shell executes the user's individual startup scripts. For the C shell, these are .cshrc and .login (in that order) in the user's home directory. The Bourne and Korn shells both execute .profile in the home directory; the Korn shell then executes the script pointed to by the ENV variable, if it is defined.

The purpose of these startup scripts is to create command aliases, define important environment variables, and perform other housekeeping functions, such as setting the terminal type. If an error occurs in one of the scripts, the user's environment will not be set up properly. If the error is a serious one, such as illegal command syntax, there will at least be an error message. However, if there is a problem where a command is legal but doesn't do what is intended, it can be a little harder to troubleshoot. A useful technique in this case (or in debugging any shell script) is to use the "-x" shell option, which is available in all of the standard shells. Setting this option (with "set -x") in a script file will cause the script to echo each command line after wildcard expansion and variable substitution, but before the command is actually executed.

A common mistake in shell login scripts is to use command syntax appropriate to a different shell. The C shell is significantly different from the Bourne and Korn shells; the latter two are a lot alike, but the Korn shell provides more flexibility and functionality. Something to be especially wary of is using Korn shell syntax in files that may also be read by the Bourne shell, such as /etc/profile. For example, to set an environment variable in /etc/profile, use the following syntax:

```
MANPATH=/usr/man:/usr/local/man; export MANPATH
```

rather than:

```
export MANPATH=/usr/man:/usr/local/man
```

In the Korn shell, both commands produce the same result. However, because the second is not a valid command in the Bourne shell, setting and exporting environment variables in one statement may cause an error at login and, more important, not achieve the desired result of setting the MANPATH environment variable.

4.1.3.2 Environment Variables

Many programs and system utilities use the values of certain shell environment variables. If a variable isn't set properly (either because a startup script terminated without setting it or because the wrong syntax was used), such programs won't function properly. For example, if the PATH variable is set incorrectly, the shell may not be able to locate a command that it tries to execute. Table 4.1 shows some of the common environment variables that may cause problems if not set properly. Some of these are set automatically by the shell, but others need to be defined in the user's login scripts.

Table 4.1 *Selected Shell Environment Variables*

Environment Variable	Description
DISPLAY	Default display for X Windows applications
EDITOR	Default editor
HOME	Home directory
LOGNAME	Login name
MAIL	Primary incoming mailbox (/usr/spool/mail/<username> by default)
MANPATH	List of directories that the man(1) command searches for man pages
PATH	List of directories to search for command executables
SHELL	Pathname of the shell
TERM	Terminal type
USER	User name
VISUAL	Default visual (full-screen) editor [e.g., vi(1)]

Environment variables (or rather the lack of them) can also be a problem with cron jobs. When cron runs a job, it does not execute the user's login scripts. Only a minimal environment is provided: the variables HOME, LOGNAME, SHELL, and PATH. If the command to be run requires other environment variables, it will not work properly. This problem can be avoided by defining the cron job as a shell script that executes the appropriate login script (e.g., ". $HOME/.profile" in sh/ksh or "source $HOME/.login" in csh) and then runs the desired commands.

4.1.3.3 Process Limits

A number of process resources are restricted by limits imposed by the command shell or the Tru64 UNIX kernel. If a process attempts to exceed one of these limits, it will fail with an appropriate error code, such as EMFILE (too many open files). Some of these errors are specific in indicating which limit has been reached, while others are more ambiguous. For example, ENOMEM (not enough memory) indicates that a memory-based limit has been reached (or possibly that the system is low on swap space). However, there are three memory-based limits: stack segment size, data segment size, and virtual memory size. Determining which of these has been exceeded requires knowing something about what the program is trying to do—or if nothing else, trial and error.

When a process exceeds one of the resource limits, the straightforward response is to raise the limit in question. The current process limits can be displayed by using the built-in shell commands "limit" (csh) or "ulimit" (ksh). Each limit has both a "soft" and a "hard" value. Soft limits can be raised, using the limit or ulimit command, up to the corresponding hard limit; hard limits, once set, cannot be increased. The limits for some resources—though not all of them—are derived from kernel parameters in the "proc" (process) subsystem. Table 4.2 contains information about each resource limit.

Table 4.2 *Process Resource Limits*

Resource	limit Field Name	ulimit Field Name	"ulimit" Switch	Derived from
CPU time	cputime	time	-t	(none)
File size	filesize	file	-f	filesystem type and quotas
Data segment size	datasize	data	-d	(soft) per_proc_data_size (hard) max_per_proc_data_size
Stack segment size	stacksize	stack	-s	(soft) per_proc_stack_size (hard) max_per_proc_stack_size
Core dump size	coredumpsize	coredump	-c	(none)

Table 4.2 *Process Resource Limits (continued)*

Resource	limit Field Name	ulimit Field Name	"ulimit" Switch	Derived from
Resident set size (physical memory in use)	memoryuse	memory	-m	Physical memory in system
Number of open files	descriptors	nofiles	-n	(soft) open_max_soft (hard) open_max_hard
Virtual memory size	addressspace	vmemory	-v	(soft) per_proc_address_space (hard) max_per_proc_address_space

A UNIX process includes a text segment, which contains executable code and other constants; a data segment, which contains defined data storage; and a stack segment, which contains the program stack. The data and stack segment sizes are limited as shown in Table 4.2, while the text segment is not specifically constrained. However, the *total* size of the text, data, and stack segments is limited by the virtual memory size limit. (There is one further constraint in older versions of Tru64 UNIX: the total size of the text, data, and stack segments, as well as all shared memory segments attached to the process, is limited by kernel parameter "vm_maxvas" in the vm subsystem. This limit was removed in V5.0.)

An additional limit (imposed by the kernel, not the shell) is the "max_proc_per_user" parameter in the proc subsystem. This parameter, which defaults to 64, defines the maximum number of processes that a nonprivileged user can execute at any one time. This limit prevents a nonprivileged user from accidentally or maliciously creating a huge number of processes, which could consume all of the system's available process slots. The default value of 64 is not enough for some applications; to increase it, change the value of max_proc_per_user with dxkerneltuner(8) or sysconfigdb(8), and then reboot the system.

There is also a hidden limit involving max_proc_per_user. Because a single user can't run more processes than the entire system is allowed to run at one time, max_proc_per_user can be no larger than the system maximum number of processes (minus 10, to reserve a few slots for system processes.) If you attempt to set max_proc_per_user higher than this amount, the system will quietly reset it to the maximum possible value. For example, if maxusers is set to 32 on a V5.0 system, the system can run a maximum of 1,024 processes. If you try to set max_proc_per_user to a higher number, say 10,000, the system will lower the value to 1,014 (1,024 minus 10) without providing any warning or error message.

4.1.3.4 File and Directory Permissions

Some elements of a user's account or shell environment can lead to problems performing operations on files or directories. The most common of these is incorrect permissions on newly created files. When new files are created by the shell or commands such as cp, the file's permission bits are based on the user's current file creation mask (umask). This mask is usually defined by executing the umask(1) command in the user's shell login script. The mask is an octal number indicating which permission bits will not be set for newly created files. For example, the command "umask 022" causes the group-write and other-write bits to be cleared. The remaining bits will be set depending on whether a regular file or a directory is being created. New directories have all user, group, and other permission bits set except those specified in the umask [i.e., the resulting permissions will be 777 (octal) minus the umask]. Thus, with a umask of 022, a new directory will have permissions of 755, or "rwxr-xr-x." However, regular files will not have any execute permission bits set; their permissions will be 666 minus the umask. With umask 022, the resulting permisions will be 644, or "rw-r—r—." This difference between regular files and directories is not common to other variants of UNIX, so it often trips up new Tru64 UNIX users.

The creation of regular files without execute permission bits is usually an issue only when creating shell scripts. Script files need execute permission to run, but when first created, they don't have it. As a result, it's very common for a user to create a new script, attempt to run it, have it fail with a "permission denied" message, and wonder what the problem is. When this happens, it is necessary to use the chmod(1) command to add execute permission to the file. However, setting the execute bits may fail because of the accidental setting of a kernel parameter. This parameter, noadd_exec_access in the vfs subsystem, provides an additional level of security for highly secure systems such as firewalls. When noadd_exec_access is set to 1, non-root users cannot add execute permission to their files; this is to prevent the introduction of Trojan horse programs. Although this feature is disabled by default, it's easy to set it accidentally while running the security configuration utility, secconfig. On secconfig's System Configuration Options menu, the option "Execute bit set only by root" is the middle of three options. Because the options on either side are checked by default, some administrators check the middle option as well without fully understanding the consequences. When this happens, there are two ways to disable the feature and enable nonroot users to set execute permission bits:

1. Run "sysman secconfig," clear the "Execute bit set only by root" option, exit secconfig, and reboot the system.
2. Using sysconfigdb(8), change the "noadd_exec_access = 1" line in /etc/sysconfigtab to "noadd_exec_access = 0," then reboot.

Users sometimes have problems performing operations on files because they don't understand the way permissions affect directories. As mentioned earlier, in order to access any file, a user must have the appropriate access to the file itself, as well as search (execute) access on every directory in the path to the file. It's also necessary to have search access to a directory in order to set it as the current directory with cd. However, to list the contents of a directory or perform wildcard operations on its files, read access to the directory is required. A common error is trying to access a file in a directory that has read access, but not execute access. Table 4.3 shows the effects of the four possible combinations of read and execute access on a directory.

Table 4.3 *Effects of Read and Execute Permission Bits on Directories*

Read	Execute	Allowable Operations
No	No	None
Yes	No	List directory contents; perform wildcard operations
No	Yes	cd to directory; access files in directory
Yes	Yes	All of the above operations

On a similar note, it seems straightforward to most users that they can't create a new file in a directory unless they have write access to the directory. However, it may not be so obvious that write access to the directory is required to delete or rename a file—even if the user has write access to the file itself. This is because deleting a file removes its directory link, while renaming a file requires modifying its link. Because both operations require writing to the directory structure, write access to the directory is necessary.

One last file-related problem occurs when users try to perform wildcard operations on large numbers of files. Because the shell expands all wildcards before executing a command, a large number of files can cause the expanded command to exceed the maximum shell command length, which is 38,912 characters (ARG_MAX in /usr/include/sys/syslimits.h). This error generates the message "arg list too long." For example, the command "rm *" in a directory containing thousands of files is very likely to experience this problem. In some cases, this can be worked around; in this example, the command "rm -r ." would do the trick (assuming there were no subdirectories that should not be deleted) because the "rm -r" command would work its way through the directory structure rather than having all the file names expanded by the shell.

However, not all cases have a similar workaround; in these other cases, the find(1) command and possibly the xargs(1) command can be used. For example, if the desired result were to delete all files whose names start with the letter "a," the command "rm a*" would fail if there were too many such files. In this case, "rm -r" wouldn't help, because that would delete all other files as well. But the task could be accomplished in a couple of different ways with the find command:

```
# find -name 'a*' -exec rm {} \;
```

or

```
# find -name 'a*' | xargs rm—
```

Using xargs, as in the second example above, would probably be faster, but it might also run into a command-length limit. The first example, although slower, would work no matter how many files were involved.

4.1.4 Account Maintenance Problems

Account maintenance includes the tasks of adding, modifying, and deleting user accounts or groups. Problems with these tasks fall into two main areas:

1. Inability to perform the task (an error prevents the task from being completed)
2. Ineffectiveness (the task is performed, but the results are not as expected)

The latter problem is almost always due to the hashed password database not being updated properly or being corrupt. This problem is discussed in section 4.1.2.3.

The most common cause of inability to perform account maintenance is the existence of one or more lock files. Tru64 UNIX uses various lock files to prevent more than one person from modifying the password and group files at the same time, a situation that could lead to corruption of those files. For example, Account Manager creates a lock file named /etc/.AM_is_running. If this file exists when Account Manager starts up, it exits with a message such as "The password and group files are currently locked by another user." In recent versions of Tru64 UNIX, this message has become progressively more informative; in V5.1A, Account Manager will identify the lock file by name, attempt to list the process ID of any other Account Manager processes, and even offer the option to override the lock and proceed anyway.

If you encounter this error briefly, there is nothing to worry about. This indicates that another privileged user was already modifying the password file and the lock files are working as intended to prevent file corruption. However, if the error persists, there are two possibilities:

1. Someone was performing account maintenance and forgot to exit the program being used.
2. One of the account maintenance utilities did not exit normally (e.g., because of a system crash while it was running) and failed to remove the lock file it created.

The solution is to verify that nobody else is running Account Manager and then remove the lock file and try again.

In addition to /etc/.AM_is_running, there are a few other files whose existence can lock out some or all of the account management utilities:

```
/etc/passwd.dir.new
/etc/passwd.pag.new
/etc/passwd.ptmp
/etc/ptmp
/etc/ptmp.dir
/etc/ptmp.pag
/var/yp/src/passwd.AM_orig
/var/yp/src/passwd.ptmp
```

If you receive the "locked" message and /etc/.AM_is_running does not exist, check for the existence of the files listed above and remove any of them that you find.

4.2 Security Problems

One of a system administrator's primary concerns is preventing unauthorized access to the system. This is a broad topic that extends well beyond the scope of this book; for further information, see the references listed in Appendix A. As such, we won't discuss how to prevent or respond to break-in attempts. What we will discuss is problems relating to the Tru64 UNIX security configuration.

Most of the security-related problems seen in Tru64 UNIX involve the enhanced security level. This is not because enhanced security is particularly buggy (actually, it works very well) but because it contains a large number of features and options whose effects are sometimes unclear to users or administrators. In the following sections, we'll cover the following problem areas relating to Enhanced security:

- Authentication database problems
- Security configuration problems
- Login failures

4.2.1 Authentication Database Problems

Tru64 UNIX enhanced security stores all security information in a set of five databases collectively known as the authentication database. The five component databases and the types of information they contain are shown in Table 4.4.

Each component database contains a set of entries—for example, the protected password database contains one entry for each user account on the system. Each entry consists of an entry name, followed by a set of one or more fields, followed by the field "chkent," which indicates the end of the entry. The fields are separated—and the chkent field is terminated—by a colon. Fields can be strings, integers, or Boolean values. A string field has the form "field_name=value." Integer fields have the form "field_name#value." Boolean fields have the form "field_name" if they have a true value, and

Table 4.4 *Components of the Enhanced Security Authentication Database*

Database Name	File Name	Field Prefix
Protected Password	/tcb/files/auth.db and /var/tcb/files/auth.db	u_
Terminal Control	/etc/auth/system/ttys.db	t_
System Default	/etc/auth/system/default	d_ for systemwide defaults; t_, u_, and v_ may also appear
Device Assignment	/etc/auth/system/devassign	v_
File Control	/etc/auth/system/files	f_

"field_name@" if they have a false value; in other words, the "@" at the end of the field acts as a negation operator. It is not necessary for every possible field to be present in every entry. When a particular field is not specified in an individual entry, the corresponding field value from the system default database is used for that entry.

Many of the authentication database fields indicate time values, either a duration (e.g., password lifetime) or an absolute time (e.g., time of last successful login). All time values are represented in seconds. For an absolute time, the value is the number of seconds since the standard UNIX time epoch, which is the beginning of the year 1970. The value zero has a special meaning in many of the integer fields, generally indicating an infinite value or a check that will not be performed. For example, the field "u_exp#0" indicates that the password expiration time is infinite (i.e., the password will never expire).

The authentication database can be manipulated manually via the edauth(8) command, which can view, edit, and remove entries in the authentication database. For example, the following command displays the protected password entry for the root account:

```
# edauth -g root
```

To edit the entry for the root account:

```
# edauth root
```

This second command invokes the editor specified by the EDITOR environment variable, or /usr/bin/ex by default, with the protected password entry for the root account.

Corruption in the authentication database can lead to a wide variety of problems with user accounts. When you encounter difficulties while running Enhanced security, one of the first troubleshooting steps should be to run the authck(8) command. This command checks the components of the authentication database for integrity and consistency. If authck reports any problems, repair them with edauth and see whether the problem is corrected.

Tru64 UNIX version 5.0 introduced the enhanced security daemon, prpasswdd(8). This daemon coordinates writes to the authentication database files, preventing file lock contention among multiple writers, particularly in Trucluster environments. If prpasswdd stops accepting requests for some reason, logins may fail or hang. This is generally corrected by restarting prpasswdd with the command "/sbin/init.d/prpasswd restart." (Note that there is only one "d" in "prpasswd" in the restart command, although there are two in the daemon's name.) In a cluster, it may be necessary to restart prpasswdd on all members.

Also beginning in version 5, changes to the authentication database are recorded in log files under directory /var/tcb/files/dblogs. These log files can lead to some potential problems:

- Unless they are periodically trimmed, the log files will continue to grow without limit until the /var file system is full, which can cause any number of unpleasant errors. It's possible to set up a cron job to automatically trim these logs. The easiest way to do this is from "sysman secconfig"; on the Custom Options screen, click the button to configure authorization database options. This lets you trim the logs immediately or create a cron job to trim the logs at regular intervals. Note that you should always use secconfig to trim the logs rather than just removing the log files with rm, or the authentication database may become inconsistent.
- Corruption of the log files can cause logins to fail, resulting in messages such as "log_get: read I/O error" and "log_get: checksum mismatch." When this happens, simply trim the log files via sysman secconfig as described above. You may also need to restart prpasswdd.

4.2.2 Security Configuration Problems

In this section, we'll discuss problems that can arise while setting up the system's security configuration, as well as common misconfiguration errors. One of the latter (unintentionally enabling the "Execute bit set only by root" option) was already discussed in section 4.1.3.4. Another error of this type is unintentionally disabling segment sharing. Segment sharing allows the text segments (only) of shared libraries to be shared by all users, regardless of the file permissions on the library. Systems requiring a very high level of security may choose to disable segment sharing in order to prevent undesired sharing of shared library text segments. The consequence of disabling segment sharing is to cause every process to have its own copy of the text segment of every shared library that it uses. This consumes a great deal of memory, possibly leading to memory shortages and performance problems. Unless you are certain that segment sharing should be disabled on your system, leave it enabled.

There is one other area in which enhanced security can affect the performance of a Tru64 UNIX system. By default, enhanced security records successful login times and unsuccessful login attempts for each user and each terminal. If many users are constantly logging in and out (e.g., on a large university system with thousands of student users), the recording of login information can create a bottleneck on the files in which this information is recorded. If performance is more of a concern than recording login information, this feature can be partially or completely disabled. The "Configure break-in detection and evasion" option in secconfig lets you selectively enable or disable the following:

- Successful and unsuccessful logins on each terminal device
- Successful logins for each user
- Unsuccessful login attempts for each user

Disabling some or all of these options may improve performance on a system with a large number of interactive users. However, disabling them will also disable the system's ability to automatically detect and evade break-in attempts.

A number of problems can arise when converting from base security to enhanced security. The most common of these affects users with passwords longer than eight characters on older versions of Tru64 UNIX. The password encryption algorithm used in Base security encrypts only the first eight characters entered by the user; any additional characters are ignored.

Thus, a user may believe that his or her password is 10 or 12 characters long, but in reality the password is only the first eight of those characters. When the system switches to enhanced security, the entire string of 10 or 12 characters is encrypted, which results in a different encrypted password than encrypting just the first 8 characters. Thus, the previous password appears to fail. When this happens, users need to log in using only those first eight characters, after which they can change passwords and use the longer string if desired.

The problem is even worse when switching from enhanced to base security. Passwords longer than eight characters won't work at all after the conversion, so users need to ensure that their passwords are eight characters or fewer before the switch. To avoid having either of these problems affect the root user, the secconfig utility provides an opportunity to change the root password when changing the security level. The new password is encrypted with the appropriate algorithm so it will be certain to work when the system is rebooted at the new security level.

There are some additional security configuration issues to be aware of in TruCluster environments. To begin with, all members of the cluster must operate at the same security level. Having mixed security levels within a cluster will make it impossible for users to log in on some members. When converting a cluster from base to enhanced security, some extra steps are necessary. First, secconfig is used to select enhanced security with the "Upgrade" option, after which each member of the cluster must be rebooted in turn. After all members are rebooted, secconfig must be run again to finish customizing the security options.

The best way to set up a cluster with enhanced security is to set up the desired security configuration on the initial member before creating the cluster. As additional members are added to the cluster, the security configuration is automatically duplicated on the new members. This is much easier and less error-prone than converting a cluster after it's already up and running.

4.2.3 Login Failures Under Enhanced Security

Perhaps the most important feature of enhanced security is its ability to control logins. There are a large number—some might say a bewilderingly large number—of options to restrict logins for any or all users. The purpose of all this is, of course, to increase security by making it more difficult for anyone to gain unauthorized access to the system. However, it can also make it more difficult for a careless or forgetful user to gain *authorized* access. For example, typing in the wrong password a few times can cause a user account to be disabled for some period of time or until an administrator explicitly re-enables it.

An explanation of all the possible login and password controls is beyond the scope of this book; for details, see the Tru64 UNIX Security Manual or the man pages for authcap(4), prpasswd(4), ttys(4), devassign(4), and default(4). What we will do is discuss the ways in which these controls can prevent user logins. The following paragraphs describe each of the possible login failures, their causes, and how to correct them.

1. **"Account is disabled—see Account Administrator."**

   This is the most common login failure message in enhanced security. It is also the only failure that has multiple possible causes (five, to be exact) without specifically identifying the problem. The possible causes of this failure are as follows:

   a. The system administrator has explicitly locked the account; this is indicated by the presence of the "u_lock" field in the user's protected password entry. To correct this, the administrator must unlock the account with one of the account maintenance tools. A low-level method to do this (e.g., for use in a script) is to use edauth to edit the protected password entry and either remove "u_lock" or add the negation operator "@" to it (i.e., "u_lock" means the account is locked, but "u_lock@" means the account is not locked.)

   b. The user is on vacation, as defined by the "u_vacation" field in the protected password entry. If this is set in error, the fix is to remove the u_vacation field with edauth or change the vacation definition using one of the account maintenance utilities.

   c. The user's password has exceeded the allowable password lifetime. In other words, the time of the last successful password change (u_succhg) was more than "u_life" seconds in the past. To correct this, either set u_life to 0 to disable the check or set u_succhg to a time close to the present.

   d. Too much time has passed since the user's last login. That is, the time of the user's last successful login (u_suclog) exceeds the maximum login interval (u_max_login_intvl). To fix this, either disable the check by setting u_max_login_intvl to 0 or set u_suclog to a time close to the present. Keep in mind that if the user has not logged in for a very long time, both this check and the password lifetime check may come into play; it's important to check for and correct both conditions.

e. The user has too many login failures (e.g., an incorrect password was entered). That is, the number of consecutive unsuccessful logins (u_numunsuclog) equals or exceeds the maximum number of tries (u_maxtries). A successful login resets u_numunsuclog to 0. To fix this, you can use the "Enable" option in dxaccounts. For a low-level solution, either increase u_maxtries to be greater than u_numunsuclog (or set it to 0 to disable the check), or set u_numunsuclog to 0. No matter which of these solutions you choose, make sure the user knows the correct password, or assign a new one!

f. The purpose of this last check is to deflect attempts to break into an account by trying many possible passwords; after "u_maxtries" failures, the account is disabled and can't be broken into even if the correct password is guessed. This check is the only one of these five that can be set to reset automatically after a specified waiting period; after "u_unlock" seconds have passed since the last login failure, the user gets another chance to log in. However, if another failure occurs, then the waiting period starts over, and the user must wait another "u_unlock" seconds to try again.

2. **"Account is disabled but console login is allowed."**

This indicates that the account is disabled for one of the reasons given above. However, a root user login on the system console will override this error and be allowed to log in. This is to ensure that the superuser can't be locked out of the system accidentally or as a result of a denial-of-service attack. Many of the following error messages have similar variations (not listed here) indicating that login would fail except for the root-on-console override.

3. **"Account has expired—please see system administrator."**

   The account had a specified expiration date, defined by "u_expdate," which is now in the past. To correct this, set u_expdate to a future date or to 0, which disables this check.

Troubleshooting Tip

Because enhanced security includes a number of time-based checks, an incorrect system date or time can cause many of them to fail. If a number of accounts or passwords suddenly expire, check your system date and time.

---

4. **"Account has been retired—logins are no longer allowed."**

   The account is explicitly retired, indicated by the presence of the "u_retired" field in the protected password entry. To "unretire" the account, you must remove the u_retired field; negating the field by adding "@" to it will not do the trick!

5. **"Wrong time period to log into this account."**

   The user tried to log in outside the time period(s) defined by "u_tod" in the protected password entry. If the time restriction isn't correct, either modify u_tod or remove it entirely.

6. **"Template account cannot log in."**

   Someone tried to log in to a template account. Such accounts are used only as templates for creating new users and cannot be logged into directly. There is no fix for this (other than educating the offending user) because it really isn't an error.

7. **"Login aborted due to no password."**

   The user's password had expired and had to be changed immediately; however, the user did not change the password successfully. To correct this, the user must try to log in again and change the password successfully.

8. **"Not authorized for terminal access—see System Administrator."**

   The user attempted to log in from a terminal device for which that user is not authorized. That is, the entry for this device in the devassign database contains a list of authorized users (v_users) and this user is not among them. If the user should be authorized, add that user to the list.

9. **"Terminal is disabled—see Account Administrator."**

   This has two possible causes:

   a. The terminal is explicitly locked by the administrator ("t_lock" is present in the terminal database entry). This is similar to 1(a) above, and has a similar fix: either remove t_lock or negate it by adding "@."

   b. There have been too many consecutive login failures from this terminal, indicated by "t_failures" being greater than or equal to "t_maxtries." This is similar to 1(e) above, and for similar reasons; the system is detecting possible break-in attempts from a particular terminal, so it disables logins from that terminal. The fix is to set t_failures to 0, or to set t_maxtries to a larger number (or 0 to disable the check). This failure also has an automatic unlock period defined by "t_unlock," similar to the "u_unlock" field described in 1(f).

10. **"Cannot obtain database information on this terminal."**

    Either the terminal is not defined in the terminal database (check this with "edauth -dt <tty>"), or the database is corrupt. If the database is corrupt, you can rebuild it with the following commands:

```
# cd /etc/auth/system/default
# mv ttys.db ttys.db.old
# convauth -dt
```

    The convauth command will convert the ASCII file /etc/auth/system/ttys into a database (ttys.db). If this still doesn't fix the problem, it's possible that the ttys file itself could be corrupted. In that case, restore the latest version from backup and try the convauth command again. If you don't have a good backup of this file, you can use the prototype file ".new..ttys" to create a new database:

```
# mv ttys ttys.old
# cp .new..ttys ttys
# convauth -dt
```

However, you will have to readd any terminals that you had previously added to the database.

Before you call support

Before calling technical support with a user account or security problem, check the following:

- Determine how many users are affected.
- If only one user is affected, give the user a new password.
- Run pwck and grpck to verify the password and group files.
- Check the system security level.
- Run authck -a if using enhanced security.
- Use the allverify tool to verify system software integrity.
- Check the system date.

5

System Failures

It does not matter how slowly you go, so long as you do not stop.

—Confucius

One of the first principles that we introduced back in Chapter 2 was that problems vary in their severity and their range of effect. In this chapter, we'll discuss problems that are at the high end of both scales: system failures, which take an entire system out of commission until corrected. These problems can be divided into three principal classes:

1. Boot failures
2. System crashes
3. System hangs

The following sections discuss each of these kinds of failures and how to go about troubleshooting them. In some cases, the underlying problem turns out to be in another area (e.g., storage) that is discussed elsewhere in this book. In these cases, the techniques presented in this chapter should at least take you to the point of identifying the underlying problem area, at which point you can turn to the appropriate chapter.

5.1 Boot Failures

A system that won't boot can be frustrating and difficult to troubleshoot. The troubleshooting tools that come with Tru64 UNIX require (not unreasonably) Tru64 UNIX to be up and running. The troubleshooting capabilities available at the console firmware level are much more limited in scope. In many cases, a trial-and-error approach is necessary to determine the cause of the problem. However, by approaching the problem systematically, it's usually possible to isolate the cause and begin correcting the problem.

In this section, we consider failures that happen when booting from a disk (including a CD-ROM) or a disk-based storage set (e.g., a RAID-5 set). Tru64 UNIX can also be booted over a network when using dataless management services (DMS) or from a bootable tape created with the btcreate(8) command. Neither of these last two options is commonly employed; the vast majority of boot problems occur when booting from disk.

In general terms, a system can fail to boot in four different ways:

1. It gets an error message and returns to the console prompt (i.e., it crashes during the boot sequence).
2. It loops trying to boot, then crashes, tries to boot again, etc.
3. It displays an endless series of error messages until interrupted.
4. It hangs at some point in the boot sequence and never continues.

Each of these situations is discussed individually, but first here are some general workarounds suitable for all boot problems.

5.1.1 General Workarounds for Boot Problems

In any boot problem, there are certain standard procedures that frequently help to work around the problem and get the system up and functioning. These procedures, which are listed below, may also help to isolate the problem. They don't need to be tried in the order shown, although the items further down in the list require that the system be booted to single-user mode. Also, some of the items may not be useful in all circumstances. The following list should not be considered a checklist, but rather a list of possibilities from which you can choose the procedures appropriate to your situation.

1. Try power-cycling the system and attached storage.
2. Try booting from genvmunix or an alternative kernel.

3. Try booting from an alternative boot disk or an installation CD-ROM.

4. If any hardware changes were performed recently, undo them if possible.

5. Try booting only to single-user mode with the console command "BOOT -FL S."

6. Try bypassing /etc/sysconfigtab with the console command "BOOT -FL C."

7. Check the console firmware version with the console command "SHOW VERSION." Ensure that the firmware version is compatible with the version of Tru64 UNIX that you're trying to boot.

8. If the firmware was recently upgraded and your system contains any EISA buses, run the EISA Configuration Utility (ECU).

9. If the system will boot to single-user mode, but has problems proceeding to multiuser mode, you can troubleshoot the boot process step by step. Once the system reaches single-user mode, try to mount the local file systems by running /sbin/bcheckrc.

10. If bcheckrc fails, there is a problem with one of the file systems. Reboot the system to single-user mode and try mounting the file systems one at a time. First, remount the root file system in read-write mode. In Tru64 UNIX V5, use the command "/sbin/mountroot"; in older versions, use `mount -u /`.

11. If you are using LSM, start it with `/sbin/lsmbstartup`. The bcheckrc script normally does this automatically, but because bcheckrc hasn't been run yet, it's necessary to start LSM manually.

12. Try to mount each of the local (non-NFS) file systems listed in /etc/fstab one at a time. Use the mount command and specify the mount point; for example, to mount the /usr file system, enter `mount /usr`. When you reach the problem file system(s), the mount command will fail, and you can take further steps to troubleshoot the problem.

If all of the file systems mount, you can modify the scripts /sbin/rc2 and /sbin/rc3 to debug the boot process in more detail. These two scripts run the startup scripts (located in directories /sbin/rc2.d and /sbin/rc3.d) as the system transitions from single-user mode through run level 2 (multiuser mode with no network) to run level 3 (multiuser mode with network). /sbin/rc2 and /sbin/rc3 are Bourne shell scripts. The first line of each of these script files is

```
#!/sbin/sh
```

In both files, modify the first line by adding " -x" at the end of the line. The new line will be

```
#!/sbin/sh -x
```

The "-x" switch turns on echo mode in the Bourne shell. As a result, each command or script executed by /sbin/rc2 or /sbin/rc3 will be echoed to the console. After modifying the scripts, try booting the system to multiuser mode with the "init 3" command. As the commands echo to the console, observe the last command executed before the boot problem occurs. This will identify the particular startup script (in /sbin/rc2.d or /sbin/rc3.d) that is executing when the problem occurs.

To further isolate the problem, you can repeat this process by turning on echo mode inside the startup script that was just identified. Boot the system to single-user mode and mount the local file systems as described above. Then edit the startup script in question and add " -x" to the end of its first line. Continue the boot to multiuser mode with "init 3" and observe the last command that executes before the problem. This will identify the command or utility that is executing when the problem occurs. This information may help you locate the actual problem and correct it.

Alternatively, you may choose to disable the startup script (if it is not critical to system operation) as a workaround to continue booting. For example, if the problem script is "/sbin/rc3.d/S40sendmail" and mail is not a critical function of the system, you can temporarily rename the script so that its name begins with a character other than "S," such as "disable.S40sendmail." The run-level startup scripts (/sbin/rc2 and /sbin/rc3) execute only startup scripts whose file names begin with an upper-case "S." Then try booting again to see if the system boots successfully or if further problems occur later in the boot sequence. In this example, a successful boot would indicate that the problem is specifically tied to mail in some way, while a further problem in the boot sequence would indicate a wider problem.

5.1.2 System Crashes During Boot

If a system crashes during the boot sequence, there are five general types of errors. These are distinguished by the type of error message displayed before the system returns to the console prompt. Examples of these messages are shown below; the actual message may vary slightly but should be similar to one of the following five examples:

1. "Failed to open device," possibly combined with more specific error messages referring to a specific device
2. "Can't open osf_boot"
3. "Can't open vmunix" or "No vmunix module list"
4. "Machine check," "unrecoverable hardware error," or a similar hardware-oriented message
5. Any panic message other than machine check

Each of these possibilities is discussed in its own section.

5.1.2.1 Boot Disk Access Failure

The Tru64 UNIX boot process consists of the following steps:

1. The console firmware selects the boot disk from the boot command line entry or, if no device is specified, from the console variable BOOTDEF_DEV.
2. The firmware loads the primary bootstrap from block 0 of the boot disk.
3. The primary bootstrap loads the secondary bootstrap from blocks 1 to 15 of UFS file systems or blocks 64 to 95 of AdvFS file systems.
4. The secondary bootstrap loads the osf_boot program from the root file system.
5. The osf_boot program loads the Tru64 UNIX kernel file specified by (a) the command line, (b) the console variable BOOT_FILE, or (c) a default of "vmunix," in that order.
6. The kernel program initializes the system and begins running Tru64 UNIX.

A message such as "Failed to open device" indicates that the system is unable to read the disk from which it's trying to boot. When this happens, the first thing to do is to verify that the console boot parameters are set correctly. This can be done with the following command:

```
>>> SHOW BOOT*
```

which generates output similar to the following:

```
BOOT_DEV            dka100.1.0.15.0
BOOT_FILE
BOOT_OSFLAGS        A
BOOT_RESET          OFF
BOOTDEF_DEV         dka100.1.0.15.0
BOOTED_DEV          dka100.1.0.15.0
BOOTED_FILE
BOOTED_OSFLAGS      A
```

Ensure that the default boot disk (BOOTDEF_DEV) is pointing to the correct disk. BOOT_FILE defines the kernel to boot; it is usually left blank and defaults to "vmunix." BOOT_OSFLAGS defines the default boot flags as a string of zero or more characters, with each character representing one flag. Table 5.1 lists the most useful boot flags for Tru64 UNIX.

Table 5.1 *Boot Flags for Tru64 UNIX*

Flag	Meaning
A	Boot to multiuser mode
C	Do not process /etc/sysconfigtab at startup
D	Enable full crash dumps
I	Boot to interactive mode
K	Start in kdebug (remote kernel debugger)
S	Boot to single-user mode (the default if none specified)

After verifying the console boot parameters (and correcting them if necessary), check to see whether the boot disk is "seen" by the console firmware. Enter the console command "SHOW DEV" and verify that the boot disk appears in the resulting output. If the disk is not listed, there is a hardware problem preventing access to the disk. Troubleshooting hardware problems is beyond the scope of this book; however, some obvious things to try are power-cycling the system and the external storage cabinet (if any) that contains the boot disk, checking the disk for fault indicator lights, or booting from an alternative disk.

Troubleshooting Tip

If you are running a version of Tru64 UNIX older than V5.0, make sure that the boot disk has a logical unit number (LUN) of zero—that is, that the console device name (e.g., DKA100) ends in zero. Older versions of Tru64 UNIX cannot boot from devices with a LUN other than zero.

If the boot disk does appear in the "SHOW DEV" output, it might still have a hardware problem; however, there are a few other things to check before deciding this is the case. To continue troubleshooting at this point, it's necessary to boot the system from an alternative boot disk or an installation CD-ROM. The next step is to try reading the disklabel of the problem disk. This requires that you know how the disk is identified by the system. For Tru64 UNIX version 5, the command "hwmgr -view devices" (or "hwmgr -v d" for short) will list the attached storage devices. The SCSI bus, target, and LUN information in this list can be used to locate the disk.

For example, suppose the boot disk is identified at the console as DKC100, indicating that the disk is at bus 2, target 1, LUN 0. After booting the system from CD-ROM, hwmgr shows the following devices:

```
# hwmgr –view devices
HWID: Device Name           Mfg      Model            Location
 ----------------------------------------------------------------------
    3: scp                           (unknown)        (unknown)
    4: /dev/kevm
   35: /dev/disk/floppy0c            3.5in floppy     fdi0-unit-0
   45: /dev/disk/cdrom0c    COMPAQ   CDR-8435         bus-0-targ-0-lun-0
   46: /dev/disk/dsk0c      COMPAQ   BD009222C7       bus-2-targ-0-lun-0
   47: /dev/disk/dsk1c      COMPAQ   BD009222C7       bus-2-targ-1-lun-0
```

The bus, target, and LUN information for the last disk in the list identifies it as the disk in question. The full device name /dev/disk/dsk1c indicates that Tru64 UNIX knows this disk as dsk1.

Older versions of Tru64 UNIX use a different naming scheme for peripheral devices. SCSI disk names in version 4 and earlier are of the form "rzLnn," where "nn" equals ((bus * 8) + target) and L is the LUN indicator, with the letters "a" through "h" indicating LUN 0 through 7. (For LUN 0, the "a" may be, and usually is, omitted.) Using this formula, the disk at bus 2, target 1, LUN 0, would be known as rz17 (or, less commonly, rza17).

Once the device name is known, try reading the disk's label. For a disk named dsk1, try

```
# disklabel -r dsk1
```

If this fails with a message such as "I/O error," there is a hardware problem with the disk or another component leading to it, such as an adapter or cable. If the disklabel command returns "disk is unlabeled," the label (at a minimum) has been corrupted. The remainder of the disk may or may not be corrupted. The next step is to try writing a new disklabel onto the disk to see if the corruption is limited to the label.

First, write a default label on the disk. If the root file system type is UFS, enter

```
# disklabel -wrt ufs dsk1
```

If the root file system type is AdvFS, enter

```
# disklabel -wrt advfs dsk1
```

This will write a default disk label, which includes a standard partition layout. If the disk was previously using the default layout, this is sufficient. However, if the disk was using a customized partition layout, it is now necessary to edit the label using a record of the previous partition layout (which hopefully was saved in hard-copy form or on another disk). To edit the disklabel, enter:

```
# disklabel -re dsk1
```

and make the necessary changes to the partition layout. It is necessary to change only the "size" and "offset" fields for partitions that need to be modified. Other fields are calculated automatically.

If the disk was previously in use by another operating system such as Linux, older versions of the disklabel command may not be able to write a new label on the disk. In this case, reformatting the disk with the SCSI CAM utility (scu) will solve the problem. (Be aware, though, that it also destroys all data on the disk.) To reformat a disk with scu, enter the following command:

```
# scu -f /dev/rdisk/dsk0c [substitute the
                            appropriate disk name]
scu> format
scu> quit
```

After writing (and editing, if necessary) the disk label, halt the system and try booting from the problem disk. If it still fails, the most likely explanation is that the disk's primary or secondary bootstraps have been corrupted. To restore the bootstraps, boot the system from CD-ROM and escape to the shell prompt. Then use the following two commands to write new boot blocks on the disk:

```
# disklabel -r dsk1 > /tmp/label
# disklabel -Rrt advfs dsk1 /tmp/label rzxx
```

The first command reads the label and stores it in file /tmp/label. (This file is writeable when booted from CD-ROM, because /tmp is a memory file system in this situation.) The second command writes the label from the file back onto the disk, but adds the appropriate bootstrap blocks for an AdvFS root file system. If the root file system is UFS, substitute "ufs" for "advfs" in the command. This command sequence does not affect existing data on the disk. Only the label is written, and the partition sizes and offsets are not changed because the existing partition table is copied back to the disk.

After writing new boot blocks on the disk, halt the system and try booting from the disk. If this still fails, the error message will most likely have changed to "Can't open osf_boot" or "Can't open vmunix." These two possibilities are discussed in the following two sections.

5.1.2.2 Inability To Open osf_boot

The message "Can't open osf_boot" indicates that the secondary bootstrap loader is unable to load the osf_boot program, which is used to load the kernel file. There are several possible causes of this error:

- An attempt was made to boot the wrong disk (one that isn't bootable).
- The root file system (or entire boot disk) has been corrupted.
- Just the osf_boot file is missing or corrupted.
- The disk's primary and secondary bootstrap are for the wrong file system type (UFS bootstraps when the root file system is AdvFS, or vice versa).
- The disk's boot blocks have been destroyed or corrupted.

Enter the following command at the console prompt:

```
>>> SHOW BOOTDEF_DEV
```

Verify that BOOTDEF_DEV is pointing to the correct boot disk. If it is boot the system from an alternative disk or CD-ROM and try to verify the boot disk's label as described in section 5.1.2.1.

If the disk has a good label (or after you've written a new label), the next step depends on whether the disk has ever successfully booted or whether it's a new boot disk (e.g., a restoration from backup following a boot disk or root file system failure). In the latter case, the most likely explanation is that the disk's boot blocks are for the wrong file system type. This is particularly likely if the root file system is AdvFS, because the disklabel command writes UFS boot blocks by default. To correct this, rewrite the disklabel using the correct boot blocks:

```
# disklabel -r dsk1 > /tmp/label
# disklabel -Rrt advfs dsk1 /tmp/label rzxx
```

If the root file system is UFS, substitute "ufs" for "advfs" in the second command. Halt the system and try again to boot from the problem disk.

If the problem still exists, the most likely cause is a missing or corrupted osf_boot file or more widespread corruption of the root file system or the entire disk. Boot the system from CD-ROM and mount the root file system from partition "a" of the problem disk. For a UFS file system, this is accomplished by a command such as the following:

```
# mount /dev/disk/dsk1a /mnt
```

For AdvFS file systems, the process is a little more complicated. First, make a temporary domain link. For temporary mounts, the domain name doesn't need to match the name given to the domain when it was created; you must, however, know the fileset name within the domain. Then create a subdirectory under /etc/fdmns for the new domain. In this subdirectory, create a link to the disk partition containing the root file system. The domain link may be created automatically by the CD boot, but in case it isn't, here's how to do it:

```
# mkdir -p /etc/fdmns/root_domain
# cd /etc/fdmns/root_domain
# ln -s /dev/disk/dsk1a
```

Now mount the root file system:

```
# mount root_domain#root /mnt
```

If you have problems mounting the root file system (whether UFS or AdvFS), verify that all your information is correct. If it is, make sure that your current working directory is not set to the mount point; this will cause the mount to fail with a "device busy" error. Also, make sure that the file system is not already mounted; use the "mount" command with no options to list currently mounted file systems (you will not be able to use df). If the file system still won't mount, it has been deleted or corrupted, and it will be necessary to restore the root file system from backup. (For details on restoring a root file system, see the Tru64 UNIX System Administration manual.) If no backup exists, there is little alternative except to reinstall the operating system.

With the root file system from the boot disk mounted, verify that file /mnt/osf_boot exists and has the same length and checksum as /osf_boot (the boot file on the CD-ROM or alternative boot disk). If the file is missing or has an incorrect length or checksum, replace it with the copy from CD-ROM:

```
# cp -p /osf_boot /mnt/osf_boot
```

Then halt the system and try booting again. If the boot still fails with "can't open osf_boot," rewrite the boot blocks if this has not already been done. If a different failure message results, go to the appropriate section within this chapter.

5.1.2.3 Kernel Load Failure

If the osf_boot program is unable to locate the desired kernel file (usually vmunix), it will print an error message and go into interactive boot mode. This will prompt the operator to enter a new kernel name, for example:

```
Can't open vmunix
Enter: <kernel_name> <option_1> <option_2> ... <option_n>
#
```

The pound sign indicates that a new kernel name should be entered; it is not a shell prompt. The "option" arguments allow the operator to set kernel parameters interactively, a feature that can be very useful in some circumstances (but not this one). At the "#" prompt, enter a new kernel file name; osf_boot will attempt to find that kernel file and load it. In Tru64 UNIX version 5.1A and later, you can also enter "ls" at this prompt for a listing of the root directory or any subdirectory within the root file system. This is extremely useful when trying to remember the name of an alternative kernel file.

If the specified kernel file exists but isn't a valid kernel, osf_boot prints an error message similar to the following:

```
Loading vmunix...
Loading at 0xfffffc0000230000
No vmunix module list
```

The system then halts and returns to the console prompt. This indicates that the kernel file is corrupt (e.g., some other file was copied over it).

When this happens, try booting the generic kernel (genvmunix) or an alternative kernel.

5.1.2.4 Machine Checks

Machine checks, which generate messages such as "machine check" or "unrecoverable hardware error," are almost always hardware problems, such as a CPU cache read error. (Software-generated machine checks aren't completely unknown, but they are extremely rare.) If your system experiences a machine check while booting, try the standard workarounds listed in section 5.1.1 to get the system booted. This will at least give you access to some of the system utilities for error detection, which may help you to troubleshoot the hardware problem.

5.1.2.5 Panics During Boot

A "panic" occurs when the UNIX kernel detects a severe error that prevents it from operating safely. Rather than continuing to operate in an environment where data corruption may occur, the kernel chooses to bring the system down and write a crash dump to preserve information about the problem. Depending on the console parameter settings, the system may immediately try to reboot and resume operation.

When a system panics while booting, only a limited amount of troubleshooting is possible. Certain panic messages at boot may indicate specific problems that are worth checking for. These panic messages include the following:

- "ialloc: dup alloc"
- "kernel memory fault" or similar messages, such as "unaligned kernel access"
- "rmalloc"
- "simple_lock: time limit exceeded" or other lock-related panics
- "vfs_mountroot: cannot mount root"

We'll discuss these a bit further below. There are also certain panics that almost always indicate hardware problems. In addition to machine checks, these include "tb_shoot ack timeout" and "vm_swap I/O error." These should be handled similarly to machine checks (i.e., follow the appropriate hardware troubleshooting procedures for your site).

The "ialloc: dup alloc" panic is caused by UFS file system corruption. This is usually (but not always) in the root file system. The corruption can usually be corrected by the fsck(8) command. Using the techniques listed in section 5.1.1, mount each file system in order to identify the corrupted one, then use the fsck command to repair it—for example:

```
# fsck -y /dev/rdisk/dsk1a
```

Substitute the correct disk partition for "dsk1a." Normally, fsck will ask whether to correct each instance of corruption that it detects. The "-y" switch automatically answers "yes" to all of these questions. After correcting the corruption, make sure that the /etc/fstab entry for the corrupted file system contains a non-zero number in the last field. For the root file system, this number should be 1; for other file systems, it should be 2 or higher. If the number is zero, correct it.

"Kernel memory fault" is a generic panic indicating that the kernel attempted to access an invalid memory address. (A more detailed explanation is provided in section 5.2.2.1.) This panic generally requires further analysis—at a minimum, examination of the stack trace leading up to the panic. However, there is one problem known to cause this panic at boot time. If you have upgraded the console firmware on an Alpha system that contains an EISA bus (which most, but not all, models do contain), you must re-run the EISA Configuration Utility (ECU) after upgrading the firmware.

The "rmalloc" panic is seen on AlphaStations with ISA buses and is generally a result of improper or corrupted ISA configuration data. It is usually seen when upgrading to Digital UNIX V4.0 or higher for the first time. To clear the problem in most cases, enter the following commands at the console:

```
>>> isacfg -init
>>> init
```

"Simple lock" panics are generic in nature, indicating a symmetric multiprocessing (SMP) locking problem; for more details, see section 5.2.2.2. The actual cause of the panic usually requires deeper analysis. However, there is a possible workaround to prevent this panic for systems that must be restored to service as soon as possible. The workaround is to disable all but one CPU on the system, which effectively disables all SMP locking. To do this, enter the following from the console:

```
>>> SET CPU_ENABLED 1
```

CPU_ENABLED is a bit mask for the enabled CPUs. A value of 1 indicates that only the first CPU (CPU 0) is enabled, a value of 3 would indicate that CPUs 0 and 1 are enabled, and so on. The parameter is normally set to FFFF or FFFFFFFF, which are hexadecimal values with all relevant bits set, indicating that all CPUs are enabled by default.

Caution

Booting a multiprocessor system with CPU_ENABLED set to 1 will degrade system performance, possibly severely. This should be considered a temporary workaround to be used only until the problem has been properly resolved.

The "vfs_mountroot: cannot mount root" panic occurs when the kernel is unable to mount the root file system. There are several possible causes for this problem. These causes, along with brief descriptions of the appropriate corrective actions, are listed below. Because the root file system is unavailable, it's usually necessary to boot the system from an alternative boot disk or installation CD-ROM in order to troubleshoot the problem. However, in some cases, booting the generic kernel is sufficient to proceed.

Possible causes of the "vfs_mountroot: cannot mount root" panic include the following:

- The root file system is corrupted. Attempt to mount the root file system as described in section 5.1.2.2; if this fails, restore the root file system.
- The /etc/fstab entry for the root file system is incorrect. Mount the root file system on /mnt and edit /mnt/etc/fstab to correct the entry.
- The root file system is AdvFS, but AdvFS isn't built into the kernel. Boot the generic kernel, add the line "options MSFS" to the kernel configuration file (/sys/conf/<HOSTNAME>), and rebuild the kernel.

- The root file system appears to be an LSM volume, but LSM isn't built into the kernel. Boot the generic kernel, add the following two lines to the kernel configuration file, and rebuild the kernel.

```
pseudo-device    lsm      1
pseudo-device    lsm_ted  0
```

- The /etc/fdmns link to the root file domain is not pointing to the correct device. Mount the root file system on /mnt and correct the symbolic link in directory /mnt/etc/fdmns/root_domain.
- The root file system is an AdvFS domain with more than one volume. If the problem is just an extra symbolic link in /mnt/etc/fdmns/root_domain, remove the extra link. If the root domain actually contains multiple volumes (a situation that Tru64 UNIX normally prohibits, but it's possible to defeat this restriction with some misguided ingenuity), it's usually necessary to recreate the domain on a single volume and restore the root file system from backup.
- The hardware configuration has changed, causing the device numbers to change. This topic is discussed further in Chapter 8.
- The console firmware is outdated and incompatible with the current operating system version. Check the firmware version and update it if necessary.
- The root device has a nonzero logical unit number (a limitation in Tru64 UNIX versions earlier than V5.0). This is not a valid boot device for older versions of Tru64 UNIX. It is necessary to move or copy the boot disk to a device with a LUN of zero.

5.1.3 System in a Crashing Loop

When a system is in a loop where it keeps crashing while booting, it indicates that console parameter AUTO_ACTION is set to "BOOT" or "RESTART," causing the system to reboot automatically when it crashes. It is necessary to set this parameter to "HALT" so that the system will halt after it crashes. To do this, you must first break the boot-crash-boot-crash cycle and get to the console prompt.

If the crash happens after the system reaches single-user mode (i.e., after "INIT: Single-user mode" appears on the console), watch for the message "Checking local filesystems" to appear during the boot sequence. This appears just after "INIT: Single-user mode." When "Checking local filesystems" appears, repeatedly enter control-C at the keyboard. This should interrupt the currently executing script and leave you at the single-user prompt. Enter the "HALT" command to halt the system and return to the console prompt. Then enter the following console command:

```
>>> SET AUTO_ACTION HALT
```

This will prevent the system from automatically booting when it crashes.

If the system crashes during the transition from single-user to multiuser mode, it's possible that crash files won't be generated, depending on where the crash occurs in the startup process. In such cases, it's usually possible to generate the crash dump files manually. First, boot the system to single-user mode, then run "bcheckrc" to mount the local file systems; if the crash occurs during bcheckrc, follow the steps listed in section 5.1.1 to get at least the root, /usr, and /var (if separate) file systems mounted. If there are no new crash dump files in the crash directory, use the following command:

```
# /sbin/init.d/savecore start
```

This will generate the vmunix.n and vmzcore.n files in the crash directory. To create the crash-data.n file, use this command:

```
# /sbin/init.d/crashdc start
```

If the system is crashing before it gets to single-user mode, it's a little trickier to get the system halted. The halting mechanism varies considerably among Alpha system types; if necessary, consult the hardware documentation for your system. When the system halts, the console prompt will appear. Set the AUTO_ACTION console parameter to "HALT" as shown above, then try again to boot the system. When it crashes again, it should stay halted, and you can use the information in the previous sections to troubleshoot the problem.

5.1.4 Continual Boot Errors

When a system is generating an endless series of error messages during boot, try to determine the following:

- What the system is trying to do
- Where the error messages are coming from

For example, if the messages indicate some type of hardware problem, such as "I/O error," "timeout," "not ready," etc., then the problem is most likely hardware related. In such a case, there should be information in the messages to help identify the device or controller causing the problem. This might include SCSI bus, target, and LUN numbers; RAID controller numbers; or similar information. Similarly, if the messages indicate that some other component is the problem (e.g., problems mounting NFS systems), this can be used to help isolate and fix the problem. After determining what you can while the system is getting the error messages, try the workarounds listed in section 5.1.1 to bring the system up so that the problem can be further isolated and resolved.

One boot failure of this type occurs frequently enough to mention specifically. If the /usr file system fails to mount, booting to multi-user mode will generate an endless series of "INIT: Command respawning too rapidly" messages on the console. This occurs because the init daemon attempts to start a "getty" process for terminal logins on the system console. The definition of the getty command in /etc/inittab includes the "respawn" parameter so that when the getty process exits (i.e., when a logout occurs on the console), a new getty process is created to enable the next login. The getty program is located in directory /usr/bin, so if the /usr file system is unavailable, the program can't be started by init. However, the "respawn" parameter causes the init daemon to keep trying to start the process as soon as it fails. The init daemon detects this state of affairs and prints the "command respawning too rapidly" message, but it doesn't stop trying to respawn the process. To get out of this situation, halt the system and boot to single-user mode. From that point, you can troubleshoot why the /usr file system isn't mounting and take steps to correct the problem.

5.1.5 System Hangs During Boot

When a system hangs while booting, it is necessary to determine what it is doing at the time of the hang. Observe the last message that appears before the system hangs. This message could be the operation causing the hang, or it could be the last successful operation to complete before the hang. (If the system hangs immediately after the message "Jumping to bootstrap code," this is a clear indication of a hardware problem.) Once you have this information, try using the workarounds listed in section 5.1.1 to bring up the system so that the problem can be further isolated and resolved. For more information on troubleshooting system hangs, see section 5.3.

Before you call support

Before calling technical support with a boot problem, try the workarounds listed in section 5.1.1, particularly the following:

- Try booting from the generic kernel or some other kernel, particularly if this is the first boot on a new kernel.
- Try booting from an alternative boot disk or an installation CD-ROM.
- Power-cycle the system and attached storage.
- If any hardware changes were performed recently, undo them if possible.
- Try booting to single-user mode. If this works, try to isolate the problem by performing the rest of the boot sequence one step at a time, as discussed in section 5.1.1.
- Try bypassing /etc/sysconfigtab with the console command "BOOT -FL C."
- Check the console firmware version and verify that it's compatible with the version of Tru64 UNIX that you're trying to boot.
- If the firmware was recently upgraded and your system contains any EISA buses, run the ECU.

5.2 System Crashes

Most system crashes are caused by kernel panics. A panic occurs when the UNIX kernel detects a severe software or hardware error and deliberately brings the system down rather than continuing to operate in an unsafe manner. It is also possible for a system to crash without panicking. This kind of crash is almost invariably due to hardware or environmental issues, such as power or temperature problems. (In rare cases, a system may crash due to a kernel panic that doesn't leave any traces of the panic; an example of this type of problem was discussed in section 2.2.4.)

In general terms, crashes can be divided into three major classes:

1. Kernel panics that produce crash dumps
2. Kernel panics that don't produce crash dumps
3. Non-panic crashes

These three classes require different troubleshooting techniques. Before getting into these, we'll discuss how Tru64 UNIX crash dumps are created.

5.2.1 Crash Dump Creation

When the kernel encounters a severe problem that causes it to panic, it first writes a panic message to the system console, the system message file, and the binary error log. The panic routine then stops all running processes and calls a kernel routine named "dumpsys" to dump the contents of physical memory to disk, specifically to one or more of the active swap devices. (The dumpsys routine can also be invoked by entering the console command "CRASH"; in this way, a forced crash dump can be created when a system is hung.) The dumpsys routine locates the available swap partitions, checks to see whether there is enough free space to hold the contents of memory, and then writes the contents of memory to the swap disks. By default, the dumpsys routine writes a partial dump, which contains only the "interesting" parts of physical memory, rather than a full dump, which contains every last byte of physical memory. There are a number of kernel parameters that configure how crash dumps are written and what they contain; for details, see the reference page for sys_attrs_generic(5).

When the system next boots to multiuser mode, the savecore(8) program runs at the beginning of run level 2 startup. The savecore program checks the swap partitions for the presence of a memory dump. If a dump is present, savecore copies the memory contents into a crash dump file named vmzcore.n (or vmcore.n for the uncompressed dumps used in older versions of Tru64 UNIX). The savecore program also copies the currently running kernel to a file named vmunix.n. The crash dump and kernel files are stored in the crash directory defined by rc.config parameter SAVECORE_DIR, or in /var/adm/crash by default. The ".n" in the file names represents a number that keeps track of subsequent crashes on the system. This sequence number is stored in file "bounds" in the crash directory and starts with crash 0. That is, the first crash dump on a system will create vmzcore.0 and vmunix.0, the next will create vmzcore.1 and vmunix.1, and so on. Later in the boot sequence (during the run level 3 startup), the crashdc(8) program runs to create a snapshot of the crash dump. The snapshot file (crash-data.n in the crash directory) is an ASCII summary of key pieces of information from the crash dump.

There is also a system utility called dumpsys(8), which produces a "live dump" snapshot of a running system. This uses a slightly different mechanism, and the system continues running while the crash dump files are produced. Because of the transitory nature of memory, there may be inconsistencies in a live dump. As such, a live dump may not be as useful as a "true" crash dump (either a forced crash or the result of a panic) because memory is not changing during the latter type of crash dump.

For knowledgeable (or adventurous) system administrators, the dbx(1) debugger can be used to examine a crash dump in detail. dbx is also used to debug application core dumps, an operation that requires a developer's license. However, no license is needed to use dbx in kernel mode (selected with the -k switch), which is used to examine crash dumps or the kernel memory of a running system. We'll discuss some basic techniques for using dbx on a crash dump, but it should be recognized that the usefulness of crash dump analysis is severely limited without a copy of the Tru64 UNIX source code (which requires a source license). The techniques described here may help to identify a known panic described in a Tru64 UNIX patch kit, or at least narrow down the general area in which a panic occurred. However, in most cases it will be necessary to engage HP technical support to analyze a crash dump. In such cases, the crash dump files are not the only pieces of information that should be provided. The sys_check(8) utility's "-escalate" option collects a number of useful files and packages them for sending to tech support. (For more details on sys_check, see Chapter 3.)

The most important piece of information in troubleshooting a panic is the *panic string*, a brief description that uniquely identifies the panic. The panic string is the main component of the panic message written to the system console and log files. For example, in the following panic message:

```
panic (cpu 0): vfs_mountroot: cannot mount root
```

the panic string is "vfs_mountroot: cannot mount root." This identifies the cause of the panic as inability to mount the root file system while the system is booting. This particular panic string is quite specific as to the cause of the problem. Not all panic strings are so helpful; for example, "kernel memory fault" is more generic, indicating only that the kernel tried to access an invalid memory location.

A crash dump, if available, is by far the most useful piece of evidence in troubleshooting a system crash. But you can also find useful information by checking the system log files for messages around the time of the crash, as discussed in section 2.2.5. The most useful log files to look at are the following:

- The binary error log, /var/adm/binary.errlog (using a tool such as DECevent or Compaq Analyze)
- The system message file, /var/adm/messages
- The system log files under directory /var/adm/syslog.dated, particularly kern.log and daemon.log

Information in these log files may provide a clue to the cause of the panic. The following types of messages are particularly useful:

- Hardware error messages
- File system problems, such as “filesystem full,” “out of inodes,” or AdvFS domain panics
- Messages indicating network problems, such as NFS “server not found” messages
- Kernel error messages, such as “no more processes”
- TruCluster or ASE errors or status messages

Hardware error messages and the binary error log are particularly important when a “machine check” panic occurs. Machine checks are caused by hardware problems and should be handled using the hardware troubleshooting procedures appropriate to your environment (e.g., engaging HP or third-party hardware support or do-it-yourself analysis of the binary error log). If the system is part of a TruCluster or ASE configuration, it’s also worthwhile to check all the above log files on each of the other cluster members.

5.2.2 Panics with Crash Dumps

A quick look at a crash dump is provided by the crash-data file, but more extensive analysis requires examining the crash dump with the dbx or kdbx debuggers. kdbx(8) is a front end to dbx with a number of useful extensions for kernel debugging. For more information on dbx and kdbx, as well as general information on debugging crash dumps, see the Tru64 UNIX kernel debugging manual.

To analyze a crash dump with dbx, use the following commands:

```
# cd /var/adm/crash
# dbx -k vmunix.n vmzcore.n
```

where "n" is the number of the crash dump you are analyzing. dbx prints a startup message followed by this warning:

```
warning: Files compiled -g3: parameter values
probably wrong
```

followed by a "(dbx)" prompt. The warning message is something to keep in mind when analyzing crash dumps. Most of the Tru64 UNIX kernel is compiled with a high degree of optimization. This increases performance, but causes dbx to be incorrect in some of its assumptions about the contents of variables.

The panic string is saved in kernel variable "panicstr." To display the panic string in dbx (in case you haven't looked at any of the several other places it's recorded), enter the following command:

```
(dbx) p panicstr
```

which returns output similar to the following:

```
0xfffffc0000a42470 = "kernel memory fault"
```

Next to the panic string, the most useful information in troubleshooting a panic is the kernel stack trace of the thread that was executing at the time of the panic. To display the stack trace, you must first set the debugging context to the "panic thread." The command to do this varies depending on the version of Tru64 UNIX that the crash dump is from; numerous kernel data structures were changed in V5.0. For version 5 crash dumps, the command is

```
(dbx) tset processor_ptr[paniccpu].m.cpu_panic_thread
```

while for pre-V5.0 crash dumps, the command is

```
(dbx) tset machine_slot[paniccpu].cpu_panic_thread
```

After setting context to the panic thread, enter the command "t" to display the stack trace. This produces output similar to the following:

```
>  0 stop_secondary_cpu(do_lwc = (unallocated - symbol optimized away)) [."./../
../../src/kernel/arch/alpha/cpu.c":1205, 0xfffffc00005f57c0]
   1 panic(s = (unallocated - symbol optimized away)) [."./../../../src/kernel/b
sd/subr_prf.c":1252, 0xfffffc00002949f4]
   2 event_timeout(func = (unallocated - symbol optimized away), arg = (unalloca
ted - symbol optimized away), timeout = (unallocated - symbol optimized away)) [
."./../../../src/kernel/arch/alpha/cpu.c":1971, 0xfffffc00005f69f4]
   3 printf(fmt = (unallocated - symbol optimized away)) [."./../../../src/kernel
l/bsd/subr_prf.c":940, 0xfffffc0000293da8]
   4 panic(s = (unallocated - symbol optimized away)) [."./../../../src/kernel/b
sd/subr_prf.c":1309, 0xfffffc0000294b28]
   5 trap(a0 = (...), a1 = (...), a2 = (...), code = (unallocated - symbol optim
ized away), exc_frame = (unallocated - symbol optimized away)) [."./../../../src
/kernel/arch/alpha/trap.c":2262, 0xfffffc00005ea400]
   6 _XentMM(0x0, 0xfffffc00002ab090, 0xfffffc000099ab20, 0x100000003, 0x8b5f9)
[."./../../../src/kernel/arch/alpha/locore.s":2115, 0xfffffc00005e41d4]
   7 solock(0x0, 0xfffffc00002ab090, 0xfffffc000099ab20, 0x100000003, 0x8b5f9) [
."./../../../src/kernel/bsd/uipc_socket.c":1265, 0xfffffc00002ab090]
   8 tcp_handle_timers(0xfffffc008133ef00, 0x8b5f9, 0xfffffc00f6128800, 0xfffffc
0000be16d0, 0xfffffc002a697200) [."./../../../src/kernel/netinet/tcp_timer.c":10
15, 0xfffffc00004b2958]
   9 tcp_rad_slowtimo(0x0, 0x0, 0x0, 0x0, 0xfffffc0001110000) [."./../../../src/
kernel/netinet/tcp_timer.c":1136, 0xfffffc00004b2d90]
```

Each indented set of lines represents one call frame on the stack. The top of the listing (frame number 0) is the last function to execute; each succeeding frame shows the function that called the one above it. The most significant frames are the ones that include routine "panic" and the next few frames below it. The frames above the panic frame can be ignored; these show the kernel shutting down following the panic. In some cases, there are two frames containing "panic" on the stack. (In rare cases, there may be more than two; the most we have seen is 47 panics out of 117 total frames, but that was an exceptional situation.) Only the oldest (highest numbered) panic frame and subsequent frames are significant. All other panics are completely irrelevant; these represent secondary panics that the kernel encountered while trying to shut down following the initial panic and are not germane to the problem that caused the initial panic. In this example, frames 1 and 4 both contain routine "panic." Frame 4 is the highest-numbered panic frame; therefore, frames 0 through 3 represent a secondary panic and should be ignored.

The key frames in a stack trace can be matched against panics described in the Tru64 UNIX patch kits to determine whether the panic is a known (and fixed) problem. A stack trace should be considered a match if the actual routine names, in the same sequence, match for several frames following the panic. The additional information printed by dbx in each frame is not significant. This additional information is derived from addresses specific to each kernel and will almost certainly not match an example from any other system. Deciding how many frames of identical routine names are necessary to declare a match is not an exact science; it depends mostly on the type of panic and experience in crash dump analysis.

A particular problem that causes a panic may arise through a number of different code paths in the kernel. The stack traces from several occurrences of such a bug will probably show several common routines below the panic frame, but may have divergent paths thereafter. We generally consider three or more frames following "panic" to be a close match, unless the panic is a kernel memory fault or a lock problem, which we'll discuss further on. This should be considered a rough guideline, rather than an absolute definition.

It can also be helpful to examine the preserved message buffer in a crash dump. This buffer contains messages that were to be written to the system message file at the time the panic occurred. Because a panic may occur very quickly when a problem arises in the system, there may be messages in this buffer that provide valuable clues about the cause of the panic. These messages will not be in the actual message file because they had not yet been written at the time the panic occurred. The contents of the preserved message buffer can be found in the crash-data file or displayed from the crash dump as follows:

```
(dbx) p *pmsgbuf
```

The following example is part of the preserved message buffer from the crash dump of an AdvFS-related panic:

```
AdvFS I/O error:
     Domain#Fileset: seq-01#vol_01
     Mounted on: /vol_01
```

```
Volume: /dev/disk/dsk12c
Tag: 0x00000055.8001
Page: 3
Block: 51533776
Block count: 8192
Type of operation: Write
Error: 5
EEI: 0x6200
I/O error appears to be due to a hardware problem.
Check the binary error log for details.
To obtain the name of the file on which
the error occurred, type the command:
/sbin/advfs/tag2name /vol_01/.tags/85
```

This information from the preserved message buffer identifies the specific AdvFS domain and fileset that encountered problems. This kind of information is extremely helpful in identifying the problem that led to the panic.

Among the most common panic types are kernel memory faults, simple lock timeouts, and other lock-related panics. These panic types are somewhat generic, meaning that they are usually the result of some other problem within the kernel. Because of their generic nature and the fact that they are among the most common panics, they deserve some further discussion, which we'll undertake in the following sections.

5.2.2.1 Kernel Memory Faults

When Tru64 UNIX tries to access a memory location that is not mapped into physical memory, a page fault occurs to load the desired page into memory. This is perfectly normal for user mode code and is the fundamental mechanism of all virtual memory systems. However, all code and data structures in the Tru64 UNIX kernel are "wired" into memory (i.e., their pages stay in physical memory at all times). If a page fault occurs in kernel mode, it means that the kernel has tried to access a location that's not currently mapped—by definition, an invalid location for kernel access. This could occur when the kernel tries to read or write data, or when it goes to fetch the next instruction to execute. These three cases are distinguished by one of the following messages preceding the "kernel memory fault" message:

- `trap: invalid memory read access from kernel mode`
- `trap: invalid memory write access from kernel mode`
- `trap: invalid memory ifetch access in kernel mode`

Following the "trap: invalid memory…" message, the kernel prints some additional information about the kernel memory fault, as shown in the following example:

```
trap: invalid memory read access from kernel mode
     faulting virtual address:     0x0000000100000007
     pc of faulting instruction:   0xfffffc00002ab090
     ra contents at time of fault: 0xfffffc00004b295c
     sp contents at time of fault: 0xfffffe054430f960
```

The "faulting virtual address" is the unmapped (and therefore invalid) address that the kernel was trying to access. The next two lines show the addresses of the instruction that caused the fault and the return address (i.e., the instruction that the kernel would return to after exiting its current routine). The last line displays the kernel stack pointer at the time of the fault. The above information is also stored in a data structure appropriately called "kernel_memory_fault_data." This data structure can be displayed with the following command:

```
(dbx) px kernel_memory_fault_data
```

which displays the following output in this case:

```
struct {
    fault_va = 0x100000007
    fault_pc = 0xfffffc00002ab090
    fault_ra = 0xfffffc00004b295c
    fault_sp = 0xfffffe054430f960
    access = 0x0
    status = 0x0
    cpunum = 0x1
    count = 0x1
    pcb = 0xfffffe054430fa00
    thread = 0xfffffc00f612a000
    task = 0xfffffc00ffe1b500
    proc = 0xfffffc00ffe1b740
}
```

The first four elements match the four lines printed with the kernel memory fault message. The data structure also includes other information that may be useful to the serious kernel debugger.

The invalid address that causes the fault is generally the result of corruption in some kernel data structure (which in turn is frequently, though not always, caused by a kernel bug). In rare cases, the kernel address can be caused by a hardware problem (e.g., an I/O adapter returning an invalid buffer address). Although the message "kernel memory fault" sometimes causes administrators to suspect faulty memory, it is extremely unlikely that a memory error would not be detected by the error correction circuitry (ECC) in the memory hardware.

The "pc" and "ra" can be converted to addresses that indicate the faulting routine and its caller. This information can be useful in determining the general area (AdvFS, networking, etc.) in which the panic occurred. dbx will display the name of the routine that contains an instruction (among other information) when the address of the instruction is followed by "/i". In the example case:

```
(dbx) 0xfffffc00002ab090/i
  [solock:1265, 0xfffffc00002ab090]   ldl     t0, 4(a0)
(dbx) 0xfffffc00004b295c/i
  [tcp_handle_timers:1020, 0xfffffc00004b295c]   ldl
v0,   0(s2)
```

The output shows that the fault occurred in kernel routine "solock", which was called by routine "tcp_handle_timers". This matches the information printed in the stack trace shown above. Why get the information this way when it's more easily found by displaying the stack trace? In rare cases, stack corruption can make it impossible for dbx to display all or part of the stack trace. In such cases, the method just shown provides an alternative method of determining the faulting routine.

The stack trace of a kernel memory fault always resembles the above example for the first few frames following the panic frame. The relevant part of that stack trace is as follows:

```
   4 panic(s = (unallocated - symbol optimized away))
[."./../../../src/kernel/bsd/subr_prf.c":1309,
0xfffffc0000294b28]
   5 trap(a0 = (...), a1 = (...), a2 = (...), code =
(unallocated - symbol optimized away), exc_frame =
```

```
(unallocated - symbol optimized away)) [."./../../../src/
kernel/arch/alpha/trap.c":2262,
0xfffffc00005ea400]
   6 _XentMM(0x0, 0xfffffc00002ab090, 0xfffffc000099ab20,
0x100000003, 0x8b5f9)
[."./../../../src/kernel/arch/alpha/locore.s":2115,
0xfffffc00005e41d4]
   7 solock(0x0, 0xfffffc00002ab090, 0xfffffc000099ab20,
0x100000003, 0x8b5f9) [."./../../../src/kernel/bsd/
uipc_socket.c":1265, 0xfffffc00002ab090]
   8 tcp_handle_timers(0xfffffc008133ef00, 0x8b5f9,
0xfffffc00f6128800, 0xfffffc0000be16d0, 0xfffffc002a697200)
[."./../../../src/kernel/netinet/tcp_timer.c":10
15, 0xfffffc00004b2958]
   9 tcp_rad_slowtimo(0x0, 0x0, 0x0, 0x0,
0xfffffc0001110000) [."./../../../src/kernel/netinet/
tcp_timer.c":1136, 0xfffffc00004b2d90]
```

(We've left out frames 0 through 3, which displayed a secondary panic that occurred after the kernel memory fault. As noted above, secondary panics are irrelevant to the real problem and should always be ignored.)

"_XentMM" is the PALcode (firmware) routine that handles page faults. If the system is in kernel mode, the handler calls the panic routine for the reasons discussed above. As such, a kernel memory fault panic will always have the routine sequence "panic," "trap," and "_XentMM" in consecutive frames. The next frame after "_XentMM" indicates the kernel routine that was executing when the invalid memory access took place. This may be helpful in identifying the general area of the panic. The last part of each stack frame shows the kernel source file that contains the routine. Even if you don't have a source license, the name of the routine can be a useful clue. In this example, the faulting routine "solock" is found in source file "../../../../src/kernel/bsd/uipc_socket.c," while its caller "tcp_handle_timers" is in source file "../../../../src/kernel/netinet/tcp_timer.c." This is a pretty strong indicator that the crash happened in TCP networking code, specifically in something to do with sockets. The usefulness of this information varies. For example, if the system in this case were experiencing network problems (e.g., a bad network interface card), it's conceivable that the crash could be directly due to underlying network errors. In such a case, the first priority would be to correct the network problems.

A variation of the kernel memory fault occurs when the kernel attempts to access an unaligned memory address (i.e., one that is not on a longword or quadword boundary, depending on the instruction being executed). When this happens, the panic string is "Unaligned kernel space access from kernel mode," and the key part of the stack immediately follows the frames containing "panic," "afault_trap," and "_XentUna," in that order. In this type of panic, the kernel_memory_fault_data structure is not used; however, you can still find the calling routine by examining the stack frame that follows the "_XentUna" frame.

Looking at the faulting routines can provide a clue to the cause of a kernel memory fault, but that's all it is—a clue. Because a kernel memory fault can be caused by any problem that leads to kernel memory corruption, additional analysis is required to understand the cause of the fault thoroughly. In practical terms, analysis beyond matching the stack trace against known problems requires access to Tru64 UNIX source code and experience in kernel debugging. As such, the analysis of most kernel memory faults should be considered a matter for HP technical support.

5.2.2.2 Simple Lock Timeouts and Other Lock-Related Panics

Tru64 UNIX, like many other operating systems, uses a multithreaded kernel capable of executing simultaneously on multiple processors within a single computer. As such, independent threads running on different processors may require access to the same data structures. Without some form of locking mechanism to prevent simultaneous modification by multiple threads, data structures could easily become corrupted. Tru64 UNIX uses two forms of locks for this purpose: simple locks, which operate at the most basic level, and the more sophisticated complex locks. Problems with complex locks can lead to a variety of panics beginning with the string "lock_," such as "lock_write: hierarchy violation." Analysis of panics involving complex locks is well beyond the scope of this book and should be left to HP technical support.

When a kernel thread requires access to an object protected by a simple lock, it attempts to acquire the lock for the required access (read or write). If the lock is successfully acquired, the kernel thread performs some operation on the object and then releases (unlocks) the simple lock. On the other hand, if another thread is already holding the lock, the thread trying to acquire the lock will wait until the other thread releases the lock. (This is somewhat oversimplified, but it conveys the general idea.) If a thread waits on a simple lock for longer than a designated timeout period, a simple lock timeout occurs. The timeout period is defined by kernel parameter "lock-timeout" in the generic subsystem and is normally set to 15 seconds. This is far longer than necessary, because most locks should be held for no more than a small fraction of a second. A simple lock timeout indicates that something is seriously wrong, so the kernel panics with the panic string "simple_lock: time limit exceeded."

The simple lock mechanism is not entirely suited to nonuniform memory architecture (NUMA) systems, such as the AlphaServer GS80, GS160, and GS320. A different locking scheme, known as "MCS locks," is used on NUMA systems. Although the underlying implementation is different, the principle is the same. On a NUMA system, the type of panic described above would have a panic string of "mcs_lock: time limit exceeded," rather than "simple_lock: time limit exceeded."

The immediate cause of a simple lock timeout is a thread holding a lock for longer than the timeout of 15 seconds. But how can this happen? There are a few possibilities:

- A kernel thread fails to unlock a simple lock that it holds (i.e., a kernel programming bug).
- A kernel thread is blocked (waiting on some event) while it holds a simple lock.
- A CPU hangs (due to a hardware problem) while executing a thread that holds a simple lock.

Although timeouts are the most common, there are a number of other simple lock panics (e.g., "simple_lock: lock already owned by cpu"). These other simple lock panics are usually, though not always, caused by kernel programming errors.

Unfortunately, simple lock timeouts are usually even more difficult to analyze than kernel memory faults. Identifying the calling routine in the stack trace of a simple lock panic may not be particularly helpful because the problem is not the thread that's trying to get the lock; rather, it's the thread that's been holding the lock for too long. Identifying the problem thread is not always possible; when it is, the kernel debugging techniques involved are beyond the scope of this book.

As with most other panics, detailed analysis of a simple lock panic is probably best left to HP technical support. However, there are a few troubleshooting techniques that may prove helpful. When a simple lock panic occurs, the kernel prints some additional information, just as it does with kernel memory faults. This can be found in the system message file or, in some cases, in the preserved message buffer in the crash dump. Consider the following example:

```
simple_lock: time limit exceeded
     pc of caller:          0xfffffc000025ad08
     lock address:          0xfffffc0000200eb8
     lock info addr:        0xfffffc00007775d0
     lock class name:       processor.callout_lock
     current lock state:    0xd600015d0025aa91
(cpu=0,pc=0xfffffc000025aa90,busy)
```

The relevant portion of the stack trace from this panic is shown below. The top 21 frames happened after the initial panic and are therefore irrelevant, so they have been excluded.

```
  21 panic(0x0, 0xfffffc000025aa90, 0x0,
0xfffffc0000670268, 0x0) [."./../../../src/kernel/bsd
/subr_prf.c":842, 0xfffffc0000286c54]
  22 simple_lock_fault(slp = 0xfffffc0000200eb8,
state = 0xd, caller = 0xfffffc000025ad08, arg = (nil),
fmt = (nil), error = 0xfffffc00005fab70 = "simple_lock:
time limit exceeded") [."./../../../src/kernel/kern/
lock.c":2643, 0xfffffc00002b106c]
  23 simple_lock_time_violation(slp =
 0xfffffc0000200eb8, state = 0xd, caller = (nil))
 [."./../../../src/kernel/kern/lock.c":2692,
0xfffffc00002b11c8]
  24 untimeout_cpu(fun = 0xfffffc00002baa00, arg =
0xfffffc004af7fc00 = ."^ø+," rem_arg = (...))
 [."./../../../src/kernel/bsd/kern_clock.c":1915,
0xfffffc000025ad08]
  25 cur_thread_timeout_cancel(th = 0xfffffc004af7fc00)
[."./../../../src/kernel/kern/sched_prim.c":1241,
 0xfffffc00002baab0]
  26 thread_continue(thread = 0xfffffc007bb85180,
cur_thread = 0xfffffc004af7fc00)
[."./../../../src/kernel/kern/sched_prim.c":2666,
 0xfffffc00002bc83c]
  27 thread_block() [."./../../../src/kernel/kern
/sched_prim.c":2373, 0xfffffc00002bc26c]
```

```
  28 mpsleep(0x1, 0x0, 0x0, 0x0, 0x0) [."./../../../src
/kernel/bsd/kern_synch.c":577, 0xfffffc000027e6fc]
  29 nxm_idle(0x0, 0x140010a80, 0x3ffc0080310,
0x100000000, 0xfffffc0066233560)
[."./../../../src/kernel/kern/syscall_subr.c":1934,
 0xfffffc00002c04c4]
  30 _Xsyscall(0x8, 0x120058720, 0x140016820, 0x0, 0x0)
 [."./../../../src/kernel/arch/alpha/locore.s":1678,
 0xfffffc0000478734]
```

The stack trace for a simple lock timeout usually includes "panic," "simple_lock_fault," and "simple_lock_time_violation" as the first three significant frames. The next frame ("untimeout_cpu" in this case) identifies the routine that was trying to acquire the simple lock. The additional information shown above tells us which lock—or at least which type of lock—it was. The first of the following lines:

```
    lock class name:      processor.callout_lock
    current lock state:   0xd600015d0025aa91
(cpu=0,pc=0xfffffc000025aa90,busy)
```

identifies the lock as a "processor.callout_lock." The "pc" field in the second line identifies the instruction that took out the lock. To decode this, we have dbx translate it as an instruction:

```
(dbx) 0xfffffc000025aa90/i
  [timeout_cpu:1813, 0xfffffc000025aa90]     bsr    ra,
simple_lock(line 1215)      <ra=0xfffffc000047c3f0>
```

Although this identifies the locking instruction as part of routine timeout_cpu(), it does not identify the actual thread that executed the instruction. As such, this information may be of limited usefulness.

For recurring simple lock (or other lock) panics, it may be helpful to turn on kernel lock debugging. This is done by setting kernel parameter "lockmode" in the generic subsystem to a value of 4 and rebooting the system. Under normal circumstances, the kernel determines the value for lockmode at boot time, as shown in Table 5.2.

Setting lockmode to 4 will cause the kernel to perform additional checks on all locking operations. If any problems are encountered, the kernel will

Table 5.2 *Lockmode Values*

Value	Meaning
0	Single processor, no real-time preemption
1	Single processor with real-time preemption
2	Multiprocessor, no real-time preemption
3	Multiprocessor with real-time preemption
4	Multiprocessor with real-time preemption and lock debugging

panic and the crash dump will contain additional lock debugging information—the analysis of which is unfortunately beyond the scope of this book. There are a couple of cautionary notes regarding lockmode 4. First, it can have a negative impact on system performance, although this is usually minor to negligible. Second, it will not reduce the number of lock-related panics; in fact, it may cause them to increase because the kernel is being deliberately intolerant of locking irregularities. As such, we do not recommend using lockmode 4 in normal operation. It should be used only when troubleshooting lock-related panics.

Because simple lock timeouts only occur in multiprocessor environments, a temporary workaround is to disable all but one processor, as described in section 5.1.2.5. However, the performance penalty of this workaround is severe, and it should be considered only as an extreme measure.

5.2.3 Panics Without Crash Dumps

In theory, every panic, unless it occurs very early in the boot sequence, should create a crash dump. When a dump is not created, troubleshooting must focus on examining the system log files as discussed previously. If a system repeatedly crashes without producing a dump, and the cause of the panic can't be determined from log files, an effort should be made to find out why no crash dumps are being produced. There are six possible reasons for this:

1. There is not enough swap space to hold the contents of memory. If this happens, make sure you are selecting partial dumps or add additional swap space.

2. There is not enough space in the crash directory to hold the crash dump files. In this case, the savecore program will print an error message and return the system to single-user mode (unless SAVECORE_FLAGS is set to "M," in which case the dump is lost). This provides the opportunity to define a different crash directory by setting SAVECORE_DIR or to make additional space available in the existing crash directory (e.g., by deleting old crash dump files). After solving the problem with either of these methods, savecore can be run again to save the crash dump files.
3. The first swap partition defined in /etc/fstab doesn't have a type of "sw" or is not the partition defined by /sbin/swapdefault. This is a problem only for Tru64 UNIX versions prior to V5.0.
4. One or more swap disks has a LUN other than zero. Like #3, this is a problem only on pre-V5.0 systems.
5. One of more of the swap disks has a missing or corrupt disk label.
6. Kernel variable "dont_dump" is set. Check this as follows:

```
# dbx -k /vmunix
(dbx) pd dont_dump
0
```

If the value is nonzero, crash dumps will not be written. (Note: this could only have been set by someone using dbx to modify the variable in memory or patch the kernel file.) To correct it, enter the following commands:

```
# dbx -k /vmunix

(dbx) a dont_dump=0

(dbx) patch dont_dump=0

(dbx) quit
```

The "a" command assigns a new value to the variable in memory. The "patch" command patches the value in the kernel file on disk. The first changes the immediate value, while the second ensures that the change will persist when the system reboots.

If any of the preceding problems exist, correct them and verify that the system can perform a crash dump. One way to do this is by deliberately inducing a panic:

```
# dbx -k /vmunix
(dbx) a hz=0
```

This is a transient, in-memory change and will not persist after the system panics and reboots. If the system still doesn't generate a crash dump, check for the other problems listed above. If that doesn't resolve the problem, your best bet is to contact HP technical support.

5.2.4 Nonpanic Crashes

When a system crashes with no trace of a panic—not only no crash dump, but no panic entries in any log files—the problem is almost certainly due to hardware or environmental issues. If this is a one-shot occurrence, there is unfortunately little that can be done to troubleshoot the problem. For a recurring problem, it should first be verified that the system really isn't panicking. It's possible, though unlikely, that a panic could occur due to a problem that prevented any of the system log files from being written. (An example of such a problem was discussed in section 2.2.4.) The best idea in such a case is to capture the output of the serial console, either by attaching a printer or connecting the serial line to another system that logs the console output. If this isn't possible (e.g., if the system has a graphics console that is always in use), consider moving the system log files to a different file system, preferably on a different storage controller. If the panic is caused by a problem such as the one discussed in section 2.2.4, this method will bypass the problem and allow the panic to leave some evidence of its occurrence.

For systems that crash with no panic, the most common cause is power supply problems—either the external or the internal power supply. If there is reason to suspect the external power supply, consider placing a power monitor on the incoming line to monitor the consistency of the internal power supply.

5.3 System Hangs

System hangs are among the most frustrating problems for a system administrator. Unlike a system panic, there is little or no immediate evidence to guide troubleshooting efforts. The focus shifts to determining what the system is doing and why it is not responding in the expected manner, and then determining the appropriate course of action to resolve the problem. In most cases, it's not possible to recover from a hang cleanly or even to gather much information while the system is hung. A reboot is usually required to alleviate the hung condition. Unfortunately, this destroys the "live" evidence on the system, making troubleshooting more difficult. Some evidence can be preserved by forcing a crash dump before rebooting the system. The resulting crash dump files contain the contents of physical memory at the time of the hang, providing a snapshot of conditions at that instant.

Not all hangs are created equal. From a user's point of view, a hang can be any condition in which the system is not responding. This could be caused by an application not responding, a network connection problem, or a system that is truly hung (i.e., not executing at all). Users tend to be an impatient lot; a system or application that is actually responding very slowly may be reported to be hung. As such, the first step in troubleshooting a hang is to determine the severity of the hang, a process that is discussed in section 5.3.1.

Most hangs are not cleanly recoverable, and it's necessary to reset the system (after forcing a crash dump). After the system is restored to service, it's important to look for evidence in the same places as you would for a crash: the binary error log, the system message file, and other system logs. It's also important to note what the system was doing at the time—for example, running a very large or new job of some type, or experiencing an extremely high user load. For recurring problems, look for patterns to try to isolate key elements common to multiple hangs. If you find an apparent key element, try reproducing the problem if at all possible. This is always a useful troubleshooting technique, but it's particularly valuable when troubleshooting system hangs, simply because hangs frequently provide little else to work with.

5.3.1 Determining the Severity of a Hang

Determining the severity of a hang is a matter of trying various ways to elicit a response from the system. If the system fails to respond in any way, it's completely hung. When this happens, there is little alternative but to force a crash (a procedure we'll discuss in the next section) and reboot the system. The first step is to try to ping the system from another host on the network. If the system responds to the ping, it indicates that the kernel is still running and able to respond to network interrupts. In this case, the system is not completely hung but is only blocked from servicing certain threads and requests.

If there's no response to the ping command, first verify that local network links are up (e.g., make sure other nodes can ping each other). If the network is working, then either the network interface has failed locally (just on the hung system), or the system is truly hung—the kernel can't even respond to network interrupts. In either case, try to log in as root at the system console. If this also fails, there's not a lot you can do at this point other than creating a forced crash dump and rebooting the system. However, if you can log in successfully, try some simple commands such as "ls," "ps," and "vmstat." If these work, then at least the kernel is still operating to some degree. If the system appears to function normally at this point (i.e., if the problem is only that you can't log in over the network), then see Chapter 7 for information on troubleshooting network problems.

If the system is still having problems when you log in at the console, there are two likely causes: Either the kernel is blocked from performing certain activities, or there is a performance problem severe enough to make the system appear to be hung. Performance problems are quickly revealed by a few basic commands: uptime (check for high load average), vmstat (low free memory), and "ps aux | more" (processes with unusually high CPU or virtual memory usage). Chapter 6 describes troubleshooting techniques for performance issues. Use the information in that chapter to help determine whether the hang is really a performance problem, and if so, how to go about correcting it.

If certain operations succeed but others hang, the kernel (or some process) is blocked (i.e., waiting for some event or resource). The ps(1) command is invaluable in this situation. This command has a large repertoire (and two flavors) of switches, but the combination we find most useful is "ps aux," often piped to grep, head, or more. In this particular situation, check the process state field (the column labeled "S") for all processes. This consists of one or more characters, as shown in Table 5.3.

Table 5.3 *Process State Indicator Characters*

Character	Process State
R	Runnable (waiting for its turn on a CPU)
U	Uninterruptible (waiting for a kernel event)
S	Sleeping (less than 20 seconds)

Table 5.3 *Process State Indicator Characters (continued)*

Character	Process State
I	Idle (sleeping longer than 20 seconds)
T	Stopped
H	Halted
W	Swapped out
>	Exceeding memory soft limit
N	Niced (process priority reduced)
<	Process priority raised
+	Process group leader

Examine the state characters for processes of interest (e.g., system daemons or applications that aren't responding). If a process is failing to responding to user requests, and it's in the I (idle) state, something is preventing the process from seeing and responding to the requests. In this situation, stopping and restarting the process may resolve the problem. A process state of U is more serious. This flag indicates that the process is an uninterruptible wait state. This state should not persist for longer than a fraction of a second. If a particular process remains in the U state, something is seriously wrong with it. Even worse, processes in the U state usually can't be killed.

When a process—whether system or user—is not responding, the first recourse is usually to try stopping and restarting the process. This is fairly simple in principle. Use the ps command to find the process identifier (PID). (If the ps command itself hangs, try using the dbx command "kps" as an alternative.) The PID is an argument to the kill(1) command, which is used to send a signal to a process. By default, the kill command sends TERM (signal 15) to the receiving process. This is usually sufficient to terminate the process normally because most UNIX processes are designed to respond to a TERM signal by exiting gracefully. It may take a few seconds for the process to perform some final housekeeping and exit. Some daemons are also programmed to respond to HUP (signal 1) as a "warm reset," causing them to return to default conditions, reread configuration files, or perform similar initialization activities. As such, it's worth trying HUP before TERM in most cases. If HUP works, it's less drastic than actually terminating the process, and if it doesn't work, nothing is lost.

Unfortunately, some daemons will ignore the TERM signal. If TERM doesn't cause the process to exit, it may be necessary to use the "big hammer" of KILL (signal 9), which cannot be handled or ignored by a process. This should be used only as a last resort because it will not allow the process to clean up after itself before exiting. Depending on what the process was doing, you could end up with corrupted files or another undesirable result. Therefore, proper system administration practice is to try the HUP and TERM signals first and wait for a reasonable period of time before taking further action.

If a process is in the uninterruptible (U) state, even a KILL signal will not cause it to terminate. The U state is usually caused by a hardware or driver issue that prevents any further action until some kernel-level activity is completed. It's possible that the uninterruptible state is transitory, so you should wait for a few minutes for the problem to clear itself before assuming the worst. If the U state persists, you must take steps to correct the underlying driver or hardware issue. This may involve replacing hardware or installing a patched driver on the system. (If you run into this and cannot make any further progress, consider making a call to HP technical support for assistance.) It's usually necessary to reboot the system in order to clear up an uninterruptible process. To analyze the problem after the fact, it's necessary to force a crash dump (see section 5.3.2) before rebooting.

When you attempt to kill a process, it will change states and eventually become a defunct process (commonly called a *zombie*) just prior to its final exit. This state should be very short in duration and is no reason for concern in normal operation of a UNIX system. If, however, defunct processes are hanging around for a long time and seem to be growing in number, there is reason to be concerned. Although zombies no longer consume most of the resources that they once used, too many zombies can cause a system to run out of process slots, thereby preventing the creation of new processes. A zombie process cannot be killed because it is already "dead" (hence the nickname); the zombie is simply waiting to be cleaned up by the system.

Zombie processes tend to arise in either of two situations. First (and most commonly), they are the result of a poorly written application that does not correctly handle exiting child processes. Luckily, this situation is easy to spot and correct; simply find the zombie's parent process using the PPID (parent process ID) field of the "ps -ef" command. Then kill the parent process, if you can do so without creating additional problems. When the parent process terminates, the defunct child processes are cleaned up automatically. The next step is to find the person responsible for the program and ask that individual to fix the programming error. Sometimes this happens in a commercial application; in that case, you should contact the vendor and open a problem report.

The second cause of zombie processes is (hypothetically) a kernel problem that prevents the zombies from exiting. This could be a hardware issue or a problem with the operating system itself. In this case, you should contact HP technical support and report the problem.

5.3.2 Forcing a Crash Dump

If a system is unresponsive to the extent that root can't even log in at the system console (or can't accomplish anything useful after logging in), the only recourse is to reset the system. However, it is very important to force a crash dump first! Rebooting the system clears the contents of physical memory, while forcing a crash dump preserves the contents of memory at the time of the hang. The resulting crash dump files can be analyzed to try and determine the cause of the hang. This level of analysis usually requires technical support or considerable expertise in kernel debugging and is generally beyond the scope of this book. However, we will mention a few basic techniques that may provide clues to the general problem area.

In order to force a crash dump, you must first halt the system. Don't press the reset button or cycle power, because this will clear the contents of physical memory. The actual halting mechanism varies depending on the processor type and usually involves a halt button, the Control-P key sequence, or a command interpreter. Whichever method is appropriate for your system, use it to bring the system to the console prompt. If the halt mechanism doesn't produce a console prompt, there is almost certainly a hardware problem, and you should troubleshoot the problem accordingly.

At the console prompt, enter the command "CRASH." This will start the crash dump process described in section 5.2.1. When the system returns to the console prompt, enter the boot command, and crash dump files will be generated by the savecore utility. The resulting crash dump files can be packaged (along with other useful system files) by the "sys_check -escalate" command for submission to technical support. The crash dump can also be examined using the techniques discussed in the following section.

5.3.3 Analyzing a Forced Crash

In broad terms, the techniques for troubleshooting a forced crash are the same as those for a crash caused by a panic. For both types of crashes, it's important to look at system logs and other circumstantial evidence, and to use dbx or kdbx to examine the resulting crash dump. However, the information to be gained from a crash dump is different for a forced crash than for a panic dump. For example, there's not much point in looking at the panic string in a forced crash dump; forced crashes always have a panic string of "hardware restart." Similarly, looking at the panic thread in a forced crash may or may not be useful. If you're fortunate, the stack trace of the thread that was executing may provide a clue as to what is blocking the kernel from proceeding. However, it's just as likely that the executing thread is completely unrelated to the actual problem.

In most cases, analyzing forced crash dumps from system hangs is even more difficult than analyzing panic dumps, and we strongly recommend submitting them to HP technical support. However, there are a few data structures that may be of interest to amateur crash dump analysts. One of these, the preserved message buffer, has already been mentioned. This buffer is displayed by the following dbx command:

```
(dbx) p *pmsgbuf
```

This data structure contains messages that had not yet been written to the system message file at the time of the crash. These often provide valuable clues—for example, messages indicating that the root file system was full (a situation that usually causes a system hang).

A Tru64 UNIX system will hang if free memory is depleted to the point of exhaustion (less than 10 free pages). To check for this possibility, examine the free-page count in the crash dump. The relevant data structures, like many others, changed between Tru64 UNIX versions 4 and 5, so the appropriate dbx command depends on which version the crash dump is from. For version 4 or earlier, it is

```
(dbx) pd vm_perfsum.vpf_freepages
4227
```

If the number of free pages is significantly less than the value of vm subsystem parameter "vm_page_free_target," the system is short of memory. However, it probably won't hang (at least for this reason) unless the free page count is down to around 10 or less. In this example, the system had 4,227 pages of free memory at the time of the hang, so memory exhaustion was definitely not the problem. To find the value of vm_page_free_target directly from the crash dump, use the following command for version 4 or earlier:

```
(dbx) pd vm_page_free_target
128
```

The version 5 command is as follows:

```
(dbx) pd vm_tune.vt_vm_free_target
256
```

Tru64 UNIX version 5 introduced the concept of resource affinity domains (RADs) to support NUMA systems. Consequently, it's necessary to check the free page count in all RADs within a system. Non-NUMA systems have only one RAD, which is RAD 0. To check the free page count, the command is

```
(dbx) pd ((struct rad *) rad_ptr[0]).rad_mad.md_vm.vm_free_count
23031
```

In this example from a non-NUMA system, there were 23,031 free pages. For NUMA systems, it would be necessary to repeat this command for each RAD in the system, replacing the "0" in the command with each RAD number.

Before you call support

Before calling technical support for a system crash or hang, try the following:

- For repeated problems, try undoing any recent changes (adding hardware, using a new kernel, etc.) and see whether that resolves the problem.
- If the problem is so severe that the system won't stay up, try the troubleshooting ideas for boot problems listed in section 5.1.
- For an apparently hung system, try logging in as root at the system console. It may be that the problem is limited to network access.
- Don't reset a hung system without first forcing a crash dump.
- Check the console firmware version and verify that it's compatible with the version of Tru64 UNIX that you're running.
- If you're going to send a crash dump (forced or otherwise) to technical support, run "sys_check -escalate" to collect the necessary files into a single package. See Chapter 3 for more information on using the sys_check tool.

6

System Performance

Performance is your reality. Forget everything else.

—Harold Geneen

The performance of a computer system can best be defined as the system's ability to accomplish its assigned tasks. Good performance means that the system is performing its workload in an acceptable amount of time and with acceptable usage of system resources. This can be difficult to quantify because it depends on a variety of factors that are both objective (performance indexes) and subjective (user perception). On the other hand, it's usually pretty obvious when a performance problem exists: things don't happen within acceptable (objective or subjective) time or resource constraints.

Managing system performance has two primary aspects: maximizing performance (proactive) and responding to specific performance problems (reactive). Maximizing system performance is an ongoing task of evaluating current performance, making adjustments, and observing the effects. This is a subject about which much has been written, and it is really beyond the scope of this book. Because our focus is on troubleshooting, we'll concentrate on the second aspect of performance management: responding to specific performance problems.

Among the many resources available on the subject of performance and tuning, we especially recommend the Tru64 UNIX System Configuration and Tuning Manual. This document has improved with each successive version, and the current edition is clear, informative, and practical—a fine example of what computer manuals should be like. Anyone interested in system performance should spend some time going through this manual; the time spent will be a worthwhile investment.

6.1 General Principles

At the most basic level, performance problems are really very simple. All activities require certain amounts of one or more resources. If sufficient resources aren't available, the activity can't be performed as desired. This is true not only with respect to computers but in all aspects of life. For example, if you'd like to take a two-week vacation to Hawaii, you need two primary resources: money to pay for the trip, and time off to take the trip. If either resource is lacking, you can't take the desired vacation. Such resource shortages often lead to workarounds. For example, you could choose to work within the available resources by taking a less expensive or shorter vacation. Alternatively, an extra amount of one resource sometimes makes a tradeoff possible. If you have plenty of money but only a week of paid vacation, you might be able to take a week of unpaid leave in order to have the full vacation. Such tradeoffs aren't always possible; in this example, the tradeoff doesn't work in the other direction. If you don't have enough money to go to Hawaii, it doesn't really matter whether you have enough time off.

With regard to computer systems, a resource is any component (hardware or software) needed to accomplish a particular task. For practical purposes, the main resources are the three principal components taught in every introductory computer class: CPU, memory, and I/O. Every computer job needs a certain amount of each of these three resources. Some activities require more of one resource than another; the actual amounts needed obviously depend on the type of work being performed. Therefore, understanding a system's workload is extremely important when it comes to identifying potential resource bottlenecks. Unfortunately, the trend toward consolidating multiple functions onto a single large server complicates this understanding. If a system is responsible only for serving Web pages, it's pretty clear that I/O (particularly network connections) is likely to be the most critical resource. But if the system also runs an Oracle database and serves as a development platform for mathematical models, good system performance will require a different mix of resources depending on the workload mix at any particular time.

6.1.1 Understanding System Performance

There are a variety of factors that affect the performance of a Tru64 UNIX system, some of which are nontechnical and beyond the ability of a system administrator to change. Understanding the nature of these factors is a fundamental part of performance management and troubleshooting. Of these, perhaps the most important factor to understand is the system's normal environment and workload. It's difficult to identify abnormalities without first knowing what is normal. This understanding is gained over time by monitoring a system to determine its average throughput and behavior. Knowing a system's typical workload also allows an administrator to see short- and long-term trends in system activity, and to predict the effects of changes to the system configuration, applications, or usage patterns.

As a starting point for understanding a system's performance, the following questions should help the effort to characterize and understand the normal workload:

- What are the types of applications running on the system (for example, database server, program development, Web server)?
- What is the average number of users on the system at each time of day?
- What are the busiest times of operation?
- Which jobs run at which times of the day?
- What are the known resource-intensive jobs?
- What is the average response time at various times of the day?

The answers to some of these questions are best obtained by logging into the system and monitoring its behavior. Tru64 UNIX provides tools and utilities that allow the system administrator to view the usage of various system resources. We discuss several of these tools in more detail at appropriate places throughout this book, but a short list would include vmstat, uptime, iostat, advfsstat, netstat, swapon, collect, and sys_check. All of these are part of the Tru64 UNIX distribution. In addition, there are also some popular (but unsupported) performance monitoring tools available on the Internet, such as "monitor" and "top."

Over time, a system administrator should gain an understanding of what is normal for a particular system. "Normal," though, is a relative term and assumes a reasonably stable workload. This isn't always the case in real life; for example, a financial management system may be quite speedy during the first part of the month, but become nearly unusable toward the end of the month as the system is under stress to complete an end-of-month close-out. In this case, both situations are normal as long as it is understood what the system is being asked to do and when. If, however, the system's response gets suddenly worse in the middle of a month, such behavior would most likely be considered abnormal and worthy of investigation. The "historical mode" feature of the collect(8) utility is quite useful for understanding a system's performance over time.

Some of the characterization questions listed above are best answered by working closely with the user community and understanding their needs and perceptions. Users tend to accept an average response time as normal, and jobs are expected to finish in about the same amount of time every time they run. These expectations aren't always valid, but they exist nevertheless. In a time-sharing system such as Tru64 UNIX, an individual user's response time can vary greatly depending on other work going on at the same time. Users that come from a PC-only background may not understand this, and it is up to the system administrator to educate them rather than to effect a change to the system's behavior.

In addition, you may discover that a user's perception of reduced response time or increased execution time is due to factors outside your control. For example, a user may be connected to the system via a slower connection than usual, resulting in slower response to that user only. The system may be performing well within acceptable parameters but still seem slower to that particular user. A system administrator needs the proper skills to interpret user complaints; one of the most important skills is patience. You will occasionally receive feedback that "the system seems slow." When this happens, work with the affected users to quantify their perceptions and enlist their help in collecting basic troubleshooting information, such as the following:

- What is the user's measured response/execution time versus normal?
- Are reported hung processes truly hung?
- Did the problem occur suddenly or did it degrade over time?
- Is this the first time this behavior has been experienced?
- Can the problem be duplicated?
- How many (and which) users were on the system at the time of the problem? What were they doing?
- Is the problem on the local system or a remote system?

Going through this process with users will help to educate them and (hopefully) impress upon them the importance of collecting useful data rather than just complaining that the system is slow. That way, you will be making them part of the process of identifying the problem and finding the solution.

6.1.2 Troubleshooting Guidelines

In the following sections, we'll discuss each of the three main resources (CPU, memory, and I/O) with respect to common performance problems and possible corrective actions. Before getting down to that level, though, we'll present some general principles in the form of a "top 10" list of performance troubleshooting guidelines. These guidelines are based on recurring themes from performance problems that we've investigated in our experience as support personnel.

Guideline 1: Every situation is unique.

Don't assume that a solution that worked for one problem or one system will necessarily work in another situation. Similar problems often have similar causes, but not always. It's certainly worth looking for similarities and patterns when troubleshooting, but don't focus on one particular solution just because it worked in the past—at least not until you perform further analysis.

Guideline 2: Work on one problem at a time.

Sometimes a problem with one resource is caused by problems in another area. Fixing the primary problem may resolve others as well. The trick is to determine whether multiple problems are related and, if so, which one is the fundamental problem. We'll discuss some common problem interactions in the later sections of this chapter.

Guideline 3: Look for memory problems first.

Memory is the resource for which adjustments usually provide the best return. This applies both to tuning—small adjustments can yield large results—and to adding more physical memory. Adding memory to a system is much less expensive than adding CPU or I/O resources.

Guideline 3.5: But don't assume memory is a cure-all.

Insufficient memory is not the cause of every performance problem. When it isn't the cause, throwing memory at the problem won't solve anything (and, in rare circumstances, can actually make the problem worse). Check for memory problems first, but if you don't find any, look for other resource issues.

Guideline 4: CPU bottlenecks can be caused by problems in other areas.

Shortages of memory or I/O bandwidth can cause the system to use extra CPU time trying to compensate. Resolve memory and I/O problems first, and CPU bottlenecks may disappear.

Guideline 5: A motor scooter will never win the Indianapolis 500.

It comes as no surprise that some systems are more powerful than others. If a system has inadequate CPU power to perform its tasks, it will never perform well—no matter how well it is tuned.

Guideline 6: You can't put 11 gallons in a 10-gallon hat.

Inadequate memory, like inadequate CPU resources, will prevent a system from performing well, despite the best tuning efforts in the world. If you've tried tuning and the system still has a memory bottleneck, strongly consider adding more physical memory. This principle has a corollary: a small increase in workload can reduce performance dramatically if the system is near capacity. (If the 10-gallon hat contains 9.5 gallons, everything is fine. But add one more gallon and the hat overflows.)

Guideline 7: A fast system with one slow part is a slow system.

Good system performance requires that all necessary resources perform adequately. If one resource has problems or doesn't have sufficient capacity, it doesn't matter if the other resources are blazingly fast. Anyone who has ever surfed the Internet via a slow dialup connection has experienced this principle firsthand. It doesn't matter how powerful your home computer is; connection speed (bandwidth) is the limiting factor when it comes to Web surfing.

Guideline 8: Swapping is bad.

Swapping is one of the worst things that can happen to system performance. Data access is reduced from memory speed to disk speed, which is orders of magnitude slower. Avoid swapping at all costs; if this means buying additional memory, it's well worth the investment.

Guideline 9: Write-back cache is good.

Disk writes can be extremely slow, particularly in mirrored or RAID-5 configurations. Write-back cache improves throughput significantly and should be considered a necessity.

Guideline 10: Know when to quit.

Remember the law of diminishing returns. Significant performance problems should certainly be resolved, but further work to squeeze out the last few percentage points of performance can take more effort than all that has gone before. If your situation absolutely requires the maximum level of performance, this effort may be worthwhile. In most situations, it's not.

6.2 Memory Resources and Performance

In order to understand how memory resources affect system performance, it's necessary to understand how memory is managed by the Tru64 UNIX kernel. In broad terms, memory resources are needed for three main functions. First, all processes require memory to run their executable code and to hold their data. Similarly, the kernel requires memory for its own instructions and data structures. Finally, a dynamic Unified Buffer Cache (UBC) is used to hold data blocks that have been read from I/O devices that contain file systems. All of these uses must be considered when looking at the overall memory usage of a Tru64 UNIX system.

The basic unit of memory is called a page. The standard size of a page in Tru64 UNIX is 8,192 bytes (8 KB). In all versions of Tru64 UNIX up to and including V5.1A (the current version at the time this book was written), the page size is fixed and can't be changed. However, it's possible that future versions may be less restrictive in this area.

At boot time, the Tru64 UNIX kernel instructions and key data structures are "wired" into memory, which means that they will always be resident in physical memory and can never be paged out. As such, the wired memory set aside for the kernel is permanently assigned and can never be used for processes or the UBC. The remainder of physical memory becomes "managed" memory [i.e., it is placed under the control of the kernel's virtual memory (vm) subsystem]. A managed page can be in one of two states:

active pages belong to either a running process or the UBC; free pages don't belong to either. In addition, active pages are either clean (unmodified) or dirty (modified). Finally, the oldest active pages belonging to processes are known as "inactive," while the oldest UBC pages are called "least recently used" (LRU) pages. These pages are the first to be selected by the vm subsystem for page reclamation, which we'll discuss further in the next section. (This terminology can be a little confusing, because the "active list" of pages includes both the inactive and LRU pages.)

6.2.1 Paging and Swapping

The virtual memory subsystem attempts to maintain the number of free pages above a designated threshold. This threshold is defined by parameter "vm_page_free_target" and defaults to 128 pages (1 MB) in older versions of Tru64 UNIX. In version 5, the kernel chooses an initial value for vm_page_free_target based on the amount of physical memory in the system. The relationship between physical memory and vm_page_free_target is shown in Table 6.1.

Table 6.1 *Default Values for Free Memory Target (Tru64 UNIX Version 5)*

Physical Memory in System	Default Value of vm_page_free_target (pages)
Less than 512 MB	128
At least 512 MB but less than 1 GB	256
At least 1 GB but less than 2 GB	512
At least 2 GB but less than 4 GB	768
4 GB or more	1,024

When the number of free pages falls below the threshold defined by vm_page_free_target, the vm subsystem goes through a series of memory reclamation steps in order to get free memory back above the threshold. These steps are progressive in nature; the quickest and easiest are performed first. If these don't reclaim a sufficient number of free pages, successively stronger steps are applied. The first step is to prewrite dirty pages to disk. These pages remain active, but because they are now clean, they can be reclaimed very quickly if necessary. The next step is to find clean pages that the UBC has borrowed from processes and return them to the free list. Again, since these are clean pages, they can be reclaimed quickly. If this doesn't reclaim enough memory, dirty inactive and LRU pages are written to disk and moved to the free list. If this still doesn't do the trick, the system begins swapping out entire processes in order to reclaim their resident pages. (This is obviously a very brief overview of the memory reclamation mechanism. For more information, see the Tru64 UNIX System Configuration and Tuning Manual, which contains a very detailed discussion of memory management.)

Nonwired memory pages must be backed by disk storage of one form or another. Readonly pages, such as program text and shared libraries, are backed by the file from which they were read. Because these pages can't be modified, they can always be reread from the original disk blocks if necessary. Modifiable data, however, must have a "home" to which the dirty page can be written. Such data could be backed by a file (such as a database) that is being modified by a running program. Alternatively, it could be "anonymous" memory, which is backed by swap space. Anonymous memory includes process data segments (i.e., program variables), shared memory segments, and memory that is dynamically allocated by a process.

When paging occurs, individual pages are selected for reclamation as described previously. The selected pages are written to disk if necessary (i.e., if they're dirty) and then unmapped. Swapping is far more drastic than paging because swapping operates on entire processes rather than individual pages. When a process is selected for swapping, all of the process's resident pages are written to disk and unmapped. Obviously, swapping results in much more disk I/O than paging does. Because disk I/O is far slower than memory operations, swapping should be avoided if at all possible.

Tru64 UNIX has two modes of swap space allocation. The default is immediate (also called "eager") mode. In immediate mode, whenever a process is created, enough swap space is reserved to hold all of the process's modifiable virtual memory. If there isn't enough unreserved swap space, the process will fail to start, and it will generate an error message such as "unable to obtain requested swap space." If sufficient swap space is available, the process keeps it reserved throughout the process lifetime, but uses the swap space only if paging or swapping actually becomes necessary. Immediate mode provides a level of safety by ensuring that a process always has enough space available for paging or swapping. The downside is that it requires the system to have at least as much swap space as physical memory, preferably more. (For average systems, swap space should be at least two or three times the size of physical memory.) In Very Large Memory configurations, this may result in a big waste of storage because it's quite possible that little or no swap space will ever need to be used.

The alternative to immediate mode is deferred (or "lazy") mode. In this mode, processes don't reserve swap space when they start up; instead, they attempt to allocate swap space only when they actually need it for paging or swapping. Deferred mode has the advantage of not requiring as much swap space as immediate mode. The potential disadvantage is that if a process needs to swap and there isn't enough swap space to hold its pages, the process is terminated. In most cases, this is not a risk worth taking for critical applications unless it's certain that swap space will never be exhausted.

Paging and swapping (particularly the latter) are detrimental to system performance because they add the overhead of disk I/O to memory access. While it's best to avoid paging and swapping completely, it's possible to minimize the performance degradation by configuring swap space for maximum I/O performance. This entails the use of multiple swap partitions on multiple disks in a one-to-one relationship (i.e., configuring a single, entire disk as one swap partition). Don't put multiple swap partitions on a single disk or put swap space on a disk that's also used for other purposes. On the other hand, don't stripe or otherwise combine multiple disks into a single swap space. The memory management subsystem uses a special algorithm to interleave swap I/O among multiple disks. This algorithm performs better than striping at a hardware or LSM level, so it's best to take advantage of it. Finally, from a hardware point of view, use only fast disks for swap space, and spread them across multiple I/O buses if possible.

6.2.2 The Unified Buffer Cache

As mentioned previously, the UBC is used to cache file system data blocks. Because processes often require repeated access to the same data in a short period of time, caching data in the UBC makes it likely that the data will still be in memory for subsequent operations, preventing extra disk I/O operations. Although the UBC provides a general method of caching that is transparent to user applications, some applications choose to manage their own data caches. There are a couple of methods by which such applications can bypass the UBC. The first is to use "raw" disk partitions (i.e., partitions that don't contain file systems) and perform I/O directly to the disk device. This can improve I/O throughput (although it doesn't always, because the file system code performs some optimization of disk I/O), but has the disadvantage that raw disk partitions are harder to manage than file systems.

The second method of bypassing the UBC is direct I/O, an AdvFS enhancement that was introduced in Tru64 UNIX V5.0. Direct I/O can significantly improve disk I/O performance for applications that rarely reuse data. Direct I/O is enabled on a per-file basis by opening a file with the O_DIRECTIO flag on the open(3) system call. There are a couple of performance considerations to keep in mind when using direct I/O:

- For optimum performance, direct I/O operations should start on a disk sector boundary and should be a multiple of the disk sector size (generally 512 bytes).
- By default, direct I/O operations are synchronous, but an application can also use asynchronous I/O (aio) operations to issue direct I/O requests without waiting for them to complete.

It's a fairly straightforward conclusion that the more data there is in a cache, the more likely it is that subsequent reads will find the desired data in the cache (a "cache hit"). For this reason, as more data is read from file systems, the UBC expands to hold the additional data. Without some constraints, the UBC would eventually consume all of a system's memory. This would clearly be too much of a good thing, because it would leave no memory in which to run processes! For similar reasons, processes like to keep as many pages active as possible in case their pages will be referenced again. Therefore, there are two factions competing for physical memory: processes and the UBC. The virtual memory subsystem maintains a balance between the two that fluctuates based on the system's current workload. If lots of I/O is occurring, the UBC tends to grow toward a maximum limit. If the currently running processes require more memory, the UBC tends to shrink toward a minimum.

Two vm subsystem parameters, "ubc_minpercent" and "ubc_maxpercent," constrain the minimum and maximum size of the UBC. A third parameter, "ubc_borrowpercent," lies between the minimum and maximum; UBC memory above this limit is considered to be borrowed from process memory. These three parameters are defined in terms of available (managed) physical memory—for example, the default ubc_maxpercent value of 100 theoretically allows the UBC to consume 100 percent of available memory. The default values for ubc_minpercent and ubc_borrowpercent are 10 and 20, respectively.

In practice, the UBC can't really grow to consume 100 percent of available memory. When free memory drops below the threshold defined by vm_page_free_target, the memory management subsystem begins using the page reclamation techniques described above. This will result in inactive pages being freed; however, if the I/O demand continues, the free pages will quickly move back to the UBC. In addition, running processes will continue to need new pages. As a result, the free memory count will bounce above and below the target threshold while pages are shuffled among process memory, the UBC, and the free page list. This behavior, which is called "page thrashing," is detrimental to system performance. Not only does the kernel spend unnecessary overhead time moving pages around, but as dirty pages are reclaimed, they must be written to disk.

Page thrashing can be detected by watching the size of the free-page list and the UBC. To check the free-page count, use a command such as "vmstat -w 2 10" and observe the "free" column. If its values are bouncing above and below the value of vm_page_free_target, check the UBC size. The "vmstat -P" command displays various statistics about physical memory. The UBC size can be determined from the "Managed Pages Break Down" section of the resulting output. Here's an example:

```
# vmstat -P
:
Managed Pages Break Down:
          free pages = 16495
        active pages = 27910
      inactive pages = 0
         wired pages = 6001
           ubc pages = 12355
           ==================
               Total = 62761
```

In the above example, the "Total" line indicates that there are 62,761 pages (490 MB) of managed memory. The system actually contains 512 MB; the remaining 22 MB is used by the kernel's wired memory. ubc_maxpercent is set to the default value of 100, so the UBC could conceivably grow to 100 percent of the available (managed) memory, or 490 MB. The "ubc pages" line shows that at the time the vmstat command executed, there were 12,355 pages (96 MB) in the UBC. This is less than one-fifth of the UBC's maximum possible size, so it's clear that the UBC is not being heavily used. In general, page thrashing occurs only if the UBC is close to 100 percent of its maximum possible size.

It's also useful to check the UBC hit rate (i.e., the percentage of page lookups that are actually found in the UBC). A high hit rate indicates that the UBC is being used effectively; every page found in the cache is a page that doesn't have to be read from disk. To determine the hit rate, it's necessary to use dbx to examine the number of attempted page lookups and the number of hits. The ratio of the second number to the first is the UBC hit rate.

Unfortunately, the relevant data structures (like many others) changed between versions 4 and 5, so the appropriate command syntax depends on which version you're running. Note that these commands display a rather large data structure. Only the two lines of interest are shown in the following examples; the remainder has been omitted. In version 4, the command is

```
(dbx) pd vm_perfsum
        :
 vpf_ubclookups = 61973362
 vpf_ubclookuphits = 16100351
        :
```

The version 5 command is somewhat more complex:

```
(dbx) p *(struct vm_perf *)processor_ptr[0].vm_perf
        :
 vp_u_lookups = 13405605
 vp_u_lookuphits = 13360878
        :
```

These numbers are cumulative since the last boot, so they may not necessarily reflect current system activity. To calculate the current hit rate, it's necessary to gather two samples over a short time and compute the changes in the two parameter values. For example, here's a later look at the version 4 system shown above:

```
 vpf_ubclookups = 62804369
 vpf_ubclookuphits = 16257136
```

In the time between these two samples, the memory management system attempted (62,804,369 - 61,973,362) = 831,007 page lookups, and had (16,257,136 - 16,100,351) = 156,785 cache hits. The UBC hit rate is (156,785 / 831,007) or 19 percent. This seems like a pretty low number, indicating that the UBC is probably not being used effectively. However, it's not possible to define a good hit rate in absolute terms because much depends on the type of data and the application. If the application doesn't tend to re-read a significant amount of data, the hit rate will naturally be low. Therefore, checking the UBC hit rate is most useful for a relative comparison of the performance of a particular system or application (e.g., before and after tuning).

For some applications, 19 percent might be a reasonable UBC hit rate. In the example system, however, 19 percent was indeed too low. After some tuning, the hit rate increased to a little over 40 percent. This still leaves considerable room for improvement, so the question naturally arises could further tuning be beneficial? One way to answer this is to look at the "fullness" of the UBC. Before the initial tuning attempts, "vmstat -P" showed that the UBC stayed at its maximum possible size, which was 40 percent of available memory. Tuning changes included raising ubc_maxpercent from 40 to 60. Although the hit rate improved (as did disk I/O throughput), the UBC was still consistently full at 60 percent of available memory, indicating that an even bigger UBC was worth a try. Unfortunately, even the 60 percent UBC took too much memory away from processes, and the system began page thrashing and even swapping. There was no "happy medium" available between processes and the UBC within the available memory resources. The only way to alleviate the memory bottleneck was to add more physical memory—a solution that was subsequently implemented with very good results.

The preceding discussion shows that if the UBC is too large, page thrashing can result. "Too large" is a variable amount; in many cases, the system workload is such that page thrashing doesn't occur even with ubc_maxpercent set to 100. In such a case, there's no reason to lower the maximum. As noted previously, the bigger the cache, the more cache hits that will result. As such, it's best to let the UBC grow as large as possible, as long as it doesn't generate other problems. However, if page thrashing does occur, the UBC should be constrained to a smaller maximum. In this situation, it's best to tune the limit in small increments. As a starting point, try decreasing ubc_maxpercent to 70 or 80 and monitoring the system further. If page thrashing still occurs, continue lowering the maximum in steps of 10 percent.

Don't go too far in this direction, however. It's possible to make the UBC too small, so we generally recommend not going below 20 percent, except under special circumstances that we'll discuss in a bit. Also, it's extremely important that ubc_maxpercent be larger than ubc_minpercent, and that ubc_borrowpercent be between the minimum and maximum (inclusive). Violating these last two guidelines is likely to result in strange (and generally unpleasant) behavior from the virtual memory subsystem.

A too-large UBC can lead to performance problems, but a too-small UBC has the same potential. Because file system I/O must go through the UBC, limiting the size of the UBC creates a bottleneck that effectively limits the system's I/O bandwidth. In addition, a smaller cache makes it less likely that a desired disk block will still be in the cache. There will be fewer cache hits, resulting in more disk read operations. Also, new reads from disk will reuse existing UBC pages; if dirty, these pages will have to be flushed to disk, increasing the number of disk writes. To determine whether the UBC is too small, check the UBC usage and cache hit rate, as shown above. If UBC size hovers near the maximum possible and the hit rate seems low, try raising ubc_maxpercent. Again, do this in small steps. If ubc_maxpercent is set to 20, try raising it in 10 percent increments until the UBC is no longer fully used or until page thrashing occurs. If thrashing begins and the UBC is still full, consider adding more physical memory to the system, as in the preceding example.

It should also be remembered that some system configurations don't need a significant UBC. For example, if you are using a database that uses only raw disk devices or AdvFS direct I/O, the UBC serves little purpose. In such cases, it's reasonable to limit the UBC to a very small percentage of physical memory. However, it's important to limit the UBC in this way only in situations in which it is justified—for example, where the system's primary applications are all using direct I/O or raw devices. If any conventional (i.e., nondirect) file system I/O is done by applications, don't use a very small UBC; performance of conventional file system I/O will suffer dramatically.

As an alternative to adding physical memory, it may be possible to tune some kernel parameters. If you have adjusted the UBC size but still appear to have insufficient memory (e.g., page thrashing or swapping is occurring), tuning may provide some relief. The virtual memory subsystem provides a significant number of parameters that govern page reclamation and other aspects of memory management. These parameters provide the system administrator with a great deal of control over system memory behavior. Examining each of these parameters is beyond the scope of this book. For information on them, please consult the Tru64 UNIX System Configuration and Tuning Manual, which discusses these parameters in detail, including their side effects, potential benefits, and tradeoffs. It should be recognized, however, that the potential performance gains from tuning these parameters are fairly limited.

6.3 CPU Resources and Performance

The amount of available CPU resources is perhaps the most important factor in system performance. The type, speed, and number of CPUs define the system's processing power. In most situations, more or faster CPUs will perform a given set of tasks more quickly. There are some exceptions to this rule. Some jobs aren't suited to multiprocessing environments, in which case additional processors will provide no benefit. Also, if memory or I/O is a limiting factor, additional CPU power will make little or no difference. In some cases, it can actually make a problem worse, which is why it's important to understand the cause of a performance problem before attempting to correct it.

Information about a system's CPU resources can be obtained with the "psrinfo -v" command, which produces output such as the following:

```
% psrinfo -v
Status of processor 0 as of: 06/09/02 15:13:42
  Processor has been on-line since time unknown
  The alpha EV5 (21164) processor operates at 250 MHz,
     and has an alpha internal floating point processor.
Status of processor 1 as of: 06/09/02 15:13:42
  Processor has been on-line since time unknown
  The alpha EV5 (21164) processor operates at 250 MHz,
     and has an alpha internal floating point processor.
```

This information is important to understanding the available CPU resources. It can also reveal whether a processor is unexpectedly off-line, which is one possible cause of performance problems. Something to look for in particular is the unintentional disabling of one or more CPUs by kernel parameters or console variables. The console variable CPU_ENABLED and the kernel parameter "cpu_enable_mask" allow individual CPUs to be disabled. In addition, setting kernel parameter "lockmode" to a value less than 2 will disable multiprocessing—that is, it disables all but the primary CPU. These parameters are sometimes used as workarounds for boot failures or recurring system crashes, as discussed in section 5.1.2.5, but by reducing the available CPU resources, they can cause a significant performance degradation.

CPU utilization can be displayed using that very useful command, vmstat. With no command switches, vmstat displays the percentage of CPU time spent in system mode, user mode, and idle time. We recommend adding the -w switch (undocumented in older versions of Tru64 UNIX), which separates out the portion of idle time spent waiting for I/O to complete. To examine current CPU utilization, run vmstat for several intervals (e.g., "vmstat -w 2 10") to display 10 samples at two-second intervals. A typical output is as follows:

```
% vmstat -w 2 10
Virtual Memory Statistics: (pagesize = 8192)
  procs       memory          pages                      intr         cpu
  r   w   u  act  free wire fault cow  pin pout  in  sy   cs  us  sy  id iowait
  3 337  30   77K  58K  25K 685M 139M 136M 8864 380  2K   1K   3  13  84    0
  3 337  30   77K  58K  25K  924   28   29    0 469 13K   2K   4  22  74    0
  3 337  30   77K  58K  25K  368   13   19    0 492  6K   2K   5  22  73    0
  3 336  31   77K  58K  25K  308    0    0    0 479  4K   2K   5  21  74    0
  3 336  31   77K  58K  25K  367   13   19    0 501  6K   2K   5  22  73    0
  3 336  30   77K  58K  25K  344    0    0    0 484  3K   2K   5  18  78    0
  3 337  30   77K  58K  25K  465   48   27    0 730  6K   2K   6  24  70    0
  3 336  30   77K  58K  25K  498   61    4    0 476  5K   2K   5  19  76    0
  3 336  30   77K  58K  25K  456   46   40    0 523  8K   2K   5  20  76    0
  3 336  30   77K  58K  25K  306    0    0    0 500  3K   2K   5  18  76    0
```

The last four fields display total CPU utilization for all processors: "sy" is system time, "us" is user time, "id" is true idle time, and "iowait" is idle time spent waiting for I/O. These represent percentages of the total available time, so they should add up to 100 (or something very close to it, allowing for rounding). Note that the first line in the example has significantly different numbers in these fields. The first line of vmstat output contains cumulative values since boot time, so it should generally be ignored.

In the vmstat output, system time is the percentage of time spent by the kernel doing system-related tasks, such as processing interrupts or managing memory. User time is time spent in user mode, running actual programs (both system utilities and user applications). Idle time is spent doing neither system or user work; true idle time (the "id" field) generally indicates spare capacity. I/O wait time is also idle time, but it's a sort of "forced" idle time because it's usually the case that a process will be able to resume execution as soon as its I/O completes.

User time represents the accomplishment of real work (as opposed to system housekeeping tasks) and therefore should be maximized. System time and I/O wait time represent time unavailable to do real work, so they should be minimized in order to maximize performance. (System time and

I/O wait time can't be completely eliminated because neither the kernel nor the system's I/O devices are infinitely fast.) There are no absolute criteria that define an acceptable amount of system time. Whether system time is high or low is somewhat subjective and depends on the workload mix and overall capacity of the system. In some situations, 20 percent system time is unacceptably high, whereas in other cases it's perfectly reasonable. Historical data can help to decide whether a system is performing normally. For example, if system time is at 20 percent and has always been around that level, it's probably not worth worrying about unless there are other indications of a performance problem. But if system time has historically been around 10 percent and suddenly jumps to 20 percent, the cause should be investigated.

The first three columns of vmstat output are also useful in measuring CPU workload. The r, w, and u columns display the current number of runnable (or running) processes, waiting processes, and uninterruptible processes, respectively. If the r column is significantly higher than the number of processors in the system, it indicates a backlog of jobs waiting for CPU resources.

A quick look at CPU performance is provided by the uptime(1) command. A typical output of this command is as follows:

```
% uptime
15:19  up 209 days, 52 mins,  70 users,  load average:
0.07, 0.22, 0.23
```

The last three numbers represent the system load average over the past 5, 30, and 60 seconds. Load average is the average number of jobs waiting to run at any given time. A low number (less than 1) indicates that the system is not experiencing a backlog and is performing well. A higher load average indicates an increasing backlog of jobs. More powerful systems (i.e., those with more processors) are better able to handle such backlogs without affecting overall system performance. For a workstation, a load average of 3 generally represents a heavily loaded system, while for a large server, 3 is usually an acceptable load average.

Heavily used CPUs don't always mean that the system has insufficient CPU resources. Because activities like memory management and interrupt handling consume system time, memory or I/O problems can cause CPU utilization to increase. As such, it's important to eliminate memory and I/O as the cause of a performance problem before looking at CPU usage. In such cases, fixing the actual underlying problem may free up significant CPU resources.

If a system really does have insufficient CPU resources, there's not a lot that can be done in terms of tuning. Some possible ways to alleviate CPU bottlenecks include the following:

- Use the nice(1) or renice(8) commands to run the most important jobs at higher priorities.
- Use the class scheduler [see the class_admin(8) reference page] to allocate CPU resources among users and applications.
- Shift work to off-peak times to reduce the maximum workload.
- Look for inefficiencies in user applications.
- Use hardware RAID instead of LSM to relieve the CPU from the overhead of some disk I/O operations.
- Stop unnecessary system daemons that may consume CPU time. A prime candidate for this is the AdvFS daemon, advfsd, which is needed only if you use the AdvFS GUI.
- If all else fails, add more CPUs and/or upgrade your existing CPUs to faster speeds, if available. Note that prior to Tru64 UNIX V5.1A, all processors in a system had to be at the same speed. In V5.1A, mixed-speed configurations are allowed, with some restrictions.

6.4 I/O Resources and Performance

When looking at I/O resources, it's useful to separate storage (disk and tape) resources from network resources. Although there are common elements between the two, there are significant differences in the ways that they affect system performance. Each type of I/O resource is discussed in its own subsection.

6.4.1 Storage I/O

In modern computer systems, storage devices are generally the slowest components. CPUs, memory, and network devices all have greater throughput than storage devices. Therefore, maximizing storage I/O performance is often the key to overall system performance. In discussing storage I/O, we are primarily concerned with disk I/O. Tape devices typically have few uses other than backup/archiving in Tru64 UNIX systems. In addition, there's not a lot that can be done to improve tape performance. However, there are a few guidelines for optimizing tape I/O performance:

- Don't mix disks and tapes on the same I/O bus. An even better idea, if the configuration permits, is to isolate each individual tape device on its own bus.
- Perform backups during off-peak hours.
- Use the highest available tape drive density.
- Use hardware compression if the tape device supports it. If the device doesn't support hardware compression, use software compression (e.g., the -C switch on the vdump command). Don't use both hardware and software compression at the same time.

When more I/O operations are directed to an I/O device than it can process, an I/O bottleneck results. This causes processes to wait longer than necessary for I/O to complete, which, in turn, causes the jobs to take longer to complete. A bottleneck can occur on a single disk or at the bus/controller level if there are a large number of requests to multiple devices on the bus or controller.

The key to troubleshooting I/O performance problems involves the following three steps:

1. Detecting that an I/O problem exists
2. Locating the cause of the problem
3. Identifying corrective action

Detecting an I/O problem is usually a matter of an I/O-intensive application taking too long to complete. "Application" here includes any program that requires a significant amount of I/O. This could be a user-written program, third-party software (e.g., a database application), a system utility such as vdump, or a shell command such as "cp." When you suspect an I/O problem, the first thing to check is whether processes are spending significant time waiting for I/O to complete. Use the command "vmstat -w 2" to gather statistics at two-second intervals. If there is a significant amount of idle or I/O wait time, but jobs are waiting to run, an I/O bottleneck exists.

As a general guideline, a bottleneck probably exists if the numbers in the id and iowait columns consistently total more than 20 or so and the number in the r column exceeds the number of processors by more than 1 or 2.

When an I/O problem is suspected, the next step is to try to locate the cause of the problem. First, check the error log for disk errors and correct any problems that you find. Then use the "iostat" and "collect" commands to gather statistics on disk activity. The iostat command is adequate for simple configurations with just a few disks, but it is too limited to be useful for larger setups. If you find that a single disk or a small subset of disks is having significantly more I/O transactions than the others, this is the natural place for further investigation.

If the disk(s) in question contain an AdvFS file domain, fragmentation of the domain can have a significant impact on performance. Use the command "defragment -vn <domain_name>" to see how fragmented the domain is. The -n switch tells the defragment command to just gather statistics and not perform any actual defragmentation. For example:

```
# defragment -vn data_domain
defragment: gathering data for domain 'data_domain'
        Extents:                   266295
    Files w/extents:            95474
    Avg exts per file w/exts:    2.79
    Aggregate I/O perf:           65%
    Free space fragments:       16596
                     <100K     <1M     <10M    >10M
      Free space:      17%     60%      21%      2%
      Fragments:     12675    3661      258       2
```

The file domain in this example is significantly fragmented. Generally, if the aggregate I/O performance number is below 90 percent, the domain should be defragmented. For more information on defragmenting, as well as other AdvFS performance considerations, see the Tru64 UNIX AdvFS Administration Manual.

The next step in troubleshooting an I/O bottleneck is to determine how the heavily-used disks are used. Are the disks used for swap space, a database, mail spool files, user home directories, or something else? Characterizing disk usage is necessary to perform the next step, which is to distribute the I/O load among multiple disks. The primary method for distributing the load is to stripe data across multiple disks to allow faster I/O access.

Either hardware RAID or LSM (or both) can be used for this purpose. LSM allows the load to be distributed across multiple buses, but at the cost of additional CPU overhead.

Another useful technique is to distribute heavily used file systems among multiple disks, preferably on different I/O buses. For example, if you have a large number of user home directories on a very active disk, consider dividing them into smaller groups (by organization, alphabetically, or whatever makes the most sense) and putting each group on its own disk. Distributing the I/O load may be more difficult in some situations; for example, a large database file may need to remain as a single file. But even in such situations, there is usually some action that can be taken to distribute I/O. It might be possible to move index or log files associated with the database to other disks. Also, if the file is on a multivolume AdvFS domain, the stripe(1) command can be used to stripe the file across the disks within the domain, which will improve I/O throughput to the file.

6.4.2 Network I/O

Network interfaces are technically I/O devices, but they are so different from storage I/O devices that they really need to be considered separately. Problems with network performance have a wide variety of causes. Many of these are external to the system experiencing the problem and in some cases you may be able to identify a problem, but corrective action is the responsibility of some other person or organization. In such cases, all you can do is to notify the responsible party and wait for that person to resolve the issue.

Chapter 7 discusses the troubleshooting of network problems, including network performance issues, so we won't duplicate that information here. In addition, there are a number of tuning options that may improve network performance in certain configurations. One important parameter is "netisrthreads" (in the net subsystem), which specifies the number of network interrupt handler threads. By default, this parameter is set to 1 on a single-processor system; on multiprocessor systems, the default value is one more than the number of processors. This allows incoming network interrupts to be handled in parallel fashion by threads running independently on each CPU. If you have a multiprocessor system, verify that netisrthreads is set to the proper value.

There are quite a few other network parameters that can be tuned to optimize performance in various situations. These parameters have various trade-offs and may not be suitable for all configurations. If your system experiences heavy network usage, check out the discussion of managing network performance in the Tru64 UNIX System Configuration and Tuning Manual. This section of the manual contains a detailed discussion of each network tuning parameter, including when it should be modified and the possible side effects.

6.5 Checking System Performance

In the preceding sections, we talked about the ways that shortages of different resources can lead to performance problems. In this section, we'll look at how these pieces fit together. The procedure listed below will provide a quick, high-level look at system performance in order to identify general problem areas. After identifying the problem areas (if any), you can use the techniques discussed previously to narrow down the problem and take the appropriate corrective action.

Monitoring system performance should be an ongoing, iterative process. After making any changes, start over from the beginning in case the changes have had unintended side effects. Even if you don't make any changes, consider going through this procedure on a regular basis or when the system workload changes. By keeping a log of the results, you will create a historical record of system performance. Running the collect tool regularly will also help to build a record of historical performance data.

In addition to the quick-look procedure described in the following subsections, we also recommend running the sys_check utility with the -perf switch and looking at its performance and tuning suggestions. The sys_check output may immediately identify potential problems and suggest possible corrections. However, it should be remembered that while sys_check is very useful, it's not perfect. A performance issue may be subtle enough that sys_check fails to detect an obvious problem. In addition, sys_check occasionally generates tuning suggestions that may or may not actually do anything to help performance, although they are unlikely to hurt it. Consequently, it's important to understand the basis for sys_check's tuning suggestions before implementing them.

6.5.1 Looking at Memory

When examining system performance, the first item to monitor is free memory. Use the vmstat tool to gather memory statistics for a short time. For example, the "vmstat -w 2 10" command returns 10 samples at two-second intervals. In the first line of vmstat output, several (though not all) fields contain values that have accumulated since the system was last booted.

Therefore, the first line may not be representative of the system's current performance and so should be ignored. A sample vmstat output is as follows:

```
% vmstat -w 2 10
Virtual Memory Statistics: (pagesize = 8192)
  procs       memory         pages                    intr        cpu
  r   w   u  act  free wire fault cow  pin pout  in   sy   cs  us  sy  id iowait
  3 337  30  77K  58K  25K 685M 139M 136M 8864 380   2K   1K   3  13  84    0
  3 337  30  77K  58K  25K  924   28   29    0 469  13K   2K   4  22  74    0
  3 337  30  77K  58K  25K  368   13   19    0 492   6K   2K   5  22  73    0
  3 336  31  77K  58K  25K  308    0    0    0 479   4K   2K   5  21  74    0
  3 336  31  77K  58K  25K  367   13   19    0 501   6K   2K   5  22  73    0
  3 336  30  77K  58K  25K  344    0    0    0 484   3K   2K   5  18  78    0
  3 337  30  77K  58K  25K  465   48   27    0 730   6K   2K   6  24  70    0
  3 336  30  77K  58K  25K  498   61    4    0 476   5K   2K   5  19  76    0
  3 336  30  77K  58K  25K  456   46   40    0 523   8K   2K   5  20  76    0
  3 336  30  77K  58K  25K  306    0    0    0 500   3K   2K   5  18  76    0
```

The free column displays the current number of free memory pages. This should be compared with the system's free memory target, which is defined by parameter "vm_page_free_target" in the vm subsystem. In older versions of Tru64 UNIX, this parameter has a default value of 128 pages. In version 5, the parameter (if not specified in /etc/sysconfigtab) is set dynamically based on the amount of physical memory (see section 6.2 for details). To determine the current free memory target, examine the parameter value with the following command:

```
# sysconfig -q vm vm_page_free_target
vm:
vm_page_free_target = 256
```

The preceding example is from a version 5 system. In version 4, use hyphens instead of underscores in the parameter name—that is, "vm-page-free-target" instead of "vm_page_free_target."

There are three possible results from comparing the free-page count with the target value:

1. If free memory consistently stays above the target value, there is not a memory problem.
2. If free memory is bouncing above and below the target, it's likely that page thrashing is occurring. Check and tune the UBC as described in section 6.2.2.
3. If free memory consistently stays below the target, the system is probably swapping. Check the pout column in the vmstat output; a nonzero value (except in the first line) confirms that swapping is occurring. Check and tune the UBC. If this doesn't help, look for some of the other memory issues discussed in section 6.2.

If free memory stays low, monitor the amount of system wired memory (the "wire" field) over a reasonably long period of time—hours or even days. If the amount of wired memory consistently increases, the system may be experiencing a memory leak. This type of problem should be reported to technical support. If you tune memory, but problems still remain, it may be time to add physical memory to the system. However, it's worth checking for performance problems in other areas first. Some problems can have effects in multiple areas; for example, an overloaded network can cause the system to use a large amount of memory to hold incoming network packets.

6.5.2 Looking at CPU Utilization

The vmstat command also provides a quick look at CPU utilization. The last four fields ("us," "sy," "id," and "iowait") display the percentage of CPU time spent in user mode, system (kernel) mode, idle, and waiting for I/O to complete. (Without the -w switch, I/O wait time is included in idle time.) The number of runnable processes (the first field in the vmstat output line) is also useful. Different distributions of CPU time lead to different conclusions:

- If idle time is high and the load average (displayed by the uptime command) is low, the system is performing well.
- If idle time is high but load average is high or there are too many runnable processes (consistently greater than the number of processors plus 1 or 2), there may be an I/O bottleneck. Use tools such as iostat and collect to gather I/O statistics and check for I/O problems, as dis-

cussed in section 6.4. It's also possible that the UBC is too small; check for this using the method described in section 6.2.2.

- If idle time and system time are low, but user time is high, check the load average and the number of runnable processes. If these look reasonable, the system is probably performing well. If either is too high, there may be a CPU bottleneck. Check for CPU problems as discussed in section 6.3.
- If idle time is low and system time is high, it's likely that either a memory or I/O bottleneck exists. Check the free memory usage as described previously; if there isn't a memory bottleneck, check for I/O problems as discussed in section 6.4.
- If user time is high, run the "ps aux" command (piped to "head" or "more") to identify the processes consuming the most CPU time. If a process is using an unreasonable amount of CPU resources, it should be investigated.

The foregoing suggestions contain some fairly vague terms like high, low, and reasonable. Unfortunately, CPU utilization is not as easily quantifiable as memory utilization, which is a simple matter of comparing the amount of free memory to an objective target. Whether system time or user time is high or low is somewhat subjective and depends on the workload mix and overall capacity of the system. In some cases, 20 percent system time is unacceptably high, while in other cases it's perfectly reasonable. Historical data can help to decide whether a problem exists.

6.5.3 Looking at I/O Performance

It takes a little more work to look at I/O performance than it does for the other two components, simply because I/O performance can be affected by many factors. Consequently, there are several things to look for. The following steps don't need to be performed in the order listed; if any seem more applicable to your situation, check them first.

- Check the binary error log using tools such as DECevent or Compaq Analyze. Correct any errors in the I/O subsystem. (*Note*: a high number of device errors can also lead to excessive system-mode CPU time.)

- Check AdvFS domains for fragmentation, as described in section 6.4.1.
- Check for a too-small UBC (see section 6.2.2) and correct if necessary.
- Gather I/O and file system statistics using tools such as iostat, advfsstat, and collect. Look for heavy I/O loads to a single device or I/O bus.

If an I/O bottleneck exists, look for ways to improve the I/O configuration as it affects the problem devices. Some possible actions to take include the following:

- Enable write-back cache if it's available and not currently used. This can provide a dramatic performance improvement.
- Distribute the I/O load if possible. Avoid having tape and disk devices on the same I/O bus. If possible, multiple heavy-usage disks on a single bus should be distributed to different buses.
- Check the swap configuration, as described in section 6.2.1.
- Look for ways to optimize the storage configuration. Consider using RAID 0+1 instead of RAID 5. Try to stripe across multiple buses if possible.

Before you call support

Before calling technical support for a performance problem, take the following actions:

- Examine the error logs for hardware errors. If any errors are occurring, correct the problem and check performance again.
- Go through the performance quick-look procedure discussed in section 6.5 and try to identify (and correct, if possible) the problem.
- Look for unusual events, such as network problems, that may be related to the performance problem.
- Check the system workload (number of users and jobs) to see whether it is unusually high.
- If performance is so poor that you must reboot the system, preserve the contents of memory first by using the "dumpsys" command (available on V5.0 and higher) or forcing a crash dump. For instructions on forcing a crash dump, see section 5.3.

7

Networking

From error to error, one discovers the entire truth.

—Sigmund Freud

Creating a network can be as simple as connecting two Tru64 UNIX systems with a single cross-connect cable. If that was all there was to it, there really wouldn't be very much to troubleshoot. In real life, even the average home office worker has a much more complex setup, often consisting of multiple hubs, a router, and a firewall. Any decent-sized organization today has a very sophisticated and complex set of communications gear and host systems to contend with. Networking, by its very nature, tends to involve a number of diverse people and organizations, all with their own sets of expectations and desires. In this type of environment, troubleshooting a network problem can be a very complex and involved process. It would be easy to spend many pages discussing different networking troubleshooting topics; whole books have been written on just this topic. To stay within the scope of this book, we'll confine our discussion to network issues that are directly related to Tru64 UNIX.

When the users on your system report a network problem, it would be nice to know first, if the problem is on your system, and second, if there is something you can do about it. If your investigation of a problem reveals that the issue is with another network or host, then your task is essentially done once you have forwarded the issue to the responsible person or organization. Your remaining involvement may simply be to monitor the issue to make sure it actually gets resolved and possibly to forward the resolution to the affected users.

In this chapter, we focus on detecting and correcting networking issues that may arise on your Tru64 UNIX system. These problems tend to fall into two main categories: networking hardware and software issues. In the sections that follow, we'll cover each of these two categories in greater depth.

7.1 Networking Hardware Problems

In this section, we will familiarize you with ways to recognize a networking hardware problem. Dealing with hardware problems—once they are identified—is usually a straightforward process, because you simply need to fix or replace the broken piece of equipment. For our purposes, a broken piece of networking hardware can include a network interface card (NIC), a cable, or a hub. Broken routers, firewalls, and other complex networking gear are beyond the scope of this text and are not discussed.

7.1.1 Intermittent Failures

Hardware problems can manifest either as total failures or intermittent problems. While it would be preferable not to have hardware problems at all, it's better (from a troubleshooting perspective) to have a total failure than an intermittent one. Total failures are much easier to diagnose because the problem is static; it isn't going anywhere. Intermittent failures, on the other hand, can be very difficult to troubleshoot. In most cases, however, intermittent hardware failures will leave at least some clues that will help to track down the faulty component.

Troubleshooting Tip

When an intermittent networking hardware failure is suspected, it may be possible to deal with it by replacing all of the possibly faulty hardware, including the NIC, cable, and hub. If the problem doesn't return, this approach can spare you long hours of troubleshooting a problem that only occasionally shows up. This is sometimes known as the "shotgun" approach because it is not very elegant. Because the exact cause of the failure is never known, it's impossible to be completely certain that the problem won't return.

One of the most important tools in troubleshooting a networking hardware problem is the netstat(1) utility. The first step in narrowing down a network hardware problem is to determine which of your network interfaces (if you have more than one) is experiencing the problem. In this case, the "netstat -i" command provides an overview of all network interfaces and a simple count of the errors encountered by each interface. This command displays the number of outgoing and incoming errors seen by the interfaces (under the Oerrs and Ierrs headings). If any of these counters are greater than zero, you can then drill down to get more information on the errors. The netstat utility can display more detailed counters for an individual port on a NIC. It also allows you to reset the counters so that it's easy to see whether the errors are continuing to increase.

The netstat utility provides access to counters kept by the link layer level of the network stack, which are most useful when diagnosing network hardware problems. The link layer contains the specific interface driver that interacts most closely with the network interface hardware; consequently, the link layer driver is the most likely to be exposed to any hardware layer errors that occur. A typical command to get the link level counters for a particular interface on a Tru64 UNIX system is the following:

```
# netstat -I ln0 -s
```

In this example, "ln0" is the UNIX name for the first Ethernet interface on a system. This command will display a plethora of statistics about the various types of errors detected by the network interface. This includes information about collisions, which are a normal occurrence for certain interconnects, such as Ethernet. (Although collisions are not errors as such, an excessive number of collisions can indicate a problem in the form of a swamped network.) In this output, the key phrase to look for is "receive failures, reasons include:" and the subsequent list of reasons. These are typically hardware-related problems that should be investigated.

Instead of watching these counters interactively (especially because they eventually overflow if not zeroed periodically), you may wish to create a cron script that runs daily to record these counters and then zero them. This approach will make it easier to detect trends, such as errors that happen only at particular times of day or under other specific conditions. If the problem occurs with some regularity, you could adjust the time for the cron job to run just before and just after the time the event typically occurs. This would provide the further evidence you need to support (or disprove) any theories as to the cause of the problem.

As an example of a problem that at first didn't look as though it would end up as an intermittent hardware issue, we started with a symptom that presented as an NFS problem. Periodically, the user's sessions would appear to hang and the following message appeared on the screen each time:

```
NFS3 server guru not responding still trying
NFS3 server guru ok
```

This message would normally indicate a problem with the server or possibly an RPC issue; hardware would not seem to be a likely suspect. Other services such as telnet were still working, so the problem would seem to be isolated to NFS. After further investigation, however, we found that errors were appearing on the main system NIC. This was discovered using the netstat command as previously described. The tu1 interface was showing both Ierrs and Oerrs as follows:

```
# netstat -i
Name  Mtu   Network      Address             Ipkts Ierrs   Opkts Oerrs  Coll
fta0  4352  <Link>       00:60:6d:d5:da:54       0     0     326     0     0
fta0  4352  DLI          none                    0     0     326     0     0
tu0   1500  <Link>       00:00:f8:1a:de:7b       0     0     324   324     0
tu0   1500  DLI          none                    0     0     324   324     0
tu1   1500  <Link>       00:00:f8:1a:d5:4a  970600   708    5283    32   388
tu1   1500  DLI          none               970600   708    5283    32   388
tu1   1500  violet-net   beach              970600   708    5283    32   388
sl0*  296   <Link>                               0     0       0     0     0
lo0   4096  <Link>                           12861     0   12861     0     0
lo0   4096  loop         localhost           12861     0   12861     0     0
```

Next, in order to figure out whether the counters were increasing, we used the netstat command again, this time specifying a five-second interval and examining only a single interface. The choice of what interval to use is fairly arbitrary, although five seconds is usually long enough to see whether errors are increasing or not. If you don't look at the counters based on an interval, it may be that the errors occurred some time in the past and are not indicative of an ongoing problem.

```
# netstat -I tu1 5
   input     (tu1)       output             input    (Total)     output
 packets  errs  packets  errs colls    packets  errs  packets  errs colls
  985099   757     5943    32   411     998087   757    19587   359   411
     513     1        5     0     0        513     1        7     1     0
     551     0        5     0     0        566     0       20     0     0
```

```
562   1   18   0   2   562   1   18   0   2
530   0   25   0   0   537   0   32   0   0
529   0   12   0   0   529   0   12   0   0
518   0   12   0   0   525   0   19   0   0
519   5   13   0   1   519   5   13   0   1
548   1   21   0   0   557   1   30   0   0
611   1   12   0   0   611   1   14   1   0
```

Finally, we needed to find out the nature of the errors on tu1. As we mentioned before, the netstat command can be used to look at the link layer statistics to help characterize the problem as a hardware issue or not. The result was the following:

```
# netstat -I tu1 -s

tu1 Ethernet counters at Wed May  8 13:41:55 2002

        11819 seconds since last zeroed
    185621263 bytes received
       919489 bytes sent
       994983 data blocks received
         6190 data blocks sent
    176092764 multicast bytes received
       983931 multicast blocks received
        46525 multicast bytes sent
          341 multicast blocks sent
          258 blocks sent, initially deferred
           76 blocks sent, single collision
          172 blocks sent, multiple collisions
           33 send failures, reasons include:
            0 collision detect check failure
          766 receive failures, reasons include:
                 Block check error
                 Framing Error
                 Frame too long
            0 unrecognized frame destination
            0 data overruns
            0 system buffer unavailable
            0 user buffer unavailable
```

Here we see that the errors are "Block check error," "Framing error," and "Frame too long." All of these messages indicate a hardware problem, but to determine whether the problem is with the NIC, the cable, or the hub, we had to do some further investigation. In this case, the first thing that was tried was to move the primary interface over to tu0, because that wasn't currently being used. These were on two different DE500 cards, so this would indicate whether tu1's NIC was bad. However, once the interface was switched, the errors returned. Next, the cable was switched out and moved to another free hub port, but those didn't help either. Finally, a longer cable was obtained and plugged into another hub a little farther away; the errors immediately stopped, and the NFS errors didn't return. This conclusively proved that the hub was failing and needed to be replaced. Once this was done, the longer cable was eventually removed and the former cable put back in place to the new hub.

This example shows how a problem that first displayed as a possible software problem with NFS turned out to be an intermittent hardware issue. This was far from clear when the investigation first started, so try to keep an open mind with regard to intermittent hardware issues. If all services stop working, then it is pretty evident the problem involves a total failure of some kind, and it would be reasonable to start an investigation with hardware in that case. The next thing we want to illustrate with this example is a methodical approach for troubleshooting a problem like this. It may seem hopeless at first, but if you follow logical steps using the tools available with Tru64 UNIX, you will eventually succeed in discovering the root cause of the problem.

In addition to using "netstat" to keep track of counters, you may want to keep an eye on the system's binary error log to help discover the nature of a networking hardware problem. If a driver encounters a hardware issue, it will typically record the issue in a log file, and the binary error log is one such place. It's necessary to use a tool such as Compaq Analyze (or another of the tools discussed in Chapter 3) to format the binary error log information into a readable form.

7.1.2 Total Failures

In contrast to intermittent NIC failures, total failures tend to be quite obvious in the way they affect multiple network services. For example, when a NIC fails completely, one user may report problems accessing a Network File System (NFS) served by your system, while another user complains about not being able to telnet to the system, and a third is unable to access the system's Web pages. Further investigation is needed to identify the particular NIC common to all three problems. If the system has only a single NIC, this is pretty obvious. More complex setups can be trickier. For example, the system may contain more than one NIC, with networks located on different subnets. The problem may be further complicated if a dynamic routing daemon, such as gated(8), is in use; it could be masking the true nature of the problem. It may even be that the host is working as intended by masking the problem from your users. While this is good for the users, it can make troubleshooting more difficult.

7.1.2.1 Identifying the Failing NIC

The first step in troubleshooting a total failure situation is identifying the NIC most affected by the problem. Many systems today have multiple NICs, possibly running different sets of networking protocols. A typical system may contain a single 10/100-Mb Ethernet adapter; on the other end of the complexity scale, a single system might have multiple 10/100 Ethernets, a gigabit Ethernet, X.25 WAN, and a Token Ring interface—or even more. In most cases, the process of troubleshooting a failed NIC is not affected by the underlying technology. The first step is to use the "netstat" command (as discussed in section 7.1.1) to examine the link layer statistics and determine if any error counters are increasing.

Troubleshooting Tip

Before your system has trouble, it is worth the time to do a little pre-emptive troubleshooting. To simulate various failures, try removing the network cable from each active port on all NICs (one at a time) when the system can be used for testing. This is sometimes known as the "cable pull" test. Following each cable removal, you should observe how the different services behave. This will provide valuable experience for understanding how the system might react during a real failure. As an added bonus, you might also see a way to redesign the network to reduce the impact of a network hardware failure.

The total failure case differs from the intermittent case in that for every outgoing packet, the error count will increase by one. In the intermittent case, there probably won't be such a one-to-one correspondence; there may be many packets successfully sent for each failed packet. For this reason, the total failure case is much more straightforward to troubleshoot. We recommend setting up one window with a running netstat output. In another window, start up a ping that you know will follow a given interface. Start with the list of interfaces in the netstat output and work your way down the list until you find an interface for which the pings fail. There may be more than one failing, so be sure to try them all. The result of this exercise will be a list of one or more failed interfaces that require further investigation.

7.1.3 Determining the Broken Component

Once you've narrowed the problem down to the affected NIC, the next step is to determine whether the problem component is the affected NIC itself, the hub or switch to which the NIC is connected, the interconnecting cable, or some other hardware between the two. In some cases, software-based troubleshooting is not sufficient to make this determination. It's frequently necessary to replace suspect components systematically with known good parts until the faulty one is discovered. We recommend starting with the cable itself because it is probably the most easily replaced, then trying another port on the hub or switch to which the host is connected, and finally replacing the NIC itself. If the cable involves complicated building-level wiring, see whether you can switch to another circuit or use a patch cable. Because the problem is not intermittent, you should know very quickly whether the problem has been resolved or not after each component replacement.

There is a wide variety of possible hardware problems that can lead to a total network interface failure. These problems include the following:

- Broken NIC or single NIC port
- Cable cut
- Broken cable connector
- Faulty wiring
- Unsupported NIC
- Incorrect system console parameters for the NIC
- Bad or powered-off hub/switch
- Failed hub/switch port
- Bad transceiver
- Bad or powered-off repeater
- Bad or improper cable tap
- Bad terminator

The last four of these pertain mostly to older configurations. With some older configurations, such as 10Base2 or 10Base5, there may be a transceiver connected from the NIC to the cable, as well as another device known as a cable tap, or possibly even a repeater such as a DELNI, DEREP, DESPR, or DEMPR in the mix.

The authors have experienced problems with cable taps that have gone bad when exposed to moisture or simply when placed too close together. For example, a new tap on a 10Base5 cable may cause problems elsewhere on the backbone due to reflections in the signal. Similarly, a bad or misconfigured transceiver could cause failures along the entire cable. It is very common for the heartbeat setting to be incorrect on a transceiver, which causes strange issues for the host connected to it.

When troubleshooting networking hardware problems, it is usually helpful to come up with a simple problem reproducer, such as pinging a host one hop away from the affected NIC. Another host or router on the same physical network is ideal for this; your network's default gateway is a good first choice. Alternatively, if the host is a member of a cluster or a group of systems performing the same function, you can try one of its peers. Be sure to use the Internet Protocol (IP) address or a hostname that exists in the local /etc/hosts file so that the problem will not be complicated by possible DNS or NIS issues. If you're not sure what the hostname resolution order is on your system, consult the /etc/svc.conf file on your system and look for the hosts entry. If local is not listed first, use the IP address and forgo attempting to use network names for this. (For more information on issues related to hostname resolution, see section 7.2.5.3.)

Some NICs, such as the DE504 and the DE602, have more than one Ethernet interface or port within the same card. In such cases, the problem you're troubleshooting may affect more than one of these ports. Sometimes you get lucky and the affected NIC fails in such a way that the problem manifests itself simultaneously on another port on the same NIC. We consider this to be a good thing because it almost invariably indicates that the problem is with the NIC itself, not a bad cable or hub/switch port. This obviously streamlines the troubleshooting process.

Auto-negotiation is an Ethernet feature (described in clause 28 of the 1998 IEEE 802.3 standard) by which two adjacent interfaces, such as a NIC and a hub, decide what speed to use to communicate with each other. Because Ethernet supports multiple different speeds, autonegotiation uses a very low-level protocol that works at the hardware level to determine the highest possible speed at which the two devices can communicate.

Troubleshooting Tip

Remember that in a critical network-troubleshooting situation, DNS or NIS services may not be available. Keep a list of your system names and IP addresses, along with a sketch of the network topology, in a separate location, such as a notebook or a file located on another system. This will prevent loss of valuable troubleshooting time looking this information up when you're under the gun.

In rare cases, autonegotiation doesn't work properly (usually because of some misbehavior in one of the devices) and you may need to set one of the devices explicitly to use a specific speed setting. There is usually a way to set the speed on a host NIC port or hub/switch port. On an Alpha system, you can set the speed of each port on each NIC via a console parameter. For example, to change the port speed characteristics for the first port on a DE602, you need to look for the parameter "eia0_mode" and change it to the desired mode. The default setting is "Auto-Negotiate," but other speed settings, such as "Half-Duplex," "Full-Duplex," and "Twisted-Pair" are also valid. See the documentation for your network card for a complete description of these settings.

Troubleshooting Tip

Some hubs have ports that are used only for uplink ports and should be used only to connect to other upstream hubs. If you attempt to use one of these ports to connect to a host system, the port will not auto-negotiate correctly and your system will not be able to communicate on the network. For this reason, the uplink port should never be used to connect a host to the network.

Administrators configuring the port speed on hubs or switches should consult the documentation for that device. In the long run, an Ethernet device that does not autonegotiate properly should be considered broken and should really be repaired or replaced. However, setting the console parameter could be a workaround until a permanent replacement part can be procured.

Although problems with multiple ports on a NIC usually indicate that the NIC itself is the problem, this might not be true if both ports were connected to the same hub or switch. This type of configuration is uncommon, though because it's usually the case that the ports are connected to different subnets, which requires them to be connected to different hubs/switches. Similarly, if a bus technology (e.g., 10Base2 or 10Base5) is being used and both ports are connected to the same bus, the problem could still be with the network itself. Once again, this type of design is rare, and it is much more likely that the ports will be configured on separate subnets on different physical networks. Designing a network with this principle in mind (multiple ports on the same NIC should be connected to different subnets) will make troubleshooting easier, as well as making the network more robust.

Network Design Tip

The Tru64 UNIX feature known as NetRAIN can save many hours dealing with network problems. This feature allows you to set up multiple network interfaces to the same physical network and make them perform as a single logical connection. If one of the network connections breaks, another one takes over automatically. This configuration can make your network more robust and utilize unused NIC ports.

Troubleshooting Tip

NICs and cables are relatively cheap today compared with other components. We recommend keeping spare NICs and cables of each type used on your critical systems available to be "popped into" a system when a problem is encountered. This can save lots of time waiting for a new part while the system is in a degraded condition.

7.2 Networking Software Issues

Software tends to be more complex than hardware and can fail in strange and unpredictable ways. Therefore, tracking down networking software problems tends to be trickier than with their hardware cousins. Although the symptoms may seem strange (e.g., failure to connect to a given service on a given machine; some services working while others are not), it is possible to troubleshoot such problems in a logical manner.

The first step is to determine whether the problem can be isolated to a single system. If so, is only one service or more than one failing? When these questions have been answered, look for common elements among the failing services. If all services have failed, make sure you've ruled out hardware problems by following the steps discussed in section 7.1. Usually, if pings to the box are working, then the system has basic network connectivity; the system itself is working at a lower level, and the problem is at a higher layer in the protocol stack. At this point, you need to define the problem by determining the services and protocols that aren't working properly.

In this section, we start with a discussion of simple system configuration issues that can keep the network from working properly and then move on to improperly configured interfaces and routing issues. Finally, we discuss some of the common network services and how they can fail. In the following section, we list some of the more common and identifiable problems and symptoms to help you either solve them or rule them out. We also discuss some of the tools needed to identify and correct new problems that arise.

7.2.1 Network Configuration Problems

The first step in tracking down a potential software problem is to examine any configuration issues that may be preventing the network from operating properly. The three main areas to be checked are the following:

1. Are there any system-related issues that prevent networking?
2. Is the interface configured properly for the network it is connected to?
3. Is the routing correct, and are the packets going where they should?

7.2.1.1 Basic System Issues

The most important question to ask regarding system problems is "what changed between the time the network worked and when it stopped working?" In this area, the most likely culprit is something that was changed in the system configuration that has inadvertently caused the network to stop working. This is where your system change log shows its usefulness. Check the log to see whether the system time was recently changed; for example, is it possible you entered the incorrect year? An incorrect system date could trigger a loss of networking services if it caused a license to expire prematurely. Another change that could adversely affect the network is alteration of the system startup parameters in the /etc/rc.config file without using the rcmgr(8) command.

It's possible to edit the /etc/rc.config file and make changes using a standard editor, such as vi, but this can be dangerous. A standard editor will not prevent multiple (privileged) users from editing this file, nor will it perform any consistency checking on the file. Therefore, it's possible for the file to become corrupted. Even worse, the corrupted file may not become apparent until the next time you reboot the system, so the change that broke the network might have been made months earlier. Your system change log should have the change documented, which would give some indication of when the problem was created.

One of the first things to check is whether a valid OSF-USR or OSF-SVR license is loaded and active. One of the main symptoms of this type of license problem will be that network operations will not function. Use the lmf(8) command to list the status of the licenses and verify that your license is valid. If the license is loaded but not active, you may be able to correct this quickly by entering the "lmf reset" command to reload and activate the license database. Other possible reasons the license may not be working are that it may have expired (especially if it was a temporary license) or that you have a less powerful instance of the same license loaded. For more information on license issues, see the lmf reference page or Chapter 11 of this book.

Another system issue that could prevent network activity is simply that the system is not in run level 3 (multiuser mode with networking). If, for some reason, the system was booted up only to level 2, the system would still be in multiuser mode, but without network services. The simplest way to check this condition is with the "who -r" command, which displays the current run level. If the system is not at level 3, enter the command "init 3" and it should come up to the right level. To prevent this problem from happening again, make sure the "initdefault" line in the /etc/inittab file looks as follows:

```
is:3:initdefault:
```

The second field defines the system's default run level and should always be 3. If the field contains anything else, correct the problem by editing the file, changing the field to 3, and rebooting the system.

On a similar note to the run-level problem, any boot problem that prevents the system from coming all the way up to run level 3 could also prevent the network from starting. It would be impossible to list every possible boot problem, but here are some possibilities that could prevent network access to the system:

1. File system corruption in /usr or /var
2. Disk failure
3. LSM failure to start properly
4. fsck(8) failure
5. Missing or corrupt system files

The key to troubleshooting system boot problems is to keep an eye on the console messages while the system is booting. These will usually give you a good indication of what is failing. You may need to connect a printer or other mechanism (e.g., a console manager or PC) to the serial console of the system to capture the boot messages before they scroll off the screen. For more information on troubleshooting boot problems, see Chapter 5.

Next, check whether the NIC is operating at all. If, when you check the "netstat –i," you don't see the interface you're expecting, then perhaps the card simply is dead. You can further verify this by taking the system to console mode and issuing a "show device" command similar to the following:

```
P00>>>show device e
eia0.0.0.2004.0          EIA0            00-02-A5-DA-D6-BC
eib0.0.0.2005.0          EIB0            00-02-A5-DA-D6-BD
ewa0.0.0.2000.1          EWA0            00-06-2B-01-0C-88
ewb0.0.0.2001.1          EWB0            00-06-2B-01-0C-89
ewc0.0.0.2002.1          EWC0            00-06-2B-01-0C-8A
ewd0.0.0.2003.1          EWD0            00-06-2B-01-0C-8B
```

If the interfaces in question are listed, the card is responding to some degree. If not, then the problem is a hardware issue and you'll need to consider replacing the broken card.

Finally, you need to verify that the NIC you are using is properly configured in the kernel. This is usually not a problem, particularly with HP-supplied NICs; the driver will dynamically load at boot time when the kernel detects the NIC. For third-party NICs, this may not be the case, so it will be up to you to make sure that the appropriate driver software is installed and built into the kernel, if necessary. For example, a memory channel card (which is technically not a NIC, but can function as one) will not be seen by the kernel until the appropriate TruCluster subsets have been installed and built into the kernel. Some third-party NICs that are not supported by HP may operate on the same principle.

7.2.1.2 Interface Configuration Issues

Once you've eliminated system problems as being the cause of a networking problem, you'll need to examine the network configuration itself. At a minimum, you'll need to check and correct any issues arising from the following:

1. Verify that the IP address, netmask, and broadcast address are correct.
2. The IP address must be unique on the network to which it is connected.
3. An appropriate default route has been configured.

These three items must be configured correctly for the system to have even minimal connectivity on the network. This assumes that the networking hardware is correctly configured and in proper working order. If the hardware has not been validated, then even a minimal network configuration may not operate. We recommend taking a look at the discussion in section 7.1 on network hardware troubleshooting if you're not sure that your hardware is operating correctly.

The appropriate method in most UNIX systems—and Tru64 UNIX in particular—for examining network interface parameters, such as the IP address, netmask, and broadcast address, is the ifconfig(8) command. This command can display the current interface configuration for a single interface (in this example, tu0):

```
# ifconfig tu0
```

or for all configured interfaces:

```
# ifconfig -a
```

If the IP address, netmask, or broadcast address values are not correct, use the ifconfig command to specify the desired values. For example, to set the interface address for tu0 to IP address 192.168.1.102 with a netmask of 255.255.255.0 and a broadcast address of 192.168.1.255, the command would be:

```
# ifconfig tu0 192.168.1.102/24
```

If the IP address parameters are correct, but the host is still not communicating on the network, make sure that a default route has been configured. This can be verified by using the netstat command as follows:

```
# netstat -rn | grep default
default          16.141.96.1       UG          0       0  tu0
```

This shows that a default gateway has been configured. If this were not present, you would need to define one by using the route(8) command or configuring a dynamic routing daemon. We'll discuss dynamic routing in the next section, but for now you could at least set a default gateway manually to see whether the connectivity problem improves. In general terms, a default gateway tells the system where to send packets that are bound for a network that is not directly reachable from the local host. Without this information, the network interface will not know where to send those nonlocal packets, and they will simply vanish into the bit bucket. This would be a serious problem for remote users of the system, but it might not even be noticed by users of any host connected to the local network.

One issue that can cause serious—and often maddeningly intermittent—problems with network connectivity is a duplicate IP address on the same local network. Depending on the network configuration, this situation can lead to very strange problems for both your host and the one using the same IP address. This situation can also be very difficult to diagnose, particularly on a large network. The best thing to do if you suspect this is happening is to take your system off-line and then use another system to ping your IP address. If you can still successfully ping even with your host off the network, you can be pretty sure that someone has "borrowed" your IP address. It is usually a good idea to get your networking people involved at this point, because the rogue host is best tracked down using low-level networking gear (and possibly some political skill).

It may be that the duplicate host is another UNIX system and you can telnet to it, thus helping to track it down by means of the information in its login banner. More likely, however, it will be an unauthorized PC, which won't respond to telnet or otherwise help you determine its location. If this situation takes your host off the air for an extended length of time, it may be best to work with your networking team to acquire a new IP address, and have them change the DNS and/or NIS settings so that other network hosts will be aware of the change.

Finally, in addition to making sure that the foregoing items are configured correctly, be sure to alter the appropriate system files to ensure that any changes survive a reboot. Remember that a manual "route" or "ifconfig" command will change the settings on a currently running system, but they won't make the change permanent so that it will survive the next reboot. Consequently, you must make the changes permanent by altering the appropriate system file (e.g., /etc/rc.config for the IP address, netmask, and broadcast addresses, and the /etc/routes file for the default gateway). Whenever you change one of these parameters manually, it's a good idea to make the appropriate system file changes and immediately test those changes by rebooting the system. This is a good system administration practice in general, and it might save many hours of troubleshooting down the road.

No matter how skilled an administrator might be, it's always possible to make an error that might not be caught until the next system reboot occurs, which might be months away or not under controlled conditions. If you make the changes and immediately reboot during a scheduled outage, you can either troubleshoot the issue at that time or back out your changes and decide to proceed another time after you've had a chance to do further research. Even if you don't have time to reboot the entire system to verify your changes, you can at least bounce the network on the system by using the rcinet(8) command (rcinet restart" or by switching to run level 2 and then back to 3 using init(8).

7.2.1.3 Routing Issues

If you've verified the basic system and network configuration, but the host still has a problem communicating on the network, the next logical thing to check is the system's routing configuration. If routing is not configured properly, some hosts might be unable to connect to your system, while others might have no problem. In the previous section, we discussed setting up a basic default gateway. The default gateway is a special route that should exist on every system, but there can be other routes, which could become numerous and complex. Your system can operate simply as an end point on the network, or it can act as a routing node by forwarding packets on to other hosts or networks.

When diagnosing a routing problem on your system, you need to know whether the host is an end node or a routing node. An end node would have a simple configuration similar to the one discussed in the previous section. A routing node may utilize static routing, but it is more likely that a dynamic routing scheme is being used.

When troubleshooting a routing issue, there are three main issues to consider:

1. Is static routing correct?
2. If dynamic routing is used, has it been configured properly?
3. Is dynamic routing used properly in the framework of the rest of the network?

The "netstat -r" command can be used to verify that routing (whether static or dynamic) is correct on the running system. This will display a list of the routes that are currently configured on the system, regardless of how they got into the routing table. Verify that the static routes (if any) are set up correctly; if they are not, investigate why they weren't set. If the /etc/routes file is properly configured, the static routes should be set up at boot time. Try manually issuing the route commands from /etc/routes and see whether an error is reported. If no error is reported and the route is correctly configured, either the route was somehow removed or there was a problem when the system tried to set the routes at boot time. Most likely, the /etc/routes file syntax is incorrect and needs fixing. Failing that, start looking at whether some kind of boot error is at fault. As usual, common sense will dictate what should come next in the investigation of the problem. See the section on troubleshooting boot problems in Chapter 5 for additional information on fixing boot problems.

Determining whether a dynamic routing daemon is operating correctly is more complicated than the static routing case. Once again, the first thing to check is the routing table by using the netstat command. If the routes are incorrect, the dynamic routing daemon should be checked for proper operation. There are two main routing daemons: routed and gated. If dynamic routing is being used, one or the other of these daemons will be in use, but not both. Which of these two is to be used depends on the protocols used on your network. If you're in doubt about the protocols that your network is using, check with the network administrator at your site. With either of the dynamic routing daemons, follow the troubleshooting techniques discussed in section 7.2.1.3.

When you need to verify whether a route is working properly, the traceroute(8) tool can be invaluable. Suppose that you cannot reach a destination any longer by ping or other network protocols. The traceroute command can be used to help determine where in the network the trouble lies by sending ICMP packets to each intervening hop on the journey to a destination. Some locations on the Internet may be many hops from your location and a problem could crop up on any leg of the journey. The syntax to trace the route to a host named gatekeeper.dec.com, for example, would be as follows:

```
# traceroute gatekeeper.dec.com
```

Normally, a problem with some link in another network somewhere wouldn't be your direct concern, but this kind of network troubleshooting can be helpful when reporting a problem to your network provider. The provider would most likely want to see your traceroute output, which can be used in the debugging efforts and consequently provide a faster problem resolution to your users. The traceroute command can also help determine whether your local routing configuration is correct. A traceroute from several systems on your local network could indicate that the problem really is local to your system and lead to an investigation of the routing configuration.

7.2.2 Problems with Services

Not all network problems are general failures affecting all network services to or from a particular host. In many cases, the problem manifests as a failure (or perhaps strange behavior) of one or more services, but not all of them. In this context, service means a high-level network protocol, such as the Network File System (NFS), telnet, or sendmail. In the realm of classic TCP/IP server-based protocols, a specialized process known as a daemon implements a network service by accepting requests from other hosts and forking a child process to service the request. Newer and more efficient methods have been developed to implement these protocols that improve on the classic design; however, the principle remains the same. Therefore, in order to troubleshoot a services-based networking problem, you must become familiar with the way each service is implemented on your Tru64 UNIX system and the tools available to troubleshoot them. An exhaustive coverage of all available services is beyond the scope of this book. Our approach in this section is to discuss the primary mechanisms for implementing network services in Tru64 UNIX, as well as the best troubleshooting tools available to examine them.

A failure of the TCP/IP higher-level protocols in Tru64 UNIX can fall into one of the four following major categories:

1. Internet services daemon (inetd) issues
2. Standalone daemon issues
3. Hostname resolution issues
4. Remote Procedure Call (RPC) issues

7.2.2.1 Internet Services Daemon (inetd) Issues

The internet services daemon, /usr/sbin/inetd, controls many of the most commonly used server protocols on a Tru64 UNIX system. These functions include telnet, FTP, remote shell, and the other "r" commands (rcp, rlogin, etc.). inetd controls these services by listening on the appropriate port for each service. When a connection is initiated, inetd forks a specialized child process to handle the request. The child process becomes the daemon that performs the actual work to service the connection according to the protocol's specifications. These daemons behave slightly differently from those in the standalone category, so you can't just make a standalone daemon operate with inetd with no modifications. Some daemons, such as the Apache httpd daemon, can operate as either a standalone daemon or in conjunction with inetd. Even such a flexible daemon as Apache must be told which of the two mechanisms is being used, or problems may occur.

Configuration Tip

Some might ask why do we need both standalone and inetd-controlled daemons? The answer is that although you give up some performance and control over the daemon when you allow it to be controlled by inetd, you have the advantage of not having to waste system resources by keeping a bunch of standalone daemons around that may not be used very often. Therefore, in situations where a choice is possible, you should configure a daemon as a standalone if it will be used frequently and performance is important. Otherwise, let the daemon be controlled by inetd in order to control and conserve system resources.

The /etc/inetd.conf file contains a complete list of the daemons controlled by inetd on your system. This file generally doesn't require any attention unless you want to add a new service or modify the settings on an existing service. The latter function is sometimes useful in debugging a problem. For example, the ftpd daemon is under the control of inetd. In order to increase the amount of debugging information for this daemon, the ftpd daemon needs to be started with the -l switch. This is accomplished by modifying the line defining the ftp service, which by default looks as follows:

```
ftp   stream  tcp   nowait  root  /usr/sbin/ftpd   ftpd
```

and adding the -l switch to the last field. The modified line will look like this:

```
ftp   stream  tcp   nowait  root  /usr/sbin/ftpd   ftpd -l
```

When the inetd.conf file is modified, the inetd daemon will not notice the change until inetd is restarted or signaled to reread its configuration file. The latter option, which is not disruptive, is accomplished by sending the daemon a HUP signal with the following command:

```
# kill -HUP `cat /var/run/inetd.pid`
```

The latter part of the above command executes the command between the back quotes ("cat /var/run/inetd.pid") and places the result into the command stream. The inetd daemon stores its current PID in file /var/run/inetd.pid, so this syntax is an easy way to retrieve the PID and use it as an argument to the kill command.

When debugging a problem that affects multiple network services, take a look at the inetd.conf file and search for common elements among the affected services. If all of the affected daemons are under inetd control, inetd itself may be the problem. Try sending a HUP signal to the daemon as described above. If that doesn't correct the problem, you may have to completely restart the daemon. This is most easily accomplished using the inetd startup script:

```
# /sbin/init.d/inetd restart
```

This will stop the inetd daemon (and any child processes) and restart it as if the system were booting up again. Be aware that this may cause active connections that are under inetd's control to drop, but should not affect connections to standalone daemons.

You can also restart all network services with the "rcinet restart" command or by switching to run level 2 and back to run level 3 using the "init" command. See the reference pages for these utilities for more information about specific switches or options. This option is more drastic than just restarting inetd, because all network connections, including standalone and RPC-based services, will be affected.

In rare cases, attempting to stop a process may cause it to go into an uninterruptible state (indicated by a U state in the output of the "ps(1)" command). The U state is usually caused by a hardware or driver issue that prevents any further activity until some kernel-level activity is completed. It's possible that the uninterruptible state is transitory, so you should wait for a few minutes for the problem to clear itself before assuming the worst. If the U state persists, you must take steps to correct the underlying driver or hardware issue. This may involve replacing hardware or installing a patched driver on the system. (If you run into this and cannot make any further progress, consider making a call to HP technical support for assistance.) It's usually necessary to reboot the system in order to clear up an uninterruptible process. To analyze the problem after the fact, it's necessary to force a crash dump (see section 5.3.2) before rebooting.

Problems will also occur if inetd exits prematurely. Like most other system daemons, inetd remains active, waiting for events, at all times. Under normal circumstances, it should never exit. If inetd is not running on your system, try to find out what happened to it. This kind of problem is frequently caused by formatting problems in the /etc/inetd.conf file. In some cases, it may simply be that the file has been removed from the system, which would prevent inetd from starting at all. If you suspect a problem with the inetd.conf file, try renaming the suspect file and copying the prototype file /etc/.proto..inetd.conf to the name /etc/inetd.conf. Then try restarting inetd and see whether it behaves properly. If it does, it's likely that your original /etc/inetd.conf file was somehow corrupted. To find the nature of the corruption, check for differences between the bad file and the prototype by using the diff(1) command.

An improperly behaving subdaemon (i.e., one of the daemons started by inetd to service a request) can also lead to problems with inetd. If this seems like a possibility, check your log book for any configuration changes that might have altered /etc/inetd.conf. Possible changes include the installation of a third-party application or device driver in addition to explicit modifications of the file. Some applications automatically alter the inetd.conf file for you during their installation process. If your problem seems to have started around the time of installing an application, for example, it's possible that the file may have been improperly updated. In addition, the application's daemon may need some additional configuration to behave correctly with inetd, so check your application's documentation for more information.

If you suspect an application but can't find anything in the documentation, try commenting out its definition in inetd.conf and sending inetd a HUP signal. If inetd starts behaving properly, it's pretty clear that there's something amiss with the application. Commenting out services can also be an effective method for isolating a badly behaving daemon. Simply work down the list in the inetd.conf file, commenting out one line at a time and sending a HUP signal after each change. When the behavior of inetd improves, you have found either a bad line in the inetd.conf file or a badly behaving daemon. In general, the daemons supplied as part of Tru64 UNIX have been thoroughly tested to operate correctly out of the box, but sometimes software problems do arise, and you may need to contact HP technical support to report the problem. If the problem is with a third-party daemon, you should contact the application vendor for assistance rather than HP.

If the inetd daemon itself is generally operating properly, but the problem is with one of the services under its control, you can focus your troubleshooting efforts on that particular daemon. As noted, it may be possible to enable additional debugging for a specific daemon by editing the inetd.conf file and modifying the line for that service. The specific change to make is dependent on the daemon itself and its defined flags and options. If the problem daemon is part of the Tru64 UNIX distribution, you can check the reference page for that daemon for possible debugging options.

For third-party applications, check the vendor's documentation to find any debugging flags and how to use them. Some freeware tools supply you with the source code, so if the program is not particularly well documented, you may be able to investigate the source code for debugging flags or options. When additional debugging is enabled, the standard location for debug output is the daemon log or system message file (unless the daemon maintains a log file of its own). If you've modified the syslog configuration, check the appropriate locations specified by syslog's configuration. See the discussion of syslog in Chapter 3 or the syslogd(8) reference page if you're not familiar with this facility.

7.2.2.2 Standalone Daemon Issues

As we have previously noted, a standalone daemon remains active at all times, usually waiting in a sleep state until an event occurs that wakes it up. Depending on the nature of the event, the daemon may then perform some action or it may fork a child process to do the work for it. Because standalone daemons stay alive all the time, they should be present in the process table at all times. If a standalone daemon is missing from the system, a problem has occurred. Standalone daemons tend to have their own startup and shutdown scripts located in the /sbin/init.d directory. Some examples of this type of daemon are sendmail, httpd, and xntpd. Space limitations prevent us from providing detailed troubleshooting information about each of the standalone daemons that might be active on a Tru64 UNIX system, but we will provide some general principles and guidelines for troubleshooting them.

When a problem occurs in a standalone daemon, the first approach should be to check to see whether the daemon for that service is running; if it isn't, try to restart it. If the daemon is behaving erratically, try stopping and restarting the daemon. (Once again, if the process has entered an uninterruptible state, you may not be able to stop it. When this happens, there isn't much you can do to correct the problem other than waiting for the condition to clear or rebooting the system.) If the daemon fails to start, check the daemon.log file for additional information as to why it may be failing. Some daemons have additional logging that can be enabled to provide more information to help track down the problem. Also, make sure there are not two or more daemons listening on the same port simultaneously. For example, if the HP-supplied xntpd daemon is active and a third-party xntpd is attempting to start up, there will be a conflict, and unusual behavior will most likely result.

Other than these general principles, anything you do to correct a problem with a standalone daemon will be very specific to that daemon. For example, a problem with the sendmail daemon could be a problem with its configuration file; therefore, correcting the problem could require some complex configuration changes. Because there are several rather thick books dedicated to the topic of sendmail (see the Bibliography), we can't possibly cover all the details involved here. Your troubleshooting activities may include consulting one of these references, and the same holds true for other standalone daemons, such as xntpd and httpd.

7.2.2.3 Hostname Resolution Issues

Hostname resolution is the mechanism by which network hostnames are translated into their corresponding IP addresses. There are generally three means by which this can be accomplished:

1. A local /etc/hosts file
2. The Network Information Service (NIS)
3. The Domain Name Service (DNS)

Tru64 UNIX can be configured on your system to use any combination of these, in any possible order of precedence. This is configured by the "hosts" entry in the /etc/svc.conf file. For example, the default configuration for a Tru64 UNIX system is as follows: first check the hosts file; then failing that, to check DNS; and finally, failing that, to check the NIS service. The hosts entry would look like this:

```
hosts=local,bind,yp
```

This indicates that a hostname will first be checked for in the local /etc/hosts file. If it is not found there, then BIND (the Berkeley Internet Name Domain service—i.e., DNS) will be queried for the hostname. If that does not return an IP address, then NIS will be queried. Naturally, if you want to use DNS or NIS, clients for these services must be configured on your system. The "sysman network" command can be invoked to configure the various network services. You may need to consult your local network administrator to determine the servers and domain names available on your local network.

Problems with hostname resolution generally fall into two categories: (1) names that don't resolve at all, and (2) names that resolve to the wrong IP address. The way to begin troubleshooting a resolution problem is by modifying the /etc/svc.conf file temporarily to use only the local hosts file. You don't have to do anything else for the svc.conf change to take effect, so you should begin to see the effect immediately. If the problem doesn't change, then the hosts file has a problem; if the problem is eliminated, you can quickly determine whether the problem is with DNS or NIS by adding them one at a time and trying to use the hostname. Once you've isolated the problem component, you can focus further troubleshooting efforts appropriately.

For DNS problems, the best troubleshooting tool is the nslookup(8) utility. When provided with a host name, this tool will attempt to look up the IP address using only the DNS servers and domain information defined in the /etc/resolv.conf file. In other words, nslookup ignores the resolver settings in /etc/svc.conf file and uses only DNS to make the name translation. As such, it is very handy for debugging DNS issues. As an example, the following command will find the IP address for host ftp.x.org (and incidentally list the DNS server from which the information was obtained):

```
# nslookup ftp.x.org
Server:  ns2.cca.cpqcorp.net
Address:  16.110.248.21

Non-authoritative answer:
Name:    ftp.x.org
Address:  192.153.166.94
```

One of two things could cause this command to give an incorrect answer. First, the host was not found in the DNS server's database. This could be true if you provided an invalid hostname by mistyping the name or perhaps by using the right hostname in the wrong domain. Alternatively, the DNS server might be inaccessible or disabled in some way. The second reason can be avoided in most cases by including a second or even third DNS server in the /etc/resolv.conf file. The resolver will try the servers in the order listed, so list the closest or most available server first, the next closest second, and so on.

One of the most common symptoms of DNS server or network problems is that a resolver request will hang. This often occurs as part of a higher-level service, so it isn't always obvious that DNS is part of the problem. For example, you might be trying to telnet to another host by name. This requires the resolver to translate the hostname to an IP address before the connection can be made. If there is a DNS problem, the telnet command will hang, and you may have to enter Control-C to break out of it. In this kind of situation, try pinging the DNS server's IP address directly to verify that it's up. If that works, try doing an "nslookup" command for the host you're trying to reach. If this succeeds, DNS is not the problem.

Unlike DNS, which is used only for hostname resolution, NIS can be used to distribute a number of different databases to clients in the same domain. (Note that an NIS domain is not the same thing as an Internet domain.) In addition to the hosts file, these databases include the password, group, and networks files as well. For NIS problems, you can use the "yp" series of tools to help troubleshoot the issue. The ypcat(8) command displays a listing of a database that is being served to the NIS clients in your domain. For example, to list the NIS-distributed hosts file:

```
# ypcat hosts
```

The output from this command should resemble a local hosts file (i.e., IP addresses paired with host names). If no output is returned, it could be that the host is not properly set up as a client for the NIS domain. Check the NIS setup and verify that the ypbind daemon is running on your system. Also, make sure the domain you are using is spelled correctly. New Tru64 UNIX administrators may not realize that NIS domain names are case sensitive. Another common mistake is to assume that the DNS domain and the NIS domain are the same. This can lead to very strange behavior, but in most cases it just means that the resolver will not be able to resolve a host name or that NIS functions will not work. The term *domain* is common in networking (not to mention other components, such as AdvFS), and care should be taken to specify the context (e.g., "NIS domain" or "Internet domain") to minimize possible confusion.

If other NIS databases are being successfully served to your host, but the hosts file is not, take a look at /etc/svc.conf and make sure that "yp" is included in the "hosts" entry. If the target host is not listed in the "ypcat hosts" output, either talk to the NIS database administrator and request that the host be added, or switch to another method (DNS or local hosts file) for resolving this hostname.

Finally, it should also be noted that NIS depends on RPC to communicate between systems. Therefore, the discussion of RPC-based problems in the next section is also applicable to troubleshooting NIS problems.

7.2.2.4 RPC-Based Services

The Remote Procedure Call (RPC) mechanism allows two networked computers to communicate with each other using a common protocol. RPC is the basis for some widely used networking protocols, including the Network File System (NFS) and the Network Information Service (NIS). In addition, the daemons used in HP's TruCluster product are heavy users of the RPC mechanism.

Problems with RPC-based services may be caused by problems with the underlying RPC mechanism, which in turn usually occur if the portmap(8) daemon (also called the "portmapper") is not running or not functioning properly. The portmapper is the "traffic cop" that accepts incoming RPC requests and hands them off to the appropriate subdaemons. In this way, portmap functions very much like the inetd daemon. However, the portmapper listens on only one TCP/IP port and uses a program identifier to keep track of its subdaemons. This conserves the use of reserved TCP/IP ports on the system.

The programs that portmap will listen for are listed in the /etc/rpc file. When these daemons start up, they register with the portmapper. If you are trying to find out why a particular program is not communicating, check this file to verify that the program is properly listed and has a unique program number assigned. If so, use the rpcinfo(8) command to verify that the subdaemon is running and has registered itself with the portmapper. To display the daemons registered with the portmapper on the local host, use the following command:

```
# rpcinfo –p
```

Alternatively, to check a host called "george" using rpcinfo, add the hostname to the command; for example:

```
# rpcinfo -p george
```

This will tell you that not only is the program properly registered, the portmapper is responding to its requests. This is a good sign that portmap is working properly.

7.3 Summary

We have discussed the troubleshooting of some of the most common networking problems that can occur on a Tru64 UNIX system. The topic of network troubleshooting is vast, and many volumes could be written about its various aspects. We've attempted to describe some of the most common issues and how to analyze and resolve them. It is our hope that this will help you to resolve most of the problems that you might encounter.

One of the most important things you can do is to thoroughly understand your network configuration and how the system looks when things are working correctly in order to compare that with how things behave when they're not working. It's also very important to understand the tools available for troubleshooting before you actually need them. Every situation is different, and you never know exactly what is going to fail and in what way. Therefore, the more experience you have, the better prepared you will be when the time comes to correct a problem.

Before you call support

Before calling technical support for a networking problem, make sure you have first checked the following:

- Is networking really the problem, or do you have a system issue that prevents network access? Check for an expired license and proper run level.
- Is your NIC seen at the console? If not, the NIC is most likely bad and should be replaced.
- Have you systematically eliminated every hardware component? Try the shotgun approach if you have spare hardware available.
- If the problem cropped up following a system reboot, check your system change logbook for changes made since the last reboot.
- Make sure that the IP address, netmask, and broadcast address are correct.
- Routes should show up in the routing table and can be checked using the "traceroute" command.
- Determine whether the problem is due to a resolver issue by using the IP address directly.
- If a standalone daemon appears hung or behaves erratically, try restarting the daemon. Check the daemon.log file for possible errors reported by an improperly behaving daemon. If an inetd-controlled daemon is failing, try restarting inetd itself.

8

Storage

Data is not information. Information is not knowledge. Knowledge is not understanding. Understanding is not wisdom.

—Cliff Stoll and Gary Schubert

Every Tru64 UNIX system is different in the way its storage is configured. There are many options available. One system may be configured to use file systems to store its data, another may use raw disks, and a third might use logical volumes created by the logical storage manager (LSM). Many administrators use tape devices for their backups, while others use a newer technique known as disk-to-disk backups. Even within a relatively narrow category, such as disk-to-disk backups, there are many different technologies one could employ to obtain the desired result. A system can even be configured to use a combination of these storage options. This flexibility is powerful and gives the system administrator many tools to accomplish a given task; however, it also greatly complicates the process of troubleshooting storage in a generic way.

Our aim in this chapter is to provide the reader with a set of troubleshooting tools and techniques to aid in solving common problems seen in the storage subsystem. Because there are so many options, we cannot hope to list all the possible ways to troubleshoot storage problems. However, what at first seems like an insurmountable problem can be broken down into simpler components. Therefore, we always start a storage troubleshooting exercise by first trying to narrow the problem down to a component of the I/O subsystem, such as a disk, tape, LSM, or AdvFS, among others. Sometimes the nature of the symptom makes it obvious which subsystem is the culprit, but most of the time the symptom does not clearly indicate the broken component. For example, a problem in which a user is unable to access his or her files might be a simple file permissions issue, but it could also be caused by any of the components in the underlying storage. The hierarchical nature of storage is powerful, but it can make it difficult to immediately determine which component is failing.

We begin this chapter at the lowest layer in the I/O subsystem: disks and tapes. These discussions include both the actual hardware devices and the kernel drivers that support them. After that, we move up to LSM, which is an optional product used on many Tru64 UNIX systems for flexibility and redundancy. Because LSM supports RAID in software, it can be an easy way to provide redundancy in the storage subsystem. Finally, we finish up the I/O subsystem in the next chapter with a discussion of file systems troubleshooting, including both the UNIX File System and Advanced File System. Each of these areas alone could fill volumes, but we will cover the most common problems we have seen.

8.1 Disks

Within the I/O subsystem, the disk layer is one of the largest and most-used components. The disk subsystem by itself can be large and complex. When a disk is failing, Tru64 UNIX logs an error to the binary error log, which you can examine with a number of tools, as discussed in Chapter 3. However, there are other useful techniques for diagnosing disk failures. These techniques are brought up in this section.

8.1.1 Detecting Disk Failures

Disk failures are most often detected by the disk driver in the Tru64 UNIX kernel, for the simple reason that the driver is the software component that is "closest" to the hardware. Disk errors are usually detected by the kernel and reported to the binary error log. The application performing I/O to the disk may possibly place an entry in the syslog as well. An application that attempts to access a file located on a failing device will usually get an I/O Error (EIO errno) return from the failed system call. (The errno mechanism is discussed in greater detail in Chapter 3.)

There are several types of hardware failures that can indicate a failed disk to the operating system. These include the following:

- Failed disk drive
- Faulty SCSI cable
- Bad SCSI or Fiber hub
- Failed RAID controller

As with most types of failures, the easiest type of device failure to troubleshoot is one where the device has failed completely. For example, this type of failure on an HP StorageWorks disk drive would most likely display itself with an amber light on the front of the drive. A correctly operating drive from HP should have green lights on while disk activity is occurring; an amber light indicates a fault of some kind. A less conclusive way to find a failure by physical inspection is to check for green lights when you know that I/O is being attempted to the device. If the light stays out, it's possible that it has simply burned out, but it could also indicate a problem with the drive.

In addition, you can confirm a suspected problem by checking for any noise coming from the drive. Active disk drives are constantly spinning; a drive that's not spinning could have failed (but it also could have been spun down by the power management subsystem). It may also be the case that a drive is intermittently failing, which is a much tougher situation to diagnose than if it had totally failed. In this kind of situation, checking the system error logs might provide a better indication of the problem.

Troubleshooting Tip

While we're on the subject of locating a hardware device, we'd like to point out the "locate" option to the hwmgr command. This option helps to identify some types of SCSI devices. This command can be used to physically locate a SCSI disk. For example, the following command flashes the light on a particular SCSI disk for one minute:

```
# hwmgr locate -id 83 -time 60
```

You can then check the disk bays for the disk drive whose light is flashing. This may or may not be helpful, depending upon how much disk activity is happening on the system because it may be difficult to distinguish your attempts to flash the light from normal disk activity. It's also not useful if the drive is behind an intelligent controller of some kind, such as an HSZ50. Naturally, if the drive has totally failed, you will not be able to flash the light.

Although it can be useful, physical inspection usually doesn't yield the first indication that a drive has failed. If physical inspection doesn't bear fruit, you can try to get some response from the disk at the system console. When the system is at the console prompt, try the following command:

```
>>> SHOW DEVICES
```

A basic indication of whether the disk is responding at all is whether it is present in the output from this command. If the disk is not listed—and assuming that the disk is normally a well-behaved device—you can be pretty confident that it has failed. In this case, the drive can be reseated or power cycled to attempt to revive it. Generally, if the drive fails to respond, the only thing that can be done to correct the problem is to replace the faulty drive as soon as possible. You can check to make sure that external power is reaching the drive and its cabinet. On the other hand, if the drive shows up at the console, but indicates errors from the operating system, you'll need to do some further troubleshooting to determine the cause.

After verifying that the console can see the device, another method for diagnosing a problem with a SCSI device is to make sure the kernel sees the device at boot time. In Tru64 UNIX version 5, the cam subsystem in /etc/sysconfigtab (you may not already have any entries there) contains a parameter that can be used to turn on the display of disk names at boot time:

```
cam:
          cam_bootmsgs = 1
```

If this parameter is set to 1, the kernel will print a list of all SCSI devices found as it boots. If the questionable disk is not in the list, it means the kernel can't see the disk, which means the disk has probably failed.

Once a system is up and running, you can use the tools from the operating system to determine whether a drive is functioning properly or not. The most important tool is the binary error log, which can be examined with various utilities, as discussed in Chapter 3. There are two types of errors recorded in the binary error log: hard errors and soft errors.

A soft error is usually a correctable medium error. An example of a soft error is a bad block replacement (BBR), which is an automatic replacement of a faulty block on a disk by the device itself without operating system intervention. When this happens, the device will let the operating system know that the BBR occurred, but was corrected; the requested data was successfully retrieved on one or more attempts of the I/O operation. The operating system will log this as a soft error.

Occasional, isolated soft errors are normal and most likely don't indicate a serious problem. However, if many soft errors appear on the same device over a period of time, it is a cause for concern and should be investigated. In our opinion, a drive logging multiple BBRs should be replaced because this indicates that the drive is most likely on the way to total failure. Most drives will not let the operating system know that a bad block has been replaced until there has been some effect, such as a retry being needed to get the data item requested. Therefore, a report of BBRs indicates that the drive has already exhausted the cache of spare blocks that it can use to replace bad blocks on its own. By the time a soft error is logged, the drive is already on the way to going bad. In addition, retries of an operation due to a soft error waste the system's time and could negatively affect system performance.

Hard errors, on the other hand, indicate that a serious, uncorrectable error occurred on the device in question. This is not good from the perspective of a user trying to access the data on the device. However, this is very good news for the person troubleshooting the problem, because it provides a strong indication of exactly which piece of hardware has gone bad. Once this identification has been made, it's usually an easy task to replace the faulty hardware and return the data to service.

8.1.2 Recovering from Disk Failure

When a SCSI disk fails, the operating system will not give the replacement device exactly the same characteristics as the failed device. For example, in Tru64 UNIX version 5, device names are tied to worldwide ID numbers (WWIDs), so the new disk will, by default, have a different device name from the one it replaced. However, you might want the replacement disk to take on the same characteristics as the original device. The "redirect" option to the hwmgr(8) command enables you to assign such characteristics. For example, if you have an HSZ (RAID) cabinet and a disk fails, you can hot-swap the failed disk and then use the "redirect" command to bring the new disk on-line as a replacement for the failed disk.

Do not use this procedure alone if a failed disk is being managed by AdvFS or LSM. Before you can swap managed disks, you must put the disk management application into an appropriate state or remove the disk from the management application. For example, a failed drive in an AdvFS domain would make the domain unusable until it was remade and the data restored in some fashion. In addition, the replacement disk must be of the same type for the redirect operation to work.

The following example shows how to use the redirect option:

```
# hwmgr show scsi
      SCSI              DEVICE DEVICE DRIVER NUM  DEVICE   FIRST
HWID: DEVICE- HOST-  TYPE   SUB-   OWNER  PATH FILE     VALID
      ID      NAME          TYPE                        PATH
  ---------------------------------------------------------------
  23:   0     clu1   disk   none   2      1    dsk0    [0/3/0]
  24:   1     clu1   cdrom  none   0      1    cdrom0  [0/4/0]
  25:   2     clu1   disk   none   0      1    dsk1    [1/2/0]
  30:   4     clu1   tape   none   0      1    tape2   [1/6/0]
  31:   3     clu1   disk   none   0      1    dsk4
  37:   5     clu1   disk   none   0      1    dsk10   [2/5/0]
```

This output shows a failed SCSI disk with hardware ID (HWID) 31 and a SCSI device ID (DID) of 3. The component has no valid paths. To replace this failed disk with a new disk that has the same device-special file name (dsk4) and device information, use the following procedure:

1. Perform the hardware steps to install the drive as described by the hardware manufacturer.
2. Use the following command for the operating system to find the new device:

   ```
   # hwmgr scan scsi
   ```

   This command probes the SCSI subsystem for new devices and automatically registers those devices. You can repeat this command and obtain the SCSI device identifier (ID) of the replacement device.
3. Use the following command to reassign the component characteristics from the failed disk to the replacement disk. This example assumes that the SCSI device id (DID) assigned to the new disk is 36:

   ```
   # hwmgr redirect scsi -src 3 -dest 36
   ```

8.1.3 Removing a Stale Path Using hwmgr

You will sometimes need to deal with multiple I/O paths, particularly in a fiber channel storage configuration. This kind of setup provides multiple data paths to a single device; when one active path fails and becomes stale, it must be dealt with. The following set of commands will remove the stale path and restore it, if necessary:

```
# hwmgr -delete component -id <did>
# hwmgr -scan scsi
# dsfmgr -m <new devname>  <original devname>
```

8.1.4 Disk Label

The disk label on a UNIX disk tells the system where to find the partition table and other important information. There will be times when you need to manipulate the disk label, which is generally done using the Tru64 UNIX disklabel(8) command. This usually works correctly; however, it's possible to run into trouble, so we have a few items in this section to help you avoid problems.

8.1.4.1 Recovering a Corrupted Disk Label

When a disk's label becomes corrupted, you may have to recover the label from a known correct label that was previously saved to a file. You should always keep the labels for your disks available in case you have a problem and need to recover a label. The way to write a label into a file is with a command similar to the following:

```
# disklabel –r dsk4 > dsk4_label.out
```

Once you have this file on disk, you can easily recover it at any time. The option to recover a disk label from a disk file is -R. A sample command set to accomplish this for a corrupted disk label would be the following:

```
# disklabel –z dsk4
# disklabel –rw dsk4
# disklabel –Rr -t advfs dsk4 dsk4_label.out rzxx
```

8.1.4.2 Writing Boot Blocks to a Disk

When recovering a disk's label as shown above, it's possible to change the boot blocks for the disk inadvertently to UFS when the disk is actually an AdvFS boot disk. This happens because the default, if the -t option is not specified, is to write UFS boot block to the disk. If you recover the label but don't specify -t advfs, UFS boot blocks are written, rendering the disk unbootable. This is quickly rectified by following the above disklabel recovery procedure and specifying the correct options as follows:

```
# disklabel –Rr –t advfs <disk> <filename> rzxx
```

8.1.4.3 Partition Is Open by Another Application

Occasionally, when you try to edit a disk's label, the response from the "disklabel" command may be something like:

```
disklabel: ioctl DIOCSDINFO: Open partition would move
or shrink
```

This means that you are attempting to change or alter a partition which has an actively mounted file system. Such a modification to an on-line file system could wreak havoc on your Tru64 UNIX system, so the system will not allow you to continue, thereby protecting you. In some cases, this message occurs while editing the disk's label to make a change to the disk's "a" partition, even if there is no file system in use on that partition. This error tends to occur when using a typical disklabel command in which the disk's simple name is specified as an argument—for example:

```
# disklabel –e dsk4
```

When just the simple device name is specified, the disklabel command accesses the label (which is stored in disk block 0) by opening partition "a," which by convention always starts at block 0. In other words, the above command is equivalent to explicitly specifying the "a" partition of the disk—for example:

```
# disklabel –e dsk4a
```

If you then attempt to modify partition "a," the conflict message appears because the "disklabel" command itself already has partition "a" open. This problem is easily worked around by specifying the "c" partition instead. By convention, the "c" partition also starts at block 0 and includes the entire disk, so it also contains the disk label. The workaround in this example would be to use the following command:

```
# disklabel –e dsk4c
```

This opens the disk label via partition "c," allowing the "a" partition information to be modified.

8.1.4.4 Reusing a Disk from Another Operating System

Disks that are shipped by HP for use with Tru64 UNIX will usually be formatted correctly straight out of the box. However, when a disk has been in use on another operating system, it typically will not have a Tru64 UNIX–compatible disk label on it. The disklabel command will usually see the disk as unlabeled or as having a corrupt label and print out a message similar to the following:

```
Disk is unlabeled or, /dev/rrz20a is not in block 0 of
the disk
```

However, because of low-level formatting differences with some other operating systems, disklabel will also fail when an attempt is made to write a default label to the drive. When this occurs, the drive must be reformatted before disklabel can write a default label to it. This is accomplished by using the scu "format" command to perform the low-level formatting, then writing a new label with disklabel.

8.2 Tapes

In the previous section, we were concerned with disk devices, which have certain characteristics, such as random access and very fast read/write ability. These characteristics make them desirable for storing on-line data. Some other characteristics, such as high cost and lack of portability, make them less desirable for off-line or archival storage of large amounts of data. It is in this area that tape drives are particularly useful, given their sequential nature and relatively low cost. Once a tape drive is purchased, the storage media (tapes) have a very low cost per megabyte compared to disk drives.

Just like other storage devices, tape drives can and do fail, and when they do you will have to troubleshoot and correct the problem. Tape problems usually fall into one of the following three categories:

1. Hardware problems
2. Media problems
3. Formatting issues

Each of these areas is discussed in the following subsections.

8.2.1 Hardware Problems

Tape drive hardware problems will be obvious when you (or one of your users) attempts to read or write to a tape and receives some kind of error. As with most device problems in Tru64 UNIX, the system logs such errors into the binary error log, so you will need to examine the error log using one of the tools discussed previously. The error returned to the application performing the I/O will generally be EIO, or I/O Error. As with disks, errors from a tape drive are either hard or soft.

As with disks, a hard error indicates a real problem that needs to be investigated and corrected. Sometimes tape drives in an external cabinet can get into a hung state, and simply resetting power to them will correct the problem. For example, a tape drive that fails to eject a tape may fall into this category. If power cycling fails to reset the device, then you should also check termination and cable lengths of the SCSI bus. As in other troubleshooting situations, try to determine when the drive last worked and what has possibly changed since then.

A soft error on a tape drive usually indicates either a medium problem or a dirty tape drive. Medium problems are discussed in the following section. A dirty tape drive can cause many read errors and generally will only worsen as time goes by. Regular maintenance of the drive is recommended to prevent this. In addition to cleaning the tape drive, another form of preventive maintenance that should be performed periodically is updating the tape drive's firmware. This is accomplished in different ways on each vendor's device, but is usually done in one of two ways. The first method is with a specially formatted tape from the device vendor; when the tape is loaded, the tape drive updates its firmware and ejects the tape when it is done. The second method is by using the Tru64 UNIX scu(8) command with the "download" option. This requires that you have the correct firmware update file on a disk somewhere before you begin.

One way to isolate a tape drive problem is by moving the drive to another system. If the drive works over there, then the problem is likely some piece of hardware in the first system, such as an adapter or cable. Once you've eliminated other possibilities, the remaining conclusion is that the drive is just broken and it's time to call the vendor to get the drive repaired or replaced. Because tape drives can be expensive, it's a good idea to eliminate other possibilities, such as cabling, before calling the vendor.

Although Tru64 UNIX supports many different types of tape devices, that doesn't mean that all possible types are supported. First, there are some types of tapes drives that are very old and no longer supported by HP. Second, there are some third-party drives that don't behave like any drive supported by HP and, thus, using them requires some sort of special driver. If that special driver is not available, the drive will not function properly. In order to see a list of all the currently supported tape devices on your system, check out the tz(7) reference page.

Before you call support

If a tape drive is logging hard errors, check the following:

- Are the SCSI bus length and termination correct?
- Is the SCSI adapter functioning correctly?
- Did you try cycling power to the drive?
- Is the tape drive supported?
- If the drive requires a special driver, is it installed?
- Have you tried updating the drive's firmware?

8.2.2 Media Problems

With disk drives, even a few soft errors should be investigated as a potential indicator of a real problem. However, the threshold for the number of soft tape drive errors that should be investigated is much higher. It is fairly normal to see soft errors coming from a tape drive during a backup, for example. This indicates that the tape itself contains bad areas that failed a consistency check. Too many of these errors could indicate that a tape has been reused too many times or the tape drive heads are getting dirty. A new tape should be tried to help determine which of these could be the problem. Of course, only high-quality media should be used for critical data such as backups, near-line, and archival storage.

In addition, some other types of tape errors are best addressed by simply replacing the bad tape. These include the following:

- Bad tape mechanism
- Broken tape
- Worn tape

Sometimes you may find that a tape is incorrectly formatted for use with the tape drive you are using. This situation can usually be rectified by first degaussing the tape with a degausser before using it. A degausser will completely erase a tape by using alternating magnetic fields that scramble the data. Some very powerful degaussers are so effective that they are even approved for use by the U.S. government for declassifying information or before throwing away an old tape.

Before you call support

If a tape has excessive soft errors, check the following:

- The tape may be worn. Did you try a new tape?
- Are the tape drive heads clean?

8.2.3 Tape Formatting Issues

Tru64 UNIX supports many different tape formats. In most cases, the format of a particular tape is already known. For example, you may have a backup tape created with vdump from which you need to recover some lost files. In this case, you already know the format, so there's no problem with deciding how to read the tape. If you don't know the format, you may have to try a number of different tools to see whether you can find one that will read the tape. Table 8.1 contains a list of supported tape formats. If you try all the possible types and still can't read the tape, try to use dd(1) as a last resort. If that at least returns some data, the tape is not blank.

Data interchange between different computer systems can be problematic. If you're lucky, the source and destination are both using the same

Table 8.1 *Tru64 UNIX Supported Formats and Tools*

Format	Read Tool	Write Tool
tar	tar and pax	tar and pax
cpio	cpio and pax	cpio and pax
dump	restore	dump
vdump	vrestore	vdump
ANSI	ltf	ltf
Raw	dd or custom program	dd or custom program

operating system. In that case, you can pick any format that the operating system supports and be pretty sure it will be readable at the destination. On the other hand, if someone is sending you data on tape from a non–Tru64 UNIX system that you need to read on Tru64 UNIX, you can most likely read the tape if it is in tar or cpio format.

These two formats are the most universally supported among different UNIX vendors, so you will have the greatest chance of success if you use them. The tar format is becoming so popular that many non-UNIX systems now support it. Some other UNIX vendors also support dump; however, not all do, so you have to check to be sure that format will be readable. Also, one vendor's dump tape might not be supported by another because of internal differences in format. Tru64 UNIX's vdump format is proprietary to Tru64 UNIX and is unlikely to be readable by any other vendor's systems.

If the other system is not UNIX, your best chance of compatibility is with an ANSI formatted tape. For example, the OpenVMS operating system writes tapes in ANSI format, which can be read on Tru64 UNIX using the Labeled Tape Facility, ltf(1). The same is true for tapes you need to send to another non-UNIX operating system. Using ltf to create an ANSI tape is generally the best bet.

The "blocking factor" is the size of a record that will be read from the tape in a single chunk. Some brands of UNIX use a different blocking factor for their tar tapes than Tru64 UNIX uses by default. The blocking factor of a tape is not always obvious and some utilities, such as tar, will not function properly without this information. If this happens, you'll get a "premature end of tape" error from tar. The trick to determining the blocking factor of a tape is to read the first tape block into a file with a dd(1) command such as the following:

```
# dd if=/dev/rtape/tape_d0 of=file.out count=1 bs=512k
```

This will attempt to read a single block (up to 512 KB) from the beginning of the tape into a file named file.out. If this works, the size of the resulting file will be smaller than 512k, and the blocking factor is equal to the file size. Assuming this is a tar tape, you can specify this value as the blocking factor—for example:

```
# tar –xb <size> -f /dev/rtape/tape_d0
```

Density can also be a factor in support for a particular type of tape. If you are writing a DDS3 tape that will be read on a DDS2-compatible drive, you will need to avoid using the highest density the DDS3 drive supports if you expect to be able to share data between the two. If the amount of data to be interchanged is small, you will have the greatest chance of being able to read the tape elsewhere if you write the tape at the lowest density supported by the drive.

Before you call support

If you can't read a tape, check the following:

- Is the tape blank? Has it been degaussed?
- Did you try dd to see whether the tape contains any type of data?
- Is the tape format supported by Tru64 UNIX?
- If the tape is from a UNIX system, did you try tar, cpio, ltf, and dump?
- If the tape is from a non-UNIX system, did you try ltf and tar?
- Is the blocking factor known?
- Is the tape density supported by the tape drive?

8.3 Logical Storage Manager

In this section, we will discuss troubleshooting problems with the optional Logical Storage Manager (LSM). LSM is a powerful and complex product used to manage disks and implement some RAID options at a software level. The details of LSM setup and operation are beyond the scope of this book; for information on LSM's many features and commands, we recommend the Tru64 UNIX LSM Manual.

8.3.1 Device Failure

One of the most common troubleshooting situations in LSM is dealing with the failure of a device under its control. Ideally, you have planned ahead for this situation and have made critical file systems redundant using either RAID 1 (mirroring) or RAID 5. In that case, you will have an easy time replacing the failed device at your leisure with no crisis atmosphere involved. But if the file system storage was not redundant, you will most likely be under the gun to correct the problem quickly.

The tools to detect a failure in LSM are the volprint and voldisk commands. These tools will show which devices have failed and the general state of the configuration. In the following example, we show "voldisk list" output with a failed disk:

```
# voldisk list
DEVICE        TYPE       DISK          GROUP         STATUS
dsk1          sliced     disk01        rootdg        online
dsk2          sliced     -             -             online
-             -          disk02        rootdg        failed failing was:dsk2
```

The corresponding volprint output showing the result of the failed drive indicates that the plex containing this drive is in the "DISABLED NODEVICE" state.

```
# volprint -ht
Disk group: rootdg

DG NAME          NCONFIG       NLOG      MINORS    GROUP-ID
DM NAME          DEVICE        TYPE      PRIVLEN   PUBLEN    STATE
V  NAME          USETYPE       KSTATE    STATE     LENGTH    READPOL   PREFPLEX
PL NAME          VOLUME        KSTATE    STATE     LENGTH    LAYOUT    NCOL/WID MODE
SD NAME          PLEX          DISK      DISKOFFS  LENGTH    [COL/]OFF DEVICE   MODE

dg rootdg        default       default   0
995304195.1029.18791:19:11:43
```

```
dm disk01       dsk1          sliced    4096       17765065 -
dm disk02       -             -         -          -        NODEVICE

v  nda_vol      fsgen         ENABLED   ACTIVE     17764352 SELECT    -
pl nda_vol-01   nda_vol       ENABLED   ACTIVE     17764352 CONCAT    -      RW
sd disk01-01    nda_vol-01    disk01    0          17764352 0         dsk1   ENA
pl nda_vol-02   nda_vol       DISABLED  NODEVICE   17764352 CONCAT    -      RW
sd disk02-01    nda_vol-02    disk02    0          17764352 0         -      RLOC
```

Notice also in this example that the volume continues to be in the "ENABLED ACTIVE" state, which means it functions even with the drive in a failed state. You can correct the problem and users will be none the wiser, because their data continues to be available even after the disk failure.

8.3.2 Volnotify

One potential problem with LSM is that in most cases, it works too well. For example, you may discover that a mirrored volume has contained a failed disk for some unknown amount of time. LSM simply did its job more or less silently, perhaps only writing a message to the error log, and the system kept on running normally. It is for these situations that the volwatch and volnotify facilities were designed. They work together to inform you of events and problems that occur with LSM.

- volwatch(8) is a script that monitors LSM, waiting for exception events to occur. It then sends e-mail to the root user (by default) or to those users specified on the command line.
- volnotify(8) is a utility that displays events related to disk and configuration changes as managed by the LSM configuration daemon. volnotify displays requested event types until it is killed by a signal, a specified number of events have been received, or a specified time period has passed.

8.3.3 RAID

LSM implements RAID at a software level in order to provide increased storage redundancy and performance. For critical data, we recommend implementing RAID on the storage located under those file systems. In most cases, hardware-based RAID will perform better than software RAID, such as LSM, but the cost tends to be significantly higher.

The RAID levels supported by LSM are the following:

- *RAID 0*—Also known as striping, RAID level 0 is not redundant, hence it does not truly fit the RAID acronym. In level 0, data is distributed across drives, resulting in higher data throughput. Because no redundant information is stored, performance is very good, but the failure of any disk in the array results in data loss.
- *RAID 1*—RAID level 1 provides redundancy by writing all data to two or more drives. The performance of a level 1 array tends to be faster on reads and slower on writes compared with a single drive, but if either drive fails, no data is lost. This is a good entry-level redundant system, because only two drives are required. On the other hand, because the data is completely duplicated, the cost per megabyte is high. This level is commonly referred to as mirroring.
- *RAID 0+1*—This level was never referred to in the original Berkeley paper, but is a logical extension of it. This is a combination of mirroring and striping and provides complete redundancy along with the performance benefit of striping for each copy of the data. The cost per megabyte for this RAID level is the same as for RAID 1, but the performance tends to be better.
- *RAID 5*—RAID level 5 is similar to RAID 0 but adds an extra disk and distributes parity among the drives to gain redundancy. Redundancy is provided at a cost that is only slightly higher than RAID 0, but with a performance penalty.

8.3.4 Correcting a Failed LSM Drive

When a drive under LSM control fails, it's necessary to put a new disk in place to replace the failed drive. However, when LSM is involved, there's a little more to it than just replacing the broken drive. The following steps describe the process of replacing a failed drive in LSM:

- Put a new label on the disk and, if possible, recover the old disk label. If you don't have the label saved in a file (doing so is a good practice), see if you can find another drive of the same type used in the same way in LSM and copy its disk label to the new drive.
- Remove old references to the failed drive (as shown in "voldisk list") using the "voldisk rm" command.

- Initialize the private region of the new disk using the "voldisk -f init" command.
- Reconnect the failed drive with its old media name with the "voldg -k adddisk" command.
- If the disk was in a mirrored volume, the plexes will not be in sync at this point. Allow the plexes to resynchronize with the "volrecover -sb" command.

If the problem was not a totally failed drive but simply a transient failure so that the drive itself is still good, then use the following steps to recover it:

- Put the LSM disk back on-line by using the "voldisk online" command.
- Reconnect the drives to their disk media names with the "voldg -k adddisk" command.
- Resynchronize the mirrored volumes using the "volrecover -sb" command.

8.3.5 Failure of the Volume Configuration Daemon

The volume configuration daemon (vold) is a critical component of the LSM architecture. This daemon must be running at all times to respond to requests for configuration changes and to gather information about the status of LSM. Problems with the vold daemon do not necessarily mean that there is anything wrong with the volumes and data under LSM control. However, if the daemon fails to respond or exits for some reason, there is a serious problem that must be addressed. If your LSM configuration has been correctly set up and running for some time, the first symptom of a problem may be an error from one of the LSM commands. For example:

```
# voldisk list
lsm:voldisk: ERROR: IPC failure: Configuration daemon is
not accessible
```

If you receive such an error, check the health of the daemon with the following command:

```
# voldctl mode
mode: not-running
```

Obviously, this indicates that the daemon is not running, which you can confirm by using the "ps" command. However, it doesn't give you an idea of what the problem is or why the daemon may not be running.

If the daemon is not running, there are several possibilities:

- The daemon was killed.
- The daemon has exited prematurely.
- The daemon never started.

Naturally, if the daemon was killed, it would have been by a user on the system with root privileges; this type of problem should be dealt with administratively. There should be tight control over who has root privileges on the system for the very reason that someone could do something without your knowledge and end up causing tremendous damage.

If the daemon exits prematurely, a serious problem occurred; the daemon is designed to be running at all times and never to go away. In this situation, you should report the problem to HP technical support. They will need some information from you to aid in debugging the problem, including a core file, if it exists, and a trace output from the daemon. If the daemon created a core file, you should be able to find it in the root directory.

One mechanism for troubleshooting the volume configuration daemon is by restarting it in debug mode, using a command similar to the following:

```
# vold –k –x 9 –x tracefile=somefile.out
```

This command turns on maximum debugging (level 9) and writes the trace output to a file called somefile.out. This can be helpful in debugging a situation where the daemon is behaving erratically or is exiting prematurely. You may find that the LSM database has become corrupt or there is a hardware problem that needs to be addressed.

If, on the other hand, the daemon never started when the system booted, there are several possibilities to check. Some of the reasons this could have happened include the following:

- LSM has not been configured on the system.
- LSM is not built into the system's kernel.
- The LSM entries in /etc/inittab have been removed or are not in the correct order.
- No valid rootdg configuration copies were found.
- The system is in single-user mode.

Let's assume for a moment that the volume configuration daemon never started. As discussed in the previous section, the symptom of this problem is an error from LSM commands. The first thing to do is to try starting LSM using the following command:

```
# lsmbstartup
```

It may be that the system is in single-user mode and, in that case, LSM will not have started yet. Starting LSM by hand like this will be your first course of action. It is also possible, depending on the timing of the boot process, that the disks containing the LSM configuration copies were not accessible when LSM was trying to start. In this case, trying to start LSM should succeed the second time around. This type of timing problem should never happen in practice; if it happens more than once, it's advisable to report it to HP technical support.

It's also possible that the daemon hung up for some reason and is not responding. In this case, you see that the daemon is running, but you get a symptom that LSM commands are hanging. When this happens, try restarting the daemon with the following command:

```
# vold -k
```

This command kills off any daemons that might already be running before trying to start a new one. If this succeeds, then you have solved the problem and you should be able to use LSM commands at this point. Of course, the daemon should not hang; if it does, check the logs for possible hardware problems or errors logged by the daemon itself. If you find any errors of this type, take steps to correct the underlying problem so the volume configuration daemon doesn't hang again.

If restarting the daemon fails because it has become uninterruptible, you may need to reboot the system to clear the issue. Again, check for hardware or other problems that led to the hanging daemon. If necessary, report the problem to HP technical support for help in diagnosing the hang.

8.3.6 Diagnosing LSM Boot Failures

As we have previously noted, there may come a time when LSM doesn't behave properly on system boot. Diagnosing a boot problem in LSM can be tricky, because it may appear that some of the tools are not available, hampering the troubleshooting process. This occurs because the system typically hasn't gotten far enough in the boot sequence to mount its /var file system and start the syslogd and binlogd daemons; as a result, errors are not being logged. In this case, the first approach is to check the system configuration and verify that it is correct. If you find something that looks wrong, make an adjustment and see whether the boot process succeeds.

You can also try watching the system console on boot or connecting a capturing terminal or printer to the console to log any messages that might be coming to it. There may be a useful piece of information in the console log that points you to the real problem. Another useful technique is increasing the logging level of the volume configuration daemon, as shown in the previous section. In this situation, make sure the output from the log is sent to a file on the root file system, so that it will be accessible in single-user mode (assuming the system gets that far).

If none of these techniques reveal the problem, it's helpful to understand the kinds of LSM problems that can happen during the system boot process. Armed with this information, you can investigate those areas and see if you can find a problem in the configuration. Once again, if you have made any adjustments to the system since the last successful system boot that may impact LSM, you should also concentrate on those areas as well. Your system configuration log should tell you what was done and when.

Some of the problems that could crop up in the boot process include the following:

- Boot hang

- System disk encapsulation problem
- Volume configuration daemon fails to start
- Hardware problem

Boot hangs are difficult to diagnose because there isn't a lot of data to work with. LSM boot hangs typically happen after the system has already gotten to single-user mode, but in some cases they can happen earlier. If the system has not yet gotten to single-user mode, watch the console and see how far the system gets. Also see Chapter 5 for information on troubleshooting system boot problems.

In the case of a boot hang when the system disk is encapsulated or mirrored, check for the following possible causes:

- Check the LSM entries in /etc/sysconfigtab and make sure they are correct. The "lsm_rootdev_is_volume" parameter should be set to 1.
- If you are using UFS for your system file systems, make sure that /etc/fstab correctly shows them as LSM volumes and not as the underlying disks.
- If AdvFS is used for the system disk file systems, make sure that the links in /etc/fdmns are pointing to LSM volumes and not to the underlying disk partitions.
- If the system disk is mirrored and the first disk has failed, do you have the second disk defined in the BOOTDEF_DEV console variable so the system will automatically attempt to boot from it? An example of setting this value at the Alpha system console would be the following:

```
>>> set BOOTDEF_DEV DKA0,DKB0
```

- If the system disk is encapsulated, LSM must be able to find the swap space or it could cause the boot to hang.
- Make sure the disk label is correct and the LSMpriv region exists.

8.3.7 Recovering LSM Metadata

One of the problems you may run into with the logical storage manager is what to do if the configuration is lost. How do you get back the LSM configuration without making the situation worse by messing around with commands? Fortunately, the volsave(8) and volrestore(8) commands were designed to solve this problem. If you save your configuration ahead of time with volsave, you can later use volrestore to bring it back.

8.4 LSM Performance

Performance usually isn't the main reason that administrators choose to use LSM. The primary reasons are the flexibility and redundancy that LSM provides at a relatively low cost. However, there are a few areas where you may be able increase performance with LSM. These are discussed in the following sections.

8.4.1 Improving Mirror Synchronization Performance

The standard method of performing mirrored volume synchronization is by copying every block from one plex to another. This can take a long time and be very I/O intensive. One way to improve the performance of mirror resynchronization is by implementing a logging feature, dirty region logging (DRL). DRL was designed to reduce mirrored volume synchronization time by keeping track of the areas or regions of the disk that have out-of-sync (i.e., dirty) data. With this information, LSM needs to resynchronize only the dirty regions, thus improving performance tremendously.

8.4.2 Enhanced Round-Robin Scheduling

In Tru64 UNIX version 5, LSM introduced a feature designed to increase the performance of sequential reads by taking advantage of disk read-ahead cache. This performance enhancement introduces a new round-robin mode whereby the difference between the last block read and the next block to read is compared with a new tunable parameter in the LSM subsystem—"lsm_V_ROUND_enhance_proximity." If the difference is less than or equal to the parameter value, data is read from the same plex. This is an attempt by the LSM software to take advantage of disk caching, increasing the chance that reading the block will result in a cache hit. The result should be improved sequential-read performance. The two new tunable parameters added by this enhancement are:

1. *lsm_V_ROUND_enhanced.* This variable activates the new enhanced round-robin read policy if it is set to TRUE (1). Otherwise, the policy is deactivated. The default value is 1 (TRUE).

2. *lsm_V_ROUND_enhance_proximity*. This variable provides the proximity in which the last read and new read must lie in an attempt to read data from the disk's cache by reading from the same plex. The variable can be adjusted from 0 to 4,096. The default value for this parameter is 512.

Testing has shown that by implementing this enhanced round-robin algorithm and tuning the proximity value appropriately, it's possible to come very close to reaching the performance of the preferred-plex algorithm with sequential reads. Test results show that the performance improvement can come close to 10 percent. Naturally, your own mileage may vary. You can set up your own test for both round-robin and preferred-plex settings of a mirrored LSM volume using commands similar to the following:

```
# volstat -r
# time dd if=/dev/rvol/rootdg/vol01 of=/dev/null bs=512k&
# volstat -i 1 -vd vol01
```

In this way, you can test different values for the proximity parameter in your own environment to get an idea of the kind of performance improvement you can expect. An even better way to get an idea of how well this enhancement would improve performance in your environment is to use your own application in the above test instead of dd(1).

8.5 Summary

In this chapter, we have provided guidelines for troubleshooting storage problems on your system. In most cases, troubleshooting storage problems involves working on some kind of hardware problem. Consequently, it's important to become familiar with the tools discussed in Chapter 3 for reading and formating the binary error log, because that's where you'll find most of the useful information for troubleshooting bad hardware. We have also provided you with some techniques that can help you in other aspects of storage troubleshooting. This information should provide a good foundation for the discussion to come in Chapter 9, because file systems are totally dependent on the reliability of their underlying storage devices.

9

File Systems

If you don't ask the right questions, you don't get the right answers. A question asked in the right way often points to its own answer. Asking questions is the ABC of diagnosis. Only the inquiring mind solves problems.

—Edward Hodnett

In this chapter, we begin our discussion of the file system layer of the I/O subsystem. As before, our goal is to give you a flavor for the kinds of issues you are likely to run into and some strategies for dealing with them. There are books devoted exclusively to the topic of file systems, and we refer you to those and to the Tru64 UNIX documentation for exhaustive coverage of all the options associated with a particular command. Within this book, we will attempt to give you as much information as we can to head off problems that crop up in the area of file systems.

9.1 Generic File Systems Issues

We'll begin with generic file system problems. These are the kinds of problems that can arise no matter what type of file system is involved. Later in the chapter we discuss issues specific to particular types of file system (e.g., AdvFS or UFS).

9.1.1 File System Full

One of the most common of all file system issues—and one that almost every UNIX system administrator runs into eventually—is a full file system. Appropriate planning can make this much less likely to happen, so we believe that a proactive approach is the best way to deal with this potential problem. However, as it may still crop up despite your best efforts, both proactive steps and corrective steps are presented in this section. A full file system can become a crisis if it prevents work from being accomplished on the system. Therefore, once it does happen, it's important to deal with it quickly.

9.1.2 Detecting a Full File System

The first step in troubleshooting a full file system is detecting that a file system has, in fact, become full. This is usually not difficult on a user file system, because you'll usually get a phone call from your users complaining about it. The applications your users are running will be unable to add more files to their directories, and they will most likely return an ENOSPC (no space) errno. (If you're not sure what an errno is, see the discussion of this topic in Chapter 3.)

Here is an example of the kind of error you might receive:

```
# cp /vmunix /tmp/1.8
/: write failed, file system is full
cp: /tmp/1.8: No space left on device
# df /
Filesystem   512-blocks        Used   Available Capacity  Mounted on
/dev/rz3a        253374      252678           0   111 percent    /
```

If the full file system happens to be a system or application file system, it will probably impact all your users, and you will quickly get inundated with calls about the problem. Tru64 UNIX will also log an entry in the messages file whenever a write attempt is made to a full file system. These entries look similar to the following:

```
Jul 24 11:47:07 mightydog vmunix: /: file system full
```

It's a good idea to check your logs periodically for these errors. When you see them, check to see whether a real problem exists. It's possible the file system is actually full and requires attention. However, it may also have become full and subsequently been corrected without your involvement. For example, a user may have copied a large file to the /tmp directory and inadvertently filled up the root file system, but later realized the error and removed the file.

Regardless of how you are notified, you will most likely use the df(1) tool to find the full file system. The output from df for a typical small Tru64 UNIX system might look as follows:

```
# df
Filesystem             512-blocks       Used   Available Capacity  Mounted on
/dev/disk/dsk3a            253374     121782      106254     54 percent    /
/proc                           0          0           0    100 percent    /proc
/dev/disk/dsk3g            792124     642466       70444     91 percent    /usr
/dev/vol/volvar            386302     326262       21408     94 percent    /usr/var
export_dmn#data           4099616    1315002     2440256     36 percent    /export
```

You'll notice in this example that the /proc file system is 100 percent full. This is actually not a problem, since /proc is a pseudo file system that is inaccessible to users, and it always shows as 100 percent full. A more closely targeted use of df would make the job easier and leave out unnecessary file systems. To leave out the /proc file system from the list, use the following option to df:

```
# df -t noprocfs
```

Alternatively, you can simply specify a single file system to check, as in the following:

```
# df /
```

Using these techniques, it will be rather easy to find which file system is becoming full, so you can take action to correct the situation and possibly even prevent occurrences in the future.

9.1.3 Correcting a Full File System Condition

Once you've determined which file system is full, you need to try to figure out what (or who) is filling it up and correct the situation. As we've already said, the df command is the most useful for finding the full file system. The set of actions needed to correct the problem will vary depending on the type of file system in question. In general, we recognize three major categories of file systems on a typical Tru64 UNIX system:

1. *System file system.* If the root, /usr, or /var file systems (or their cluster equivalents) become full, this can have severe consequences, so it is important to correct the problem quickly. A full file system in

this category can cause the system to misbehave or fail to operate altogether.

2. *Major application file system.* A major application is one that takes all or a majority of a file system for its own use. Typically, these are large databases or other enterprise applications that cannot be interrupted. Again, a full file system can cause the application to misbehave or fail to operate.

3. *User file system.* A file system containing user directories will tend to move up and down in usage (but mostly up) on a regular basis. A full file system condition on a user directory will prevent users from creating new files, saving their work, or running certain applications.

These categories can be dealt with in different ways. The possible techniques for dealing with full file systems include the following:

- *Self-policing.* This option tends to be used only for user file systems. It has the benefit of relieving you from dealing with a full file system situation on some file systems. You can set up your user file systems as a free-for-all, where it's up to the users to police themselves. If there's plenty of disk space and the users mostly know each other (and behave like adults), this can be a good option. When it works, this option certainly prevents phone calls and e-mails to the system administrator to correct a full file system situation, except in the case where the entire group needs more space; in that case, you might be called upon to add more storage or reorganize the file systems. It should be noted that self-policing seldom works in practice. There are always some users who choose never to delete anything and who eventually end up hogging all the space. When that happens, you will probably end up getting involved anyway.
- *Threats and intimidation.* Once again, this method is primarily used on user directories. When the self-policing policy fails, this option gets you more heavily involved by requiring you to monitor file use and to penalize users who take up too much space. It is still up to the users to find and remove their own files, as in the self-policing method, but you become the enforcer when people don't follow the policy. The amount of success you have usually depends on the amount of power that the management of the organization allows

you to wield. Therefore, it is important to get management buy-in before implementing this option.

- *Search.* In this situation, when a file system becomes full, you need to identify the offender or offenders and take action to correct the problem. This is a manual search process which involves using one or more of the du(1), find(1), ls(1), and fuser(8) commands. This option can be used on user file systems for such things as finding an individual user who is taking up an excessive amount of disk space. For system and application file systems, you will need to check common problem areas, such as temporary directories and log files.
- *Search and remove.* Removal of offending files can be used in user directories for things such as core files that take up too much space. However, this option tends to be used mostly for the system and application file systems. If an application (such as a database program) has a designated administrator, you can work with that individual to identify and remove the files that are taking up too much space. In the case of a system file system (e.g., root or /var), you'll want to check the regular offenders, such as /tmp, /var/tmp, and the log directories under /var/adm.
- *Adding space.* One way to deal with the problem is to not deal with it at all and simply give the users more space. This is necessary if there truly is a space crunch after unnecessary files have been removed and other tactics have been exhausted. With the current trends in the price of storage, a large amount of disk space can usually be obtained at a relatively low cost.
- *Taking a proactive approach.* Proactive steps help prevent the file system from becoming full to begin with. These techniques are discussed in the following section.

9.1.4 Preventing File Systems from Becoming Full

In order to avoid dealing with full file system problems (which is certainly among the less interesting tasks for a system administrator), it's helpful to adopt a set of preventive measures to keep these situations from becoming crises. Possible preventive measures include the following:

- *Quotas.* The system can help to prevent a single user from taking up too much disk space by the use of disk quotas. This guarantees that users will be able to use only up to a certain number of blocks or files on a particular file system. For AdvFS, quotas can be set up on a fileset basis; for UFS, on a file system basis.

- *File system partitioning.* Sometimes the best approach is to move users who have a common workload pattern and who constantly run into each other onto different file systems.
- *Automated cleanup.* You can create an automated, proactive script that performs a nightly cleanup, such as removing unnecessary core files, clearing old items from the /tmp and /var/tmp directories, and checking and rotating the system logs.
- *Relocating files to other file systems.* Some log files can be relocated to other file systems, making it less likely that they could impact the entire system by filling up a file system. It's also possible to relocate where crash dumps are written so they don't fill up the /var file system—a problem that could prevent the system from booting.

Troubleshooting Tip

You can prevent a situation from deteriorating to the point of affecting users by setting up a cron script that monitors the file systems and notifies you when their usage exceeds a certain threshold. You can then deal with the situation in a calm fashion before users know that a potential problem even exists. Such a script can be written from scratch, or you may be able to modify one obtained on the Internet or from another system administrator. These can range from very simple scripts to quite fancy scripts that page you when file systems reach certain thresholds. In addition, there are commercial software packages that will perform this type of monitoring (among other types).

9.1.5 Erroneous File System Full

Sometimes you may encounter a situation where users cannot create files in a file system even though it does not appear to be full. This would seem to be an error on the part of the system, and that may in fact be the case. However, it is more likely that the file system contains one or more open, but unlinked, files. It is a common practice for applications to create a file for temporary data storage. The file is unlinked (removed from its directory) immediately after it is created. Thus, the file remains open—which occupies disk space—but no reference to it can be found in any directory. Unlinking the file means that it will be deleted when there are no more open references to the file (i.e., when the process closes it or exits). Such temporary files automatically disappear when the application exits (normally or otherwise).

This practice is one reason that the du and df tools can report different results for disk usage. The only solution is to find the application that has the open but unlinked file and somehow force the file to release the space by closing it. You may have to cause the application to exit (either gracefully or by killing it) in order to make this happen. The fuser(8) command can be used to determine which applications have open files on a particular file system. In a critical situation, if all else fails and you can't identify the application that is causing the problem, the last resort is to reboot the system.

It's also possible that a problem with the file system is causing an erroneous file system full situation to occur. Make sure you have the latest patch kit installed and all known problems have been accounted for. Once you have ruled out other possibilities, you should report the problem to HP technical support.

Before you call support

If you have a file system full situation, check the following possible causes before calling technical support:

- Is the file system really full? Use df, du, and find to identify the application that is filling up the file system.
- Check to see whether quotas are being used. Has the user just reached the limit of his or her quota?
- Are there applications with open and unlinked files on the file system? Have you tried using fuser to find the culprit? Have you tried rebooting the system?
- If the file system is AdvFS:
    - Check whether there are multiple filesets in use in the domain.
    - Check whether there are clone filesets in use.
    - Check whether there are quotas being used.
    - The df utility is sometimes unreliable on AdvFS file systems. Use vdf for a more accurate picture.
- If the file system is UFS, what is the minfree value for the file system? Nonroot users will be limited by the minfree amount.
- Are the latest patches installed on the system?

9.1.6 Issues with Mounting and Unmounting File Systems

Attempting to mount a file system is an operation that usually succeeds. Sometimes it doesn't, however, and you will need to troubleshoot the problem. Some of the more common problems are listed below. The likely error message is listed in parentheses with each possible cause:

- You are not logged in as root (Permission denied).
- The file system is already mounted (Device busy).
- Another application has the block-special-device file open (Device busy).
- The mount point specified is not a directory (Not a directory).
- An AdvFS file system has experienced a domain panic (I/O error).
- The device has encountered a hardware error (I/O error).
- The file system is not supported in the kernel (File system invalid or not installed).
- The AdvFS file system is a copy of an already mounted file system (I/O error).

One of the most common issues you may run into with unmounting file systems is that the umount command will fail with a "Device busy" message if there are open files anywhere in the file system. When this happens, the fuser command will show which users are using the file system so they can be asked to move or, if necessary, their processes can be killed. Some other problems that occur when unmounting local file systems are the following:

- You are not logged in as root (Not owner).
- The file system is not mounted (Not currently mounted).

9.1.7 Leveling Cache Flush Performance

Since early in the development of caching in UNIX, the update(8) daemon has operated in the same manner as it does today. This daemon runs every 30 seconds and executes a sync() system call to flush all dirty (i.e., modified) I/O buffers to disk. This mechanism works well for most systems, but systems with a large amount of volatile data can experience a momentary pause in system response while the cache is flushed.

The smooth sync and I/O throttling features were first introduced in Tru64 UNIX V5.0 in order to address the problem of systems pausing when large numbers of dirty pages were flushed to disk during each pass of the update daemon. In the case of very large, very active UFS and AdvFS file systems, the pauses could be frequent and disruptive to other operations on the system.

Smooth sync allows each dirty page to age for a specified time period before being written out to disk. This allows more opportunity for frequently modified pages to be found in the cache, thus decreasing the overall I/O load on the system. In addition, pages are queued to a device only after having aged sufficiently, rather than being flushed by the update daemon. Therefore, cache flushes in which large numbers of dirty pages become locked on the device queue are minimized.

In addition, the I/O throttling feature addresses the problem of locking dirty pages on the device queue. It enforces a limit on the number of delayed I/O requests on the device queue at any one time. The result of this constraint is to allow the system to be more responsive to any synchronous requests added to the device queue. This may also decrease the duration of process waits for specific dirty buffers, because pages will continue to remain available until placed on the device queue.

9.1.8 General Performance Issues

There are a few general issues that can affect file system performance, regardless of the type of file system. These are as follows:

- *Caching.* Poor use of one of the system caches can have a negative impact on the general performance of file systems. A very badly tuned cache can cause a situation known as "cache thrashing" to occur. A thrashing cache can cause the system to spend so much time managing the cache that very little normal work can be accomplished.
- *LSM mirror syncing.* If the performance of a file system that resides on an LSM mirrored volume seems slow, check to see whether the volume is synchronizing.
- *Hardware problems.* On occasion, poor performance of a file system may result from an underlying hardware issue that needs to be addressed. Check the error log for evidence of hardware errors if there

is any unexplained file system performance problem. The system could be using up resources logging the errors, which doesn't leave as much time available for normal activities.

The authors are all too familiar with complaints from system users who simply state, "The system is slow." This kind of response is not quantified and virtually impossible to troubleshoot without additional information. More investigation is required in order to determine what "slow" really means. It is important to get an idea of the degree of the slowness. Is the system 10 percent, 50 percent, or 100 percent slower than before?

It is also helpful to get the user to quantify the problem with a time frame: When did the slowness start, and is it a temporary or permanent problem? Is performance better or worse at some times or others? In order to answer these questions, it is useful to employ a tool such as collect, which we discussed in Chapter 3. The collect tool can be set up to gather system performance statistics in an ongoing fashion so that, over time, a record of historical data can be obtained. The record can be used to compare recent performance with past performance to help pinpoint when the issue arose.

9.2 AdvFS

In this section, we are concerned with problems specific to the Advanced File System. AdvFS is a complex and powerful file system with features that make it extremely useful for critical production systems. For example, the clone fileset feature is ideal for sites that cannot afford to take a file system off-line to perform backups. Because AdvFS is heavily relied on, it is critical to understand and correct file system problems quickly.

AdvFS includes some very good facilities and tools to help with troubleshooting, correction, and repair of problems. Our main areas of concern with respect to troubleshooting AdvFS are the following:

- AdvFS I/O errors
- Domain panics
- AdvFS-specific error messages
- File system corruption
- Missing or incorrect volumes
- Performance issues

9.2.1 AdvFS I/O Errors

AdvFS I/O errors are a special logging feature of AdvFS that lets you know a problem has occurred on one of the file systems. The error messages include information to help you figure out what the cause of the problem was. These messages are sent to the syslogd daemon, so they typically appear in the /var/adm/messages file. An example of an AdvFS I/O error seen on a real system is the following:

```
AdvFS I/O error:
    Domain#Fileset: CCS_domain#CCS
    Mounted on: /usr/CCS
    Volume: /dev/vol/rootdg/CCSvol
    Tag: 0x00007477.8001
    Page: 90
    Block: 2137344
    Block count: 32
    Type of operation: Write
    Error: 5
```

To obtain the name of the file on which the error occurred, type the command:

```
# /sbin/advfs/tag2name /usr/CCS/.tags/29815
```

As you can see, this message indicates that a problem was discovered when performing a write operation on a domain called CCS_domain. The specific problem encountered was an errno of 5, which (as we discussed in Chapter 3) indicates that an EIO or I/O error was returned to the application.

Troubleshooting Tip

The users of the system may not always let you know that they received one of these errors because they may not realize that it was a system error. Therefore, we suggest you check the messages file with an automated script that runs each night. This is one way to be proactive so you can take immediate action in case a disk or other hardware has begun to fail.

Troubleshooting Tip

AdvFS I/O errors usually correspond to hardware events, as in the example shown. Therefore, if you examine the binary error log file around the same time period as the I/O error occurred, you will most likely find more helpful information about the root cause of the problem. A bad block replacement (BBR) is a typical disk error that can lead to an AdvFS I/O error.

9.2.2 Domain Panic

If an AdvFS file system encounters an error so severe that it is no longer considered safe to continue using the file system, the system will take the file system off-line rather than continue with a potentially unsafe condition. This event is known as an AdvFS domain panic. A domain that has entered this state will no longer be accessible to users, but will still show as mounted. The system typically logs a domain panic to the syslog; thus, it will appear in the messages file with an entry similar to the following:

```
AdvFS Domain Panic; Domain var_domain Id
0x32e4e8d9.00073ce0
```

In addition to logging to syslog, the domain panic message will also be logged to the binary error log file. Ways to examine this file are discussed in greater depth in Chapter 3 of this book.

If a domain panic occurs on your system, you will need to deal with the situation quickly in order to get your data back on-line as quickly as possible. To recover from a domain panic, perform the following steps:

1. Use the mount command with no options to obtain a list of all the filesets in the domain. Then use the umount command to unmount all of these filesets in preparation for using the verify utility on the domain. Keep in mind that the filesets in a domain must be in the unmounted state in order to run the verify utility that checks them. [For more information, see the restrictions noted in the verify(8) reference page.] If umount fails because files are still open on the file system, use fuser to clean these up to allow the umount to succeed.

2. If the problem is a hardware issue, correct it before going to step 3. If you are not sure whether your system is encountering hardware errors, check the binary error log and make sure there are no indications of errors prior to the domain panic.

3. Use the savemeta(8) utility to collect a copy of the on-disk metadata in case a problem report needs to be filed later with HP technical support.

4. Attempt to mount a fileset in the domain or try the showfsets command on the domain. If these cause another domain panic, try using the fixfdmn(8) utility to repair the domain so that it can be mounted. Make sure the filesets are unmounted again before going on to the next step.

5. Run the verify utility on all of the filesets in the domain. See section 9.2.4 for information about how to run the verify utility to detect and correct file system corruption.

6. If the verify utility completes cleanly, mount all of the filesets that were unmounted in step 1. At this point, you can resume normal operations. However, if the verify utility indicates that there is a problem and it cannot correct it, recovery actions should be started.

7. If there is a failure that prevents complete recovery, you must first recreate the domain and restore the domain's data from backup media. Then mount all of the restored filesets in the domain and resume normal operations. You should also file a problem report with HP and provide them with the savemeta output and the results from a "sys_check -escalate" run on the system.

8. As a last resort, if there is no current backup, the salvage(8) utility can be used to attempt to recover files from the damaged domain. See section 9.2.4 for an explanation of the salvage utility.

Troubleshooting Tip

An AdvFS domain panic is usually caused by a hardware malfunction. Therefore, if you discover a domain panic message in the system messages file or binary error log file, it is a good idea to examine the binary error log for hardware failures that occurred at or prior to the time of the domain panic.

As mentioned earlier, the default response of Tru64 UNIX is to take the file system off-line in a domain panic situation. In addition, the system will create a live crash dump, which saves the system's state at the time the domain panic occurred. A live crash dump is a snapshot of the system's internal state taken at the time the problem occurred; it can be used for debugging the problem at a later time. A live dump is similar to the information obtained when a computer system crashes, except that the system doesn't reboot itself; it simply writes the information onto disk and continues operating. (For more information about the differences between a live dump and a system crash, see Chapter 5.) You can change the system's behavior to one of several responses, depending on your troubleshooting needs, with the system parameter "AdvfsDomainPanicLevel." See Table 9.1 for a list of the possible values of this parameter.

Table 9.1 *AdvfsDomainPanicLevel Values*

Level	Description
0	No live crash dump will be created during a domain panic.
1	A live crash dump will be created if a domain panic occurs in a domain that has any mounted filesets. This is the default.
2	A live crash dump will always be created during a domain panic, whether or not the domain has any mounted filesets.
3	A domain panic will be promoted into a system panic, causing the system to crash.

9.2.3 AdvFS Error Messages

AdvFS error messages are special error codes that pertain only to the AdvFS file system. They provide additional data that can be used in troubleshooting a problem with the file system. These error messages look like the following:

```
# clonefset export_dmn clone_local another_clone
clonefset: can't create clone file set 'another_clone'
of set 'clone_local' in domain 'export_dmn'
clonefset: error = E_CANT_CLONE_A_CLONE (-1125)
```

When you encounter one of these errors, you can consult the advfs_err(4) reference page for more information to assist you with debugging the problem. In this case, the error message makes it rather obvious what the problem is, but other errors may not be quite as obvious. We suggest that you scan this reference page before you have problems in order to get a feel for the kinds of errors listed there. For example, the reference page entry for the above AdvFS error is the following:

```
(-1125)
    E_CANT_CLONE_A_CLONE
    You cannot create a clone fileset from a clone fileset.
```

In this example, you would discover that there is a restriction that prevents cloning a clone fileset, and then you would take appropriate action.

9.2.4 Dealing with AdvFS Corruption

A file system corruption problem is something that nobody wants to encounter, but it can happen and should be dealt with swiftly when it does. As with most topics we cover in this book, there are methods for determining whether a problem is really one of corruption or not; and, once you've confirmed that corruption exists, there are techniques for correcting the problem. These two topics are discussed in the following subsections.

9.2.4.1 Detecting File System Corruption

In most cases, there isn't much that you need to do to find corruption in a file system. Most of the time, either users will let you know or an application will fail with a data inconsistency. File system corruption can manifest itself in many different ways, and it may not always be obvious whether the problem is really with the file system or with one of the layers underneath it. When looking at an apparent file system problem, keep in mind that it may just be the outward manifestation of an underlying device issue. For example, a failing disk could generate a symptom such as an AdvFS I/O error, followed by a domain panic. In such a case, see the procedure in section 9.2.2 for information on dealing with this kind of situation.

In general, corruption falls into one of two categories, based on the effect the problem can have on the system and the system's response to it:

1. *Metadata corruption.* This type of corruption is in the file system's on-disk internal structures. This means it can have a wide-ranging effect on the entire domain (including other filesets in the same domain). The system's response to a metadata corruption will most likely be a domain panic. In this case, follow the domain panic response steps discussed previously to troubleshoot the situation.

2. *User-level corruption.* This type of corruption occurs in user data files. It usually is not detected until users try to access the data and get an AdvFS I/O error or simply notice that their data is incorrect. If an AdvFS I/O error is logged, it's necessary to analyze the error in order to determine the best way to deal with it.

In addition, a problem with a device can lead to corruption in a file system. In that situation, it's necessary to correct the device problem before dealing with the corruption. If you try to correct the corruption first, the problem will most likely reappear later because the underlying device problem remains untreated. Once all hardware problems have been addressed, you can move on to detect (and hopefully correct) any corruption that remains.

9.2.4.2 Correcting AdvFS Corruption

In order to correct a domain that has encountered AdvFS corruption, multiple tools may need to be employed. The Tru64 UNIX system has several utilities and techniques that can be used; we discuss the best ways to use them in the following list.

- *verify(8).* The verify tool is used to detect and correct metadata corruption in an AdvFS domain. Because it must mount the filesets to perform its work, this utility cannot be used if a domain is so badly damaged that its filesets cannot be mounted. A clean run of verify (no errors returned) is a good (albeit less-than-perfect) indication that problems have been corrected. It is possible for user corruption to exist without being detected by verify.
- *fixfdmn(8).* This tool will fix certain types of AdvFS metadata corruption so that a domain can be mounted for further correction by the verify tool. Do not attempt to use a domain after correcting it with fixfdmn without first using verify to make certain no other problems still exist.

- *salvage(8)*. The salvage command is used to recover files from a domain that has been badly corrupted and for which no backups exist. Salvage has two modes: normal and sequential. The former is the default and attempts to follow the metadata structures to find lost files. The sequential mode is used to scan the volumes block by block, looking for metadata signatures. This technique tends to be much slower, but it yields better results. It is recommended that you use the normal mode first and then, if the results are not sufficient, use sequential mode.
- *Other techniques*. For certain types of isolated, user-level corruptions, it is possible, using knowledge of the on-line disk structure, to remove or isolate the corrupted files so that operations can continue with no downtime. After this kind of correction, some data may need to be restored, and it's a good idea to run the verify program on the domain to check for other corruption. We don't recommend trying this on your own without contacting HP support for assistance. Without the proper knowledge, this type of correction could make your domain inaccessible.
- *Restore from backups*. When all else fails, and once all hardware problems have been corrected, the domain can be recreated and the data restored from a known good backup. This is always the final option in any corruption situation.

9.2.4.3 Missing or Incorrect AdvFS Volumes

AdvFS stores the association of domain names to storage volumes in directory /etc/fdmns. This directory contains subdirectories named for the domains on the system. Located within each of these domain directories are symbolic links that point to the devices that compose the volumes of the domain. The benefit of this arrangement is that the domain name can be manipulated with normal UNIX commands. Unfortunately, this can also lead to problems if, for example, the /etc/fdmns directory is accidentally removed. Luckily, if that happens, the advscan(8) tool can be used to scan for and recreate the domain information.

In addition, because advscan doesn't know what the domain names were before the directories were removed, you will need to supply this information by renaming the directory to the correct name after advscan has completed its work. You can avoid having to use advscan (and having to remember this information) by keeping a good backup of the root file system. From this backup, simply restore those directories (/etc/fdmns and its subdirectories) and the problem will be solved. Once again, keeping good backups can be a great time saver.

Troubleshooting Tip

The advscan tool is useful for debugging certain types of corruptions in AdvFS domains because it can read the on-disk structure and provide some useful information even without mounting any fileset on a domain. If you attempt to use advscan on a particular volume and it fails to read useful domain information, this may indicate a serious metadata corruption.

9.2.4.4 AdvFS Performance Issues

In this section, we will briefly discuss how to deal with AdvFS performance issues. When faced with any performance problem, you need to characterize the problem with some quantifiable data that demonstrates (1) that a real problem exists and (2) that it is definitely a problem with AdvFS and not with another component of the operating system or hardware.

The advfsstat(8) utility can be used to answer some of these questions. This tool has many options and can gather many different types of AdvFS-related statistics, so we refer you to the reference page for more details. The advfsstat utility will gather statistics on a single AdvFS domain (and fileset, if specified) and can be set up to perform its data gathering at a specified interval and for a specified number of iterations. The main categories of statistics that can be collected are the following:

- Fileset statistics
- Lock effectiveness statistics
- Volume performance statistics
- Cache effectiveness statistics
- Metadata statistics

It is possible to tune some aspects of individual AdvFS file systems or of the entire AdvFS subsystem. Although there are some tuning parameters available through sysconfig, we don't recommend changing them unless you really know what you're doing. Generally, if you're having a bad enough performance problem where you may need to change one or more of these parameters, you should already be talking to HP technical support. However, there are some configuration adjustments you can make to help improve the performance of AdvFS domains under certain circumstances.

- *File striping.* An individual hot file can be striped across multiple volumes in a domain to try to improve the performance of I/O to that file.
- *Direct I/O.* This is a feature of AdvFS that allows a program to open a file and write directly to the disk, bypassing the Tru64 UNIX file system cache. This should be used only by database applications that perform their own caching; it thus reduces the double caching effect that occurs when not using direct I/O. In general, it's not a good idea to bypass caching, because it is designed to speed up application performance when data items are reused frequently.
- *I/O size.* The read and write I/O sizes for a volume in a domain can be modified using the chvol command. This may possibly improve performance.
- *User file fragmentation.* Because AdvFS is an extent-based file system, files can become discontiguous with pieces spread over the domain. Making files contiguous with the defragment(8) command can improve performance.
- *Metadata fragmentation.* Some metadata files can become fragmented in the same way user files can; however, the defragment utility will not help in all cases. When this happens, one way to relieve the fragmentation is to back up the domain, recreate it, and restore its files. Alternatively, you can do this process on-line using addvol(8) and rmvol(8) if additional disk space is available.
- *On-disk version.* The AdvFS on-disk structure was changed beginning with Tru64 UNIX V5.0 to perform better when there are a large number of files in a single directory and when there are a large number of smaller files in a file domain. Both the old AdvFS version 3 and the newer AdvFS version 4 are fully supported in Tru64 UNIX version 5. However, if you have not updated your domains, you may be missing out on some performance benefits.

Troubleshooting Tip

To examine an individual file for fragmentation, use the "showfile" command with no options, which gives a performance value associated with the file's fragmentation. A 100 percent performance number is the best, with lower numbers indicating greater fragmentation of the file. Use showfile with the -x option to examine the file's extent map and to obtain a more detailed picture of its fragmentation.

9.3 UFS

UNIX File System (UFS) troubleshooting is fairly straightforward for a couple of reasons:

1. Its structure is less complex than that of AdvFS.
2. It has been around for so long that the tools and techniques for detecting and correcting problems have been fine-tuned for most potential problems.

9.3.1 Dealing with UFS Corruption

It may occasionally be necessary to deal with corruption on a UFS file system. When this happens, the primary tool for detecting and correcting file system corruption is the file system structure checker, fsck(8). When a Tru64 UNIX system boots up, it runs /sbin/bcheckrc, which executes fsck on each UFS file system specified in /etc/fstab prior to mounting the file system. If the file system was cleanly unmounted before the boot, fsck will not need to do anything; the file system will be mounted and the process moves on.

However, if the file system was not cleanly unmounted, fsck will run with the -p switch, which is also known as preen mode. In preen mode, fsck will make some corrections that are safe to make without user interaction. In the vast majority of cases, this is perfectly fine, and the correction occurs so the boot process can continue. In a few cases, this process will not result in a file system that is mountable when the process is complete. In those cases, the boot process will stop in single-user mode, and manual interaction will be required.

The fsck tool performs an enormous number of checks on a UFS file system and can take a long time to run for very large file systems. That's one reason why HP recommends using AdvFS for very large file systems. Rapid recovery is one of the major advantages of that file system over UFS.

In addition to fsck, there are other tools available to assist with debugging or correcting UFS file system corruption. Some of these are listed below along with a short description:

- *ncheck, icheck, dcheck.* These tools are older and are used for specific types of troubleshooting or correction tasks. In general, these are all replaced by fsck today.
- *dumpfs.* This tool will provide a detailed output of all the file system structures for a UFS file system. These can be useful when debugging problems with the file system or when you need to know the current values for some of the filesystem parameters used in its creation.
- *fsdb.* This file system debugger allows changes to the on-disk structure of a filesystem to be made. The syntax is similar to that of the adb debugger, for those familiar with that tool. The fsdb tool requires very detailed knowledge of the file system to be successful.
- *newfs.* In order for fsck to do its work, it must have access to a usable superblock. Luckily, UFS stores the superblock in many locations throughout the disk. The "newfs" command with the -N option can be used to find out where all the alternative superblocks are located so they can be used by fsck with the -b option.

9.3.2 UFS Performance Issues

Due to its somewhat simplistic design, the UNIX file system tends to perform consistently in many different situations. However, there are a few things you can do to tune an individual file system's performance based on your workload. These options are discussed in the following sections.

9.3.3 Fragmentation

Fragmentation of a UNIX file system is a different situation from the one discussed earlier for AdvFS. UFS is not extent-based, so performance does not suffer if a file contains discontiguous blocks. Thus, fragmentation pertains to the use of fragments, which can still have a negative impact on file system performance. A fragment in a UFS file system is a partial data block that is used to hold the parts of files that are too small to fill a complete data block. This can be either an entire file that is smaller than a complete (8 KB) file system page or the "leftover" portion of a file that exceeds an integral number of file system pages.

The main problem with using larger blocks in file systems is that most UNIX file systems contain primarily small files. Studies of typical workloads show that a uniformly large block size tends to waste space in the file system. Wasted space is the percentage of disk space not containing user data. Conversely, another key finding has been that although smaller blocks are much less wasteful of space, performance suffers as a result. A compromise solution is to allow larger block sizes but use a smaller data structure called a fragment to store the pieces that don't fill an entire block.

Therefore, the best performance on a UFS file system can be achieved by eliminating the use of fragments on the file system at the expense of disk space. This may be a desirable trade-off for some users; for others it may not. The "optimization preference" specifies whether the file system has been set up to utilize fragments or not. The optimization preference is set on a UFS file system either when it is created with the "newfs" command or at a later time with tunefs. The two possible values for the optimization preference are "space" and "time." Space optimization means that fragments will be used, while time optimization means they will not. The default is to optimize for space.

9.3.4 Tuning UFS File Systems

The tunefs(8) command modifies the dynamic, tunable parameters of a UFS file system located in the superblock. This tool does not alter any data in the file system; it only affects the way in which future writes will be handled. The command switches that you specify indicate which parameters are to be changed. The following items can be changed using tunefs:

- The maximum number of contiguous blocks that will be written in one transfer (the cluster size)
- The rotational delay between groups of blocks in a file
- The maximum number of blocks any single file can allocate out of a single cylinder group at one time
- The percentage of free space on the file system held back from use by nonroot users (minfree)
- The optimization preference

The "tunefs" command works on mounted and active file systems, as well as those that are unmounted. However, the superblock for a mounted file system is cached in memory, so changes made while a file system is mounted will be clobbered the next time the buffers are synchronized. If you attempt to make changes to a mounted root file system, the system must be rebooted for those changes to be effective.

Troubleshooting Tip

A file system's superblock contains the values of the parameters that can be modified using tunefs. You can find out how particular UFS parameters are configured by examining the superblock with the dumpfs(8) tool.

9.4 Summary

In this chapter, we have focused on troubleshooting common file system problems. With this and the previous chapter, we have tried to give you a feel for how to find and fix problems anywhere in the I/O subsystem. Always keep in mind that a problem needs to be solved at the lowest possible layer in the I/O subsystem. A problem in the lower layers will have an impact on the upper layers, but the solution to the problem must be in the appropriate layer. For example, a disk problem can impact the LSM and file system layers. Be careful not to make the mistake of correcting file system corruption without first identifying and correcting a possible hardware problem that caused it.

10

System Configuration

To build may have to be the slow and laborious task of years. To destroy can be the thoughtless act of a single day.

—Sir Winston Churchill

In the previous chapters, we've discussed problems that generally arise during normal, everyday system usage or common system administration tasks. In this chapter, we'll look into problems that occur when performing some relatively infrequent activities—those involved in setting up and configuring a Tru64 UNIX system. Specifically, these activities include the following:

- Installing or upgrading the operating system
- Installing patches
- Configuring the kernel
- Setting the system timezone

A typical system administrator might never have to perform some of these tasks. Because they are relatively infrequent activities, there is generally less troubleshooting information available concerning them (e.g., from Internet sources). We hope to address this lack of information by describing common problems and troubleshooting techniques for these areas in the following sections.

10.1 Installation Problems

Tru64 UNIX has two principal forms of installation: full installation and update installation. Full installation does just what the name implies. It installs a new copy of the operating system from scratch. Update installation, on the other hand, upgrades an existing system to a later version of the operating system while preserving existing file systems, user accounts, and other aspects of the system configuration. There is also a third form of installation called cloned installation, which replicates an installation onto multiple similar systems. Cloned installation is not widely used, so we won't discuss it further in this book.

10.1.1 Full versus Update Installation

Before performing an installation, it's important to understand the differences between the two principal types of installation. A full installation installs a brand-new copy of the Tru64 UNIX operating system. The installation creates new file systems and swap partitions, overwriting any existing system- and user-created files on the disk partitions where the new file systems and swap partitions are installed. After installation, the system must be configured for general use by adding user accounts, setting up the network configuration, and similar tasks.

In contrast to a full installation, an update installation converts a system that is running a specific version of Tru64 UNIX to a later version of the operating system. Unlike a full installation, an update installation preserves existing disk partitions, file systems, network configuration, user accounts, and all other customizations.

It's important to realize that update installation is generally available only to the next version of the operating system, or at most to two or three subsequent versions. Upgrading to a much later version can't be done in a single update installation. Table 10.1 shows the available update installation paths in recent versions of Tru64 UNIX. For example, V5.1A can be installed via a single update from V5.0A or V5.1, but not from V5.0. Upgrading from V5.0 to V5.1A would require two update installations: one to V5.0A or V5.1 and a second to V5.1A. Obviously, larger version jumps require more updates; for example, upgrading from V4.0 to V5.1A would require at least four update installations. At some point, it becomes easier to do a full installation and reconfigure the system rather than performing multiple updates. Each update requires the appropriate distribution media, takes time to perform, and increases the risk that something may go wrong.

The trade-off point between full and update installations is somewhat subjective and depends largely on the degree of customization involved, which in turn depends on the complexity of the system configuration. We generally consider it worthwhile to perform two update installations for a simple configuration and three for a complex system. Beyond that point, it's usually easier to do a full installation.

Table 10.1 *Available Update Installations in Tru64 UNIX*

Target Version	Starting Versions
V4.0	V3.2C, V3.2D
V4.0A	V3.2G, V4.0
V4.0B	V4.0, V4.0A
V4.0C	None
V4.0D	V4.0A, V4.0B, V4.0C
V4.0E	V4.0B, V4.0C, V4.0D
V4.0F	V4.0D, V4.0E
V4.0G	V4.0D, V4.0E, V4.0F
V5.0	V4.0D, V4.0F
V5.0A	V4.0F, V5.0
V5.1	V4.0G, V5.0A
V5.1A	V5.0A, V5.1
V5.1B	V5.1, V5.1A

Although an update installation preserves the existing system configuration, a full installation does not. A full installation results in the loss of existing configuration information, user accounts, layered products, and third-party software. For the first installation on a new system, this is not an issue because there is no existing data to be lost. But if you are performing a full installation over a previously used disk, it's important to recognize this fact and be prepared for it. All user data in any of the standard UNIX file systems (such as /usr/users) must be backed up before the installation and restored afterwards. Any configuration information that you wish to preserve, such as the password and group files, must also be backed up.

Before beginning any installation operation, there is one cautionary note that can't be emphasized too strongly. It's always a good idea to back up your data before making significant changes to a system, but this is particularly true of an installation. We strongly recommend that you back up *all* existing file systems before beginning a full or update installation. The installation process is inherently destructive to existing data; if something goes wrong, restoring from backup is usually the only alternative.

Installation problems tend to be caused by one of the following:

- Out-of-date system firmware
- Invalid EISA configuration data
- Invalid operating system version
- Defective installation media
- Interrupted installation

These problems can affect both full and update installations. There are also a few problems specific to update installations:

- Insufficient disk space
- Layered product conflicts
- File-type conflicts

These problem types are discussed in the following sections.

10.1.2 Out-of-Date System Firmware

Obsolete firmware can prevent Tru64 UNIX from installing. To check the system firmware version, enter the following command at the SRM console prompt:

```
>>> SHOW VERSION
```

Ensure that the firmware version is compatible with the version of Tru64 UNIX that you're running. If it isn't, upgrade to a compatible version. If you do upgrade the firmware, be sure to run the EISA Configuration Utility (ECU) afterwards.

10.1.3 Invalid EISA Configuration Data

Many Alpha systems, particularly older models, contain EISA buses. The EISA configuration information is stored in non-volatile memory. If it becomes corrupted or is never initialized, Tru64 UNIX may not install successfully. In addition, updating the system firmware will clear the EISA configuration data, requiring that it be restored.

To restore the EISA configuration, run the EISA Configuration Utility (ECU), which is provided on a floppy diskette with the Tru64 UNIX distribution. Older versions of the ECU existed in two versions: one for Tru64 UNIX and OpenVMS systems, the other for Windows NT systems. Be sure to use only the former version, which is labeled "UNIX/VMS" on the diskette. The console command to run the ECU may vary depending on the platform type, but is usually one of "runecu," "ecu," or "run ecu." When the ECU starts up, simply choose the "Save and Exit" option. After exiting the ECU, power cycle the system.

10.1.4 Invalid Operating System Version

Not all versions of Tru64 UNIX support all Alpha platforms. Support for new hardware is added from time to time; for example, V5.1A introduced support for the AlphaServer ES45. Attempting to install an older version of Tru64 UNIX on a platform not supported by that version will fail. Booting the installation CD-ROM for the older version will cause the system to halt after displaying a warning message such as the following:

```
WARNING: proc_type 0x42 / sys_type 0x45 unknown
```

(The hexadecimal numbers 0x42 and 0x45 in the example are arbitrary; the actual numbers displayed will probably be different.)

Similarly, support for very old systems based on obsolete technologies (such as the Turbochannel-based DEC 3000 series) has been removed from recent versions of the operating system. Booting the operating system CD in such a situation will panic the system with a message such as "platform not supported."

This kind of situation can also arise by moving or duplicating a system disk from one platform type to another. For example, if you copied the system disk from an AlphaServer ES40 running Tru64 UNIX V4.0G and installed it in an AlphaServer ES45, the system would panic on boot with the "proc_type / sys_type unknown" message. An ES45 requires Tru64 UNIX V5.1A or later, and V4.0G will not run on that platform.

In this kind of situation—whether from a new installation, an update installation, or copying a system disk to another system—there is no way to work around the problem. The Tru64 UNIX kernel code needed to support the specific platform hardware architecture is simply not present in the version you're trying to install. The only alternative is to install a version that does support the platform.

10.1.5 Defective Installation Media

In rare cases, a defect in the installation CD-ROM can cause an I/O error while loading the software subsets for the new version. If the error is a "hard" error that the I/O driver can't recover from, the installation can't proceed. This kind of error is indicated by console messages such as "unable to open device," "unrecoverable hardware error," "irrecoverable media error," or similar messages. In this situation, it's necessary to start over with a new copy of the installation media. (Alternatively, you could try cleaning the problematic CD-ROM.) If this problem occurred in the middle of an update installation, it would be necessary to restore the system from its preupdate backup. This is because not all of the new version software subsets have been loaded, which means that the system will contain a mix of the original and new operating system versions. Such a mix probably won't run at all; even if it does run, correct operation is extremely unlikely.

10.1.6 Interrupted Installation

As the previous section indicated, the loading of new software subsets should not be interrupted for any reason. Unfortunately, sometimes this occurs due to power failure or operator mishap. As noted above, there is no way to recover from this situation gracefully; it's necessary to start over from the beginning. In the case of an update installation, the operating system is left in an inconsistent state (i.e., a mix of the old and new versions). In that case, it's necessary to restore the system to the preupdate state and begin again.

10.1.7 Insufficient Disk Space

The installation process for both full and update installations checks to make sure that the system has sufficient free disk space before loading the new software subsets. If there is not enough free space, the installer notifies the operator. In full installations of recent versions of Tru64 UNIX, the installer adjusts the disk partition sizes as needed, so this problem will never arise. In older versions, running out of disk space requires either selecting fewer software subsets or using the disk configuration utility to configure larger disk partitions.

During update installations, the installer provides the operator with several options to free more disk space. These options include the following:

- *System cleanup*. This option removes system crash dump files, application core dumps, and duplicate or old copies of the Tru64 UNIX kernel.
- *Remove .PreUPD files*. The update installation checks for customized system files and backs them up by copying them into files with the suffix ".PreUPD." This option displays a dialog box that allows you to select the files to remove.
- *Remove software subsets*. This option allows you to remove software subsets not currently being used. This frees some disk space immediately and also prevents these subsets from being updated by the installation process.

If you still don't have enough disk space after using these options, exit to the UNIX shell (via the File pull-down menu) and look for other files that can be removed.

10.1.8 Layered Product Conflicts

There are two types of layered software products that affect update installations:

1. Products that allow the update to proceed but may need to be reinstalled later

2. Products that must be deleted before the update installation can proceed

For the first type, the installer displays a dialog box that lists the layered products that may need to be reinstalled. You can either exit the update installation and manually remove this software or you can continue. In the latter case (continuing the update without removing the layered product), it's important to test the layered software as soon as the update installation is complete. It may also be necessary to update the layered product to a newer version that is more compatible with the new version of the operating system.

In the second case above (a layered product must be removed to continue the update), the installer provides the option to remove the problematic layered product. You can either take this option (i.e., delete the product and continue) or you can exit the update installation; it is not possible to continue without removing the conflicting software. If you choose to exit at this point, no changes are made to the system. If the conflicting software is not supported by the new version of the operating system and the software is critical to your operation, you probably shouldn't continue unless you have an alternative way to provide the critical functionality. If you do continue, note that the layered product deletion will occur immediately. The deleted software will not be automatically restored if the update installation is canceled at a later point.

10.1.9 File-Type Conflicts

All system files (i.e., those files distributed as part of the operating system) have a specific file type: regular file, directory, hard link, symbolic link, block device, or pipe. In an update installation, the installer expects to find each system file of the same type as was shipped with the currently installed version of the operating system. A file-type conflict exists when a system file has a different type. There are two types of file type conflicts:

1. Serious conflicts, which must be resolved before the update installation can continue
2. Minor conflicts, which can optionally be ignored while the update installation proceeds

In both cases, the installer identifies the conflict and informs the operator of the action required to resolve it. This feature helps to ensure the integrity of the operating system version that is being installed.

A serious file-type conflict causes the update installation to exit without updating the system. If the update were to continue, it could result in a corrupt operating system. As such, serious conflicts must be resolved manually before restarting the update installation. Serious file-type conflicts include the following:

- A directory changed to a regular file or symbolic link
- A symbolic link changed to a directory

All other file-type changes are considered minor conflicts. The installer automatically resolves minor conflicts by copying the file with the modified type to a file with the extension ".PreUPD" (e.g., /etc/hosts.PreUPD). When the new version of the operating system is loaded, the original file (e.g., /etc/hosts) is replaced by the new version—with the correct file type—that is shipped with the new operating system version. In this situation, the installer will not be able to merge the original and new files properly. As a result, any customizations in the original file must be manually merged from the ".PreUPD" version into the new version after the update installation is finished.

Before you call support

Before calling technical support on an installation issue, check the following:

- Verify that the system firmware is up-to-date.
- Run the EISA Configuration Utility (ECU).
- Make sure the operating system version is compatible with your hardware. Older systems may not be compatible with newer operating system versions (and vice versa).
- If the installation media has a problem, try another copy if one is available.
- And please back up your system before starting any kind of installation!

10.2 Installing Patches

Tru64 UNIX uses the dupatch(8) utility to install operating system and TruCluster patches. This utility keeps track of installed patches, checks for patch prerequisites and dependencies, and generally makes installing Tru64 UNIX patch kits a straightforward process. When dupatch installs a patched file, it checks the size and checksum of the existing version of the file against known values (i.e., it expects the file to come from the original operating system installation or a previously installed patch). If the size and checksum are not as expected, dupatch will display a warning and not install the patch. This is done to protect the system against accidental removal of a problem correction provided by HP technical support or another source. If a patch was installed manually (i.e., without using dupatch), then dupatch could supersede the patched file with a version of the same file from the patch kit it was installing. The file from the patch kit might not include the same problem correction, in which case superseding it would not be a good idea. On the other hand, the patch kit might include that problem correction among others, so installing the file from the patch kit would be desirable.

In such cases, dupatch has no way to tell whether superseding a "manual" patch is desirable. As such, it informs the operator of the conflict and will not install the conflicting patch until the conflict is resolved. To resolve the conflict, use the Baseline/Analysis option from the dupatch installation menu. This locates and displays any patch file conflicts and provides the option to install the patch anyway. It's a good idea to run the Baseline/Analysis option before attempting to actually install a patch kit. If any conflicts are detected, you can determine whether or not the previous file should be superseded. Your system change log should have a record of the previous patch installation and the problem it was intended to fix. Compare this with the patch kit release notes to see if the fix in question is included; if it is, you can choose to go ahead and install the patch. If the fix is not included in the new patch kit—or you can't be sure from the patch kit documentation—you should probably hold off on installing the conflicting patch (and perhaps the rest of the patch kit as well). In this situation, it's usually a good idea to contact HP technical support for further assistance.

10.3 Kernel Configuration

The Tru64 UNIX kernel includes a wide variety of options and parameters. Options are features or capabilities of the operating system (e.g., AdvFS), while parameters are values that control or limit system behavior. A typical kernel parameter is "maxusers," which defines the number of simultaneous users that the system can support efficiently. (The maxusers parameter is an important one; it's discussed in greater detail further on.)

An option is included in the kernel by statically building its supporting code into the kernel. If the option is not selected, the kernel code that provides the associated capability is left out of the kernel. Unnecessary options can be left out of the kernel in order to minimize the amount of disk space and physical memory consumed by the kernel. However, this is beneficial only for older systems that have small root file systems or limited physical memory. With newer systems, it's usually easier to just include all possible options. The extra disk space and memory consumed are relatively insignificant in a modern system.

Parameter values are also statically built into the kernel. In older versions of Tru64 UNIX, rebuilding the kernel with new values was the only way to configure parameters. V4.0 introduced a way to configure the kernel dynamically by means of the sysconfig(8) utility and the /etc/sysconfigtab file. The sysconfigtab file contains parameter values that are read by the kernel during system startup; these values supersede the static values that were built into the kernel. Thus, changing a kernel parameter value no longer requires rebuilding the kernel. Instead, all that needs to be done is to modify the parameter value in /etc/sysconfigtab and reboot the system. The new value is read at boot time and immediately takes effect. Some (but not all) parameters can even be adjusted on a running system without requiring a reboot.

Configuring the Tru64 UNIX kernel (i.e., modifying the kernel options and parameters) is almost always necessary after a new system installation; few systems are ideally configured out of the box for their ultimate environment. After a system has been in place for a while, kernel configuration is an occasional task whose frequency is highly variable. Once a system is up and running in a stable situation, you might never have to modify the kernel configuration. On the other hand, if you frequently add new capabilities or perform a great deal of system tuning, you might need to configure the kernel on a daily basis. As discussed previously, there are two ways to configure the kernel: statically (rebuilding the kernel) and dynamically (using the sysconfig utility and /etc/sysconfigtab). Each of these methods has its own set of potential problems, which are discussed in the following subsections.

10.3.1 Building the Tru64 UNIX Kernel

Tru64 UNIX uses the doconfig(8) utility to build a customized kernel. The doconfig utility reads the kernel configuration file to determine the desired kernel options, parameter values, and some hardware configuration information. The kernel configuration file is located in directory /sys/conf and has a file name of the form HOSTNAME (i.e., the system's host name in upper case letters). It's possible to have multiple kernel configuration files in /sys/conf. These can be used to build alternative kernels for the system or for other systems.

In Tru64 UNIX version 5, rebuilding the kernel is necessary only when adding new kernel options or a new type of hardware (e.g., a type of I/O adapter not previously present on the system). In version 4, it's necessary to rebuild the kernel when any new adapter is added, whether or not an adapter of the same type is already present. As mentioned previously, it's also possible to change the value of kernel parameters by rebuilding the kernel. However, dynamic parameter configuration via /etc/sysconfigtab is so much more convenient that we don't recommend rebuilding the kernel for this purpose.

If doconfig is invoked with the -c switch, it builds a new kernel from the specified configuration file. For example, "doconfig -c HOSTNAME" uses configuration file /sys/conf/HOSTNAME to build the new kernel. If doconfig is specified without -c, it first invokes the sizer(8) program to determine the system's hardware configuration and generate a new configuration file, which is then used to build the new kernel. The doconfig utility builds the kernel in a build directory named /usr/sys/HOSTNAME, which doconfig creates if it doesn't already exist. There is also a symbolic link, /sys /HOSTNAME, that points to /usr/sys/HOSTNAME. The newly built kernel is in file /usr/sys/HOSTNAME/vmunix, which must be copied to the root directory (and the system then rebooted) in order to take effect.

The process of copying the kernel to the root directory is one of the potential trouble spots in the kernel build process. In older versions of Tru64 UNIX, copying the new kernel to the root directory was usually accomplished by the "mv" command (i.e., "mv /sys/HOSTNAME/vmunix /vmunix"), because this had the added benefit of removing the kernel file from the build directory after copying it to the root directory. In version 5, "/vmunix" is a context-dependent symbolic link (CDSL) rather than a regular file. If the "mv" command is used to copy the new kernel, the new /vmunix will become a regular file, unintentionally removing the CDSL. This is not a significant problem for standalone systems, but can cause strange problems in a cluster. Therefore, it's important to always use cp rather than mv to move a new version 5 kernel to the root directory.

If the kernel build fails, there are a couple of generally useful troubleshooting techniques. The first involves recreating the temporary build directory in case some corruption or inconsistency is present in the files it contains. To do this, remove the directory and its contents with "rm -r /usr/sys/HOSTNAME" and try to build the kernel again. The directory will be automatically recreated and repopulated with the correct files. It's important to remove the actual directory (/usr/sys/HOSTNAME) rather than the symbolic link (/sys/HOSTNAME) that points to the directory. In older versions of Tru64 UNIX, /sys/HOSTNAME was the build directory, and "rm -r /sys/HOSTNAME" was the appropriate way to remove it; in version 4 and higher, however, this command removes only the symbolic link rather than the underlying build directory. The next attempt to rebuild the kernel restores the symbolic link, but its target is the original build directory with its original (and possibly corrupt) contents.

The second troubleshooting technique is one that we've suggested in a number of other situations. The doconfig utility is actually a shell script, so it's possible to edit the script file (/usr/sbin/doconfig) and add " -x" to the first line in order to echo each command line as the script executes. This identifies the command that's executing when a problem occurs, allowing you to focus on the failing command. It may be necessary to repeat this process one or more times in order to drill down further into the problem.

Rebuilding the kernel can fail in one of two main ways: Either the doconfig command never finishes, or it exits with errors. The doconfig utility normally prints a "Working" message every two minutes while the kernel is building. The build process should take no more than 15 minutes—it's usually much less on faster (i.e., newer) systems. If doconfig is still running after 20 minutes, it is probably never going to finish. This problem is usually caused by the shell trapping signal 15 (SIGTERM), which is used by the timer process that prints the "Working" message. If signal 15 is trapped, the timer process will not work properly and the kernel build will not complete. This is most likely caused by a "trap" command in a shell startup script—for example:

```
trap 1 2 3 15
```

Check the root user's shell startup files (and any other scripts called by those files) for such a command. The startup scripts to check include the following:

- /.profile and /etc/profile (if root's default shell is the Bourne or Korn shell)
- /.cshrc, /.login, and /etc/csh.login (if root's default shell is the C shell)

Single-user mode always uses the Bourne shell, so you must check /.profile and /etc/profile if doconfig hangs in single-user mode, even if root's default shell is the C shell. If you find a command that traps signal 15, comment it out by adding a # character at the beginning, then start a new shell and try again to build the kernel.

If doconfig encounters compile or link errors while building the kernel, it displays the last few errors and then exits. Typical errors include "symbol undefined," "file not found," and others. To examine the errors, check file /sys/HOSTNAME/errs, which contains a log of the commands used to build the kernel and their output. When errors are encountered, the problem is usually one of the following:

- Corrupt or inconsistent binary files
- Incorrect "make" utility
- Corrupt null device

If any of the binary files used to build the kernel are missing or corrupt, compile or link errors are almost certain to occur. Also, if some binary files are mutually inconsistent—for example, if a patch kit was incompletely installed—similar problems can result. The allverify utility (available from HP technical support) is ideal for detecting this type of problem. Run the allverify utility and correct any inconsistencies found; then try the kernel build again.

The kernel build process uses the make(1) utility to perform the necessary compile and link operations. The makefile that controls this process is very sensitive with regard to format, and only the Tru64 UNIX–supplied make utility should be used to build the kernel. If the supplied make utility is replaced by a different version (e.g., the GNU make utility), the different make utility may not handle the kernel makefile correctly, resulting in kernel build errors. If you are using an alternative make utility as the default on your system, you may need to replace it with the original Tru64 UNIX version in order to build the kernel.

Finally, very strange build errors can occur if there is a problem with the null device, /dev/null. Typical error messages include (but are not limited to) the following:

```
/usr/lib/cmplrs/cc/cfe: Fatal: Cannot open the file rm
cc: Error: no source, object or ucode file specified
/usr/lib/cmplrs/cc/cfe: Fatal: Cannot open the file vmunix
/usr/lib/cmplrs/cc/cfe: Fatal: Cannot open the file vmunix.*
```

This problem occurs if /dev/null is a regular file instead of a special device. This is almost always caused by a privileged user accidentally deleting /dev/null. The next command that redirects output to /dev/null (e.g., many of the system startup scripts) recreates /dev/null as a regular file. This doesn't really cause any problems for most subsequent operations; output sent to such a /dev/null just accumulates in the file instead of disappearing. However, the kernel build process uses /dev/null in some creative ways, and if /dev/null is a regular file, it causes errors like those shown above. Because the problem doesn't surface until the next kernel build, it may exist for some time without being noticed.

To see whether this problem exists on your system, use the file(1) command to check the null device type:

```
# cd /dev
# file null
null: empty
```

The only correct output is "null: character special (2/2)." If the result is anything else, remove the null file and recreate it:

```
# rm null
# ./MAKEDEV null
```

Now the file command should show the null device as a special device file with major and minor numbers both equal to 2:

```
# file null
null: character special (2/2)
```

After recreating the null device, remove the temporary build directory ("rm -r /usr/sys/HOSTNAME") and try the kernel build again.

10.3.2 Dynamic Kernel Configuration

Certain kernel parameters can be configured dynamically via the sysconfig utility and the /etc/sysconfigtab file. The sysconfigtab file is read by the kernel when the system boots; parameter values specified in the file override the values that were statically built into the kernel. In addition, some (but not all) parameters can be adjusted even while the system is running (i.e., without requiring a reboot). In some cases, a parameter can be adjusted in only one direction (e.g., it can be increased but not decreased while the system is running).

A detailed explanation of how to use sysconfigtab and the sysconfig utility is beyond the scope of this book; for background information, see the Tru64 UNIX System Administration Manual and the appropriate reference pages. In this section, we discuss problems that affect dynamic kernel configuration and how to resolve them. One of the most important principles to remember is always to make a backup copy of /etc/sysconfigtab before modifying it. This is a good idea when you modify any system configuration file, but it's particularly important in the case of /etc/sysconfigtab. Poorly chosen values for certain parameters can prevent a system from booting.

In this situation (changes to /etc/sysconfigtab render the system unbootable), it's possible to bypass most sysconfigtab processing by adding the "C" flag to the console boot command:

```
>>> BOOT -FL C
```

This prevents the problematic parameter values from taking effect. However, it also prevents most other entries in /etc/sysconfigtab from taking effect. Therefore, this should be used only as a temporary workaround in order to repair the problem.

The above boot command boots the system to single-user mode. Mount the root directory read/write, then copy the backed-up version of sysconfigtab back to /etc/sysconfigtab and reboot:

```
# /sbin/mountroot
```

(Note: the mountroot command does not exist in version 4 or earlier; use "/sbin/bcheckrc" instead.)

```
# cd /etc
# cp sysconfigtab sysconfigtab.problem
# cp sysconfigtab.backup sysconfigtab
# halt
```

Then reboot the system and investigate the problem. The following command provides a quick look at the differences between the two versions of sysconfigtab:

```
# diff /etc/sysconfigtab /etc/sysconfigtab.problem
```

Another guideline for modifying sysconfigtab is to always use the sysconfigdb(8) utility instead of modifying /etc/sysconfigtab with a text editor. Although editing the file is usually simpler, sysconfigdb performs basic syntax checking on the parameters being modified. Using sysconfigdb also prevents the possibility of a parameter being specified twice in /etc/sysconfigtab. If a parameter is specified more than once, only the last value found is used, with no error message. This can cause a great deal of confusion when a parameter change apparently doesn't take effect, because the same parameter is specified with a different value later in the file. Also, manually editing sysconfigtab may cause problems if the operating system version is subsequently upgraded with the installupdate utility. The update installation process merges the existing sysconfigtab file with the new version from the Tru64 UNIX distribution. The merge operation is quite sensitive to the layout of the sysconfigtab file, and unintended changes to this layout can cause problems when the files are merged.

One final problem to watch out for is an excessively large sysconfigtab file. Because this file is read very early in the boot process (before the full kernel is operating), it is constrained to a fairly small size: 32,768 characters in version 4, and 49,152 characters in version 5. (The character count excludes comment lines and white space.) This size is sufficient for all normal situations, but without much to spare. A large part of the file is occupied by hardware configuration information. Consequently, it's important to include only those kernel parameters that need to be set to nondefault values. Attempting to specify all configurable parameters in /etc/sysconfigtab will exceed the size limit. When this happens, all information beyond the size limit is ignored. The kernel displays a warning about this problem when it reads the file at boot time:

```
Warning: /etc/sysconfigtab size exceeds 49152 bytes
All attribute defaults not picked up.
```

Using the sysconfig utility to change parameter values on a running system is fairly straightforward. Assuming the parameters can be changed dynamically, there's not a lot that can go wrong with this operation. However, it's important to remember that changing a parameter value on a running system and changing it in /etc/sysconfigtab are two separate operations: sysconfig performs the former, while sysconfigdb is used for the latter. If you change a parameter value dynamically with sysconfig, and you want the change to become permanent, it's necessary to use sysconfigdb to make the change in /etc/sysconfigtab. If you don't, the parameter will revert to its previous value when the system reboots.

We'll also mention one parameter of great importance to the kernel configuration. This parameter is "maxusers" in the proc (process) subsystem. The value of maxusers is defined as the number of simultaneous users that a system can support without straining its resources. Numerous kernel data structures and internal limits are derived from the value of maxusers. For example, the maximum number of processes that can run simultaneously is calculated as follows:

```
(maxusers*8) + 20  [Version 4 and earlier]
```

or

```
(maxusers*32) rounded up to a power of 2  [Version 5]
```

To display the current value of maxusers, use the following command:

```
# sysconfig -q proc maxusers
proc:
maxusers = 64
```

The default value of maxusers is 32 in Tru64 UNIX version 4 and earlier. This value is very conservative and may be suitable for a personal workstation, but it's too low for most situations. In version 5, the kernel determines a value for maxusers (if it's not specified in /etc/sysconfigtab) based on the amount of physical memory in the system. The relationship between maxusers and physical memory is shown in Table 10.2. The minimum possible value for the parameter is 8, while the maximum is 16,384 (4,096 in version 4).

Table 10.2 *Default Value of maxusers in Tru64 UNIX Version 5*

Physical Memory Size	Default Value of maxusers
Up to 32 MB	16
More than 32 MB, less than 256 MB	128
At least 256 MB, less than 512 MB	256
At least 512 MB, less than 1 GB	512
At least 1 GB, less than 2 GB	1,024
More than 2 GB	2,048

If maxusers is too small, the most common error is a shortage of available process slots. When this happens, attempting to run a command fails with an error message such as "pid table is full," "too many processes already exist," or something similar. To correct this problem, increase the value of maxusers. In version 4, maxusers can be modified at only at boot time. In version 5, however, it's possible to raise (but not to lower) the value of maxusers without rebooting. For example, to increase maxusers from a current value of 128 to 500 on a V5.0 system, use the following:

```
# sysconfig -r proc maxusers=500
maxusers: reconfigured
```

Remember that this change will not persist after the system is rebooted, unless you also use sysconfigdb to modify /etc/sysconfigtab.

To determine whether a parameter is dynamic, use the command "sysconfig -Q <subsystem> <parameter list>." The "ops" field in the output indicates the supported configuration operations for the parameter. If this field includes the character "R," the parameter can be reconfigured dynamically. For example, the following command shows that maxusers is dynamic ("R" is present), but parameter "max_proc_per_user" is not dynamic:

```
% sysconfig -Q proc maxusers max_proc_per_user
proc:
maxusers -       type=INT op=CRQ min_val=8 max_val=16384
max_proc_per_user -      type=UINT op=CQ min_val=0
 max_val=524287
```

Before you call support

Before calling technical support on a kernel configuration issue, check the following:

- For kernel build problems, remove the build directory ("rm -r /usr/sys/HOSTNAME") and try again.
- Run the allverify utility to check for corrupt or inconsistent files.
- Ensure that /dev/null is a special device file.
- Verify that you're using the correct version of the make utility.
- If you changed /etc/sysconfigtab, try booting with "BOOT -FL C" and checking the changes you made.

10.4 Timezone Issues

The system timezone is a minor element of UNIX system configuration, but it is nevertheless an important one. In most cases, there will never be a problem with the timezone definition, nor any need to modify it (unless the system is moved to a different geographic location). However, in the rare event that a timezone problem does arise, it can be quite serious for users and applications—and quite mysterious to the unlucky system administrator who has to track down the problem and fix it. In the interest of minimizing unnecessary anguish on the part of system administrators, we're including a discussion of the most likely timezone problems and their solutions.

In order to troubleshoot timezone problems, it's necessary to understand how UNIX in general—and Tru64 UNIX in particular—handles system time and timezones. From an internal timekeeping perspective, the UNIX kernel has no concept of timezones. The kernel keeps time as the absolute number of seconds since the beginning of the year 1970—that is, since 00:00:00 January 1, 1970, Greenwich Mean Time (GMT). (GMT is also known as Universal Time, or UTC). This internal time is never adjusted for timezones or daylight saving time. The system does define a timezone, but it is used only to convert the internal time to a form convenient for users. For example, an internal time value of 1050000000 is 1,050,000,000 seconds since the beginning of 1970, or in more familiar terms, 18:40:00 GMT on April 10, 2003.

In some older versions of UNIX, the timezone definition was built into the kernel and could be changed only by rebuilding the kernel. Most modern versions, including Tru64 UNIX, are more flexible. Tru64 UNIX uses the symbolic link /etc/zoneinfo/localtime to define the system time zone. The target of this link is a time zone definition file whose name represents the timezone name, geographic region, or a major city within the time zone. For example, a Tru64 UNIX version 5 system in the Eastern timezone of the United States has the localtime link defined as follows:

```
# cd /etc/zoneinfo
# ls -l localtime
lrwxrwxrwx   1 root       system        16  Jul  1 10:30
 /etc/zoneinfo/localtime -> America/New_York
```

To change the timezone, all that has to be done is to modify the symbolic link to point to the desired zone. This can be done on the fly and does not require a kernel rebuild or even a reboot. For example, suppose the system in the above example is moved from Atlanta to Houston, which requires the timezone to be changed from U.S. Eastern to Central. All that needs to be done is to replace the symbolic link with the correct value:

```
# cd /etc/zoneinfo
# ln -sf America/Chicago localtime
```

The timezone definition files reside in subdirectories under /etc/zoneinfo, so the target of the symbolic link could be either a relative path ("America/Chicago") or an absolute path ("/etc/zoneinfo/America/Chicago") with equal validity. Each definition file defines its time zone in terms of its offset from GMT, its rules for starting and ending daylight saving time, and the abbreviation(s) used to designate the timezone. For example, the America/New_York file defines the U.S. Eastern time zone. Standard time is five hours before GMT, daylight saving time advances the clock by an hour beginning the first Sunday in April and ending the first Sunday in October, and the abbreviations "EST" and "EDT" are used for Eastern Standard Time and Eastern Daylight Time respectively.

Most (but not all) of the timezone names changed between Tru64 UNIX versions 4 and 5. For example, the U.S. Eastern timezone is "US/Eastern" in version 4, but "America/New_York" in version 5. When a system is upgraded from version 4 to version 5, the update installation procedure changes the symbolic link if the timezone name changed. If the timezone name did not change, no action is taken—which leads to one of the possible timezone configuration problems. There is a set of timezones defined strictly in terms of their offset from GMT, with no daylight saving time changes. These timezones have names such as "GMT–5," "GMT+2," etc. In Tru64 UNIX version 4, the timezone name represents the offset from GMT—for example, "GMT–6" is six hours behind GMT, or the equivalent of U.S. Central Standard Time (CST). However, Tru64 UNIX version 5 was changed to comply with the POSIX.1 standard (ISO/IEC 9945-1 ANSI/IEEE Std. 1003.1), which defines GMT-offset timezone names in terms of the number of hours that must be added to local time in order to match GMT. In this scheme, the time equivalent to U.S. CST must have six hours added to it in order to match GMT, so this timezone is now called "GMT+6." In other words, the definition change effectively swapped the plus and minus signs in the zone names; the old GMT-6 is now GMT+6, and vice versa. (In our opinion, the definition called for by the POSIX.1 standard is counterintuitive and confusing. However, it is the standard.)

When a system using one of the GMT-offset timezones is upgraded from Tru64 UNIX version 4 to version 5, the timezone symbolic link is not changed—but the definition of a timezone such as "GMT–5" *has* changed in an unexpected way. It's now a timezone that's five hours ahead of GMT instead of five hours behind, or a total of 10 hours ahead of the desired timezone. This problem usually appears as the system time "jumping" forward or backward several hours when the system is upgraded to version 5. If you encounter this behavior, check to see if you are using one of the GMT-offset timezones. If so, change it to the zone name with the opposite sign or (preferably) a timezone with an appropriate "meaningful" name.

Timezone problems can also occur if a timezone definition file becomes corrupted. This is usually caused by issuing an "ln" command to change the localtime symbolic link, but specifying the arguments in the wrong order (e.g., "ln -sf localtime America/New_York" instead of "ln -sf America/New_York localtime"). The latter command correctly defines the symbolic link "localtime" pointing to target file "America/New_York." Specifying the arguments in the wrong order defines "America/New_York" as a symbolic link, which overwrites the actual timezone definition file. If there is a problem with the underlying timezone file, Tru64 UNIX won't be able to interpret the timezone correctly. In this case, there are two alternatives. Either copy the affected timezone file from another Tru64 UNIX system or the installation CD-ROM, or rebuild it from the timezone source files.

The timezone source files are located in directory /etc/zoneinfo/sources. There is one file for each continent containing all the time zones on that continent (e.g., "europe," "northamerica," etc.). To rebuild the timezone definition files, use the timezone compiler, zic(8), on the appropriate source file. For example, if America/New_York is corrupted, the following commands will rebuild all of the North American timezone definition files:

```
# cd /etc/zoneinfo/sources
# zic northamerica
```

This replaces the corrupted "America/New_York" file with a newly built version.

If you suspect a corrupted timezone file, the "zdump(8)" command can be used to verify the timezone definition. The "zdump -v" command reads a timezone definition file and displays the GMT offset and daylight saving time transitions in each year from 1900 to 2038. This generates a lot of output, but it can be pared down by piping the command to grep for the current year. For example, the following command checks the definition for America/New_York:

```
# zdump -v America/New_York | grep 2003
America/New_York  Sun Apr  6 06:59:59 2003 GMT = Sun
Apr  6 01:59:59 2003 EST isdst=0 gmtoff=-18000
America/New_York  Sun Apr  6 07:00:00 2003 GMT = Sun
Apr  6 02:00:00 2003 EDT isdst=1 gmtoff=-14400
America/New_York  Sun Oct 26 05:59:59 2003 GMT = Sun
Oct 26 01:59:59 2003 EDT isdst=1 gmtoff=-14400
America/New_York  Sun Oct 26 06:00:00 2003 GMT = Sun
Oct 26 01:00:00 2003 EST isdst=0 gmtoff=-18000
```

Check the output from zdump to see if the timezone has the correct definition. If the output is incorrect or missing, the definition file needs to be replaced by one of the methods described above.

One final timezone issue that can arise under rare circumstances is the need to change a timezone definition. For example, the government of Mexico changed that country's timezone rules in 2001. As a result, systems in Mexico that continued to use the existing Mexican timezone definition files would not display the correct time for part of the year. In such cases, it's necessary to modify the timezone source files and build new timezone definitions. The details of this process are beyond the scope of this book, but the basic procedure is as follows:

1. Edit the appropriate source file in /etc/zoneinfo/sources and modify or create the appropriate timezone definitions.
2. Use zic to compile the new timezone definitions.
3. Change the /etc/zoneinfo/localtime symbolic link (if necessary) to point to the newly defined timezone.

For information on the timezone source files, consult the tzfile(4) reference page.

Before you call support

Before calling technical support on a timezone issue, perform the following:

- Check the current system date.
- Verify that the timezone link (/etc/zoneinfo/localtime) points to the correct timezone.
- Check the timezone definition file with zdump.
- If necessary, rebuild the timezone definition files with zic.

10.5 Summary

The system configuration activities discussed in this chapter—installation, kernel configuration, and timezone—are infrequent but important tasks for a system administrator. When problems arise in these areas, they are usually quite serious and need to be resolved quickly. Unfortunately, the relative infrequency of these tasks means that troubleshooting information is correspondingly harder to find. The information in this chapter, along with the general troubleshooting techniques provided earlier in this book, should help you to resolve these types of configuration problems quickly.

11

System Administration

To be really great in little things, to be truly noble and heroic in the insipid details of everyday life, is a virtue so rare as to be worthy of canonization.

—Harriet Beecher Stowe

In this chapter, we'll discuss problems that arise in some of the less common areas of system administration—tasks that come up occasionally, but usually not on a daily basis. These tasks include the following:

- Software license management
- Printing
- Scheduling jobs with the cron facility

Another way of looking at this chapter is that it includes the miscellaneous bits that don't fit anywhere else.

11.1 Software Licenses

In most cases, the purchase of any software package (whether it's an operating system or a layered product) requires a license agreement with the software vendor. The license agreement defines the terms and conditions under which the software package may be used legally. System administrators have a twofold responsibility with respect to software licenses. First, they must ensure that all license terms and conditions are observed. Second, they must perform the license management operations needed to install and operate the licensed software.

11.1.1 License Management

In order to troubleshoot license problems, it's necessary to understand how Tru64 UNIX manages licenses. This function is performed by the aptly-named License Management Facility (LMF). LMF creates and maintains a database of license information, which is stored in the file /var/adm/lmf/ldb. The Tru64 UNIX operating system and most layered products contain license-checking functions. These functions interact with the license database to verify that the software is properly licensed for the system on which it is running.

Most products that run under Tru64 UNIX are licensed by either an activity license or an availability license. An activity license (also called a per-user license) limits the number of users who can use a product simultaneously by requiring a certain number of license units for each user. On the other hand, an availability license (or capacity license) provides unlimited access to a software product once its license has been registered and loaded on a particular system. For some licenses, different models of hardware require different numbers of license units to allow a product to run. In general, the more powerful the hardware, the more license units are needed to run a product. License unit requirement tables (LURTs) specify how many license units are needed to run a product on a particular model of hardware.

Although there are a plethora of possible licenses that may be installed on your system, there are two of particular concern for all Tru64 UNIX installations: OSF-BASE and OSF-USR. OSF-BASE is an availability license that grants the right to run the Tru64 UNIX operating system on a particular system. A Tru64 UNIX system without a valid, active OSF-BASE license can still operate, but with limited functionality. Among other restrictions, only the root user can log in, and only from the system console.

The number of units required for a valid OSF-BASE license depends on the type and number of processors in the system, all the way from 12 units for some of the smaller systems up to 6,000 units for a fully loaded (32 CPU) AlphaServer GS320. The LURT for OSF-BASE, showing the required number of units for all Alpha systems, can be found at the following URL:

```
http://www.compaq.com/products/software/info/refmat/swl_alpha.html
```

Tru64 UNIX also accepts the UNIX-SERVER license as an alternative to OSF-BASE; however, the UNIX-SERVER license is rarely (if ever) seen in practice. By themselves, both OSF-BASE and UNIX-SERVER allow logins only by the root user; in order for nonroot users to log in, the OSF-USR license is also required. OSF-USR is an activity license that allows a specific number of non-root users to log in and use the system. Both licenses (OSF-BASE and OSF-USR) must be active for nonroot users to use the system.

OSF-USR requires 100 units for each nonroot user (e.g., a four-user license contains 400 units). As with many other parameters in UNIX, a value of zero indicates an unlimited amount, so an unlimited OSF-USR license contains 0 units. Tru64 UNIX comes with an implicit four-user (400-unit) OSF-USR license that can be used if a larger license is not purchased.

It's also possible to have a UNIX-WORKSTATION license instead of OSF-BASE and OSF-USR. This license combines the functions of both OSF-BASE and OSF-USR. It grants the right to run Tru64 UNIX on a workstation system and have two nonroot logins. Like the UNIX-SERVER license, UNIX-WORKSTATION is rarely seen in practice.

Some components of the operating system provide basic functionality without an additional license, but contain advanced features that are available only when a license is present. For example, AdvFS is provided as part of Tru64 UNIX, and AdvFS file systems can be created and used without an additional license. However, advanced AdvFS features, such as multivolume domains, require the ADVFS-UTILITIES license. Similarly, basic LSM functionality comes with the operating system, but advanced features such as striped or RAID-5 plexes require the LSM-OA license.

11.1.2 Troubleshooting License Problems

Most license problems surface when a license-dependent function suddenly stops working. In many cases, an informative error message is generated. For example, the following message at boot time indicates that a valid OSF-BASE license wasn't loaded:

```
Can't find an OSF-BASE, UNIX-WORKSTATION, or UNIX-SERVER
license PAK
```

However, some license problems aren't quite as obvious. A nonroot user attempting to log in may be denied access with the following error message:

```
Too many users logged on already.
Try again later.
```

This indicates that there aren't enough OSF-USR units available for another login. This may or may not actually be a problem. There might be a problem with the OSF-USR license, or it could be that the maximum number of licensed users is already logged in. In the latter case, the license is functioning as intended and the user is just out of luck until somebody logs out.

The most important tool for troubleshooting license problems is the lmf(8) command. When a license problem appears, the first step is to use the "lmf list" command for a quick look at the status of the license; for example, if a problem with the OSF-USR license is suspected:

```
# lmf list | egrep 'OSF-USR|Product'
Product          Status          Users: Total         Active
OSF-USR          active                   4            1
```

The above output indicates that the OSR-USR license supports a total of four nonroot user logins, of which one is currently in use. The license has a status of "active," which is the desired state. A status of "enabled" or "terminated" indicates a problem.

To get more detailed information about a license, use the "full" option with the "lmf list" command. For example:

```
# lmf list full for OSF-USR
           Product Name: OSF-USR
               Producer: DEC
                 Issuer: DEC
   Authorization Number: UNIX-SERVER-IMPLICIT-USER
        Number of units: 400
                Version:
   Product Release Date:
   Key Termination Date:
Availability Table Code:
    Activity Table Code: CONSTANT=100
            Key Options:
          Product Token:
            Hardware-Id:
         License status: active
      Cancellation Date:
        Revision Number: 0
```

```
               Comment:
     Cache Total Units: 400
       Activity Charge: 100
          Usable Units: 300
```

The above example shows the four-user implicit license that comes with the operating system. The availability code field indicates that 100 units are needed for each user. The license has a total of 400 units (four users), of which 100 units are currently charged for one login. There are 300 usable units remaining, indicating that three more nonroot users could log in at the same time. (The user license limits the number of simultaneous logins, not the total number of accounts on the system.) The "Key Termination Date" field is empty, indicating that the license will never expire. Depending on the terms of a license, it may or may not have a termination date.

When a license has a status of "terminated," it means that the license has expired. Check the termination date with the "lmf list full" command. If the termination date is indeed past, it's time to get a new license. On the other hand, if the termination date is in the future, check the system date; it's possible that the date has accidentally been set to sometime in the future. After correcting the date, enter the "lmf reset" command to activate the license. The reset option instructs LMF to rescan the license database and load the appropriate licenses into the kernel's license cache.

If a license status is "enabled," it's possible that the license has simply not been loaded into the kernel cache. The first thing to try is the "lmf reset" command. This will either activate the license—thereby solving the problem—or produce an informative error message, such as "Not enough units to load OSF-BASE."

If no licenses are activated, there's most likely a problem with the license database file. Make sure the /var file system (or the /usr file system, if /var is part of /usr) is mounted and that file /var/adm/lmf/ldb is accessible. If the database file is missing, restore it from a recent backup and enter the "lmf reset" command. If the file is present, but has somehow been corrupted, lmf will usually detect this and display an error message indicating that the file is corrupt. In this case, rename the corrupt database to a different name, such as "ldb.bad," and restore the file from backup.

Insufficient units can be a problem for both OSF-BASE and OSF-USR. When this problem arises with OSF-BASE, check the number of units with "lmf list full." Compare this with the LURT (at the URL listed in section 11.1.1) to verify that you have enough units for your system configuration.

If you don't have enough units, there are several possibilities. If you've upgraded your system to a newer model and used the license present on the older system, the old OSF-BASE license may not have enough units for the new system. In this case, you'll need to purchase additional OSF-BASE units.

Another possibility is that you've increased the number of processors on the system by adding CPUs or reconfiguring a partitioned system. As the LURT shows, multiprocessor systems generally require additional OSF-BASE units for each CPU added to the system. If you've added a new CPU, you also need to install an additional license (which usually comes along with the new processor) in order to provide the necessary additional units. If you don't have the additional license on hand, it's possible to disable the additional CPU(s) temporarily until the license can be obtained. This can be done by changing the value of the console variable CPU_ENABLED, which is a bit mask specifying which processors can be used. Setting bit 0 enables CPU 0, bit 1 enables CPU 1, and so on. The default value of CPU_ENABLED is FFFF or FFFFFFFF (hexadecimal)—that is, all bits are set, indicating that all CPUs are enabled.

For example, adding a third processor to a two-CPU AlphaServer ES45 requires an additional 50 units of OSF-BASE. If the additional license was not available, booting the system with all three CPUs enabled would result in the "Can't find OSF-BASE" error message, and system functions would be severely limited. To workaround this problem until the additional license becomes available, the third CPU could temporarily be disabled by setting CPU_ENABLED to a value of 3. This value has only bits 0 and 1 set, so the system would use only those two CPUs. After the additional license was obtained and installed, CPU_ENABLED would need to be reset to its default value in order to enable the new CPU.

When there are insufficient units for OSF-USR, the problem is usually related to the implicit user license: either it's active when it shouldn't be, or it's not active when it should be. Licenses of the same type can generally be combined in order to use all of their total units. For example, in the situation above, a new 50-unit OSF-BASE license could be combined with an existing 100-unit license in order to provide the 150 units needed for a three-CPU AlphaServer ES45. The same is true of user licenses: a 12-user license might actually be issued as an 8-user and a 4-user license, which would combine to provide the necessary 1,200 units of OSF-USR. Multiple licenses of the same type are easily detected by piping "lmf list" to the grep command, as shown previously in this section.

Problems can arise because the implicit four-user license is intended for situations in which it's the only user license needed, so it may not combine with other OSF-USR licenses. As a result, if the implicit user license accidentally becomes activated, it may override the other user licenses in the database. This can be quite disconcerting when the system contains an unlimited user license, but allows only four simultaneous logins! If fewer logins are allowed than expected, use the following command to examine all of the OSF-USR licenses on the system:

```
# lmf list full for OSF-USR | more
```

If multiple licenses are present, check their Authorization Number fields. If one contains "UNIX-SERVER-IMPLICIT-USER," it's the implicit license. Try deleting this license (it can always be recreated if necessary) with the following commands:

```
# lmf delete OSF-USR DEC UNIX-SERVER-IMPLICIT-USER
# lmf reset
```

This should remove the license conflict and resolve the problem.

The opposite problem exists when the implicit license is the only user license on the system, but it's not active. In this case, use "lmf list" to determine whether the license is present (enabled), but has not been activated. If so, the "lmf reset" command should cure the problem. However, if the license isn't present, it can be recreated and activated with the following commands:

```
# /sbin/it.d/bin/load_usr_pak
# lmf reset
```

The load_usr_pak script creates a new implicit user license. Prior to Tru64 UNIX version 4.0, the equivalent script was /sbin/it.d/bin/twouser. As the script name implies, the implicit license allowed only two logins in early versions of Tru64 UNIX.

One other license problem worth mentioning can occur while registering a new license. License information is frequently provided in the form of a product authorization key (PAK). The information on the PAK must be manually entered with the "lmf register" command. If the error message "Checksum does not validate" occurs, make sure that you entered all the information on the PAK exactly as it appears; the information is case sensitive. If this does not resolve the problem, contact the license provider.

Before you call support

Before calling technical support for a license problem, check the following:

- Use "lmf list" to check the status of the problematic licenses.
- Try the "lmf reset" command.
- Verify that the license database (/var/adm/lmf/ldb) is accessible. If it's missing, restore it from a recent backup.
- For OSF-BASE license problems, verify that you have at least the required number of OSF-BASE units for your system configuration.
- For OSF-USR license problems, check the implicit user license. If the implicit user license is active when it shouldn't be, delete it. If the implicit user license should be active but isn't, recreate it.

11.2 Printing

There are a number of ways that printing can be implemented on a Tru64 UNIX system. These include the following:

- Traditional (BSD-style) UNIX printing
- Advanced printing software (APS)
- System V printing

Of these three methods, we'll discuss only the first, BSD-style printing. APS is a separately licensed layered product, while System V printing is used only with the System V extensions available in Tru64 UNIX versions 4 and earlier.

In Tru64 UNIX, printers can be categorized by their connection type as follows:

- Local printers are connected directly to a system's parallel or serial port.
- Remote printers are directly connected (i.e., local) to another host on the network.
- Network printers are connected directly to the network with their own network interface cards.

The appropriate troubleshooting techniques for a printing problem vary based on the printer's connection type. We'll cover each type in its own subsection; first, however, we'll discuss some general principles for troubleshooting printing problems regardless of the connection type. We'll also put in a recommendation for some further reading. The Tru64 UNIX System Administration Manual contains some excellent information in its chapter on administering print services.

11.2.1 General Printer Troubleshooting

The initial step in troubleshooting a printing problem is isolating the problem to the area in which it is occurring. There are three possible areas to consider:

1. The printer itself
2. The UNIX printing subsystem
3. The connection between the printer and the UNIX system

The first thing to check is whether the printer itself is operational. If you have physical access to the printer, check its indicator lights to determine whether the printer is powered on, is on-line, and contains paper of the proper size. If so, try the printer's self-test function. If no test page appears, something is wrong with the printer, and you should consult its operating manual or built-in diagnostics.

Assuming the printer self-test works, the next step is to try sending something to the printer from a different host or by an alternative method. For locally connected printers, the best way to do this is to send a short ASCII file directly to the interface port, bypassing the UNIX printing subsystem. For example, to send a file to a printer connected to the parallel interface port:

```
# cat /etc/motd > /dev/lp0
```

For PostScript™ printers, you may need to pipe the file through a print filter on the way to the printer. To send a file to a PostScript printer connected to the first serial port:

```
# cat /etc/motd | /usr/lbin/ln03rof > /dev/tty00
```

If the file prints, it verifies that both the printer and the printer-host connection are working. The problem is isolated to the UNIX printing subsystem.

For remote or network printers, try printing something from a different host on the network. If this is successful, it verifies that the printer is operational; however, if it doesn't work, the problem could be with either the printer or the connection to it (i.e., the network). If the printer is remote and you have sufficiently privileged access to its host system, you can also troubleshoot it as a local printer from that host.

Once you've verified that the printer can print a test page, start looking at the UNIX printing subsystem. Begin by checking the printer log files for errors or other informative messages. The primary printer log file is /var/adm/syslog.dated/current/lpr.log, which logs messages from the printer daemon, lpd(8). In addition, an error log file for an individual printer may optionally be specified in the printer configuration file, /etc/printcap. For example, in the following sample printcap entry for printer "lp0," the error log file is specified by the "lf" field—in this case, /var/adm/lp0err.

```
lp0|unix.ln17a.ascii|0|lp|lp0|lpr0:\
:lf=/var/adm/lp0err:\
:lp=@unln17a/tcpprt:\
:if=/usr/lbin/ln03rof:\
:of=/usr/lbin/ln03rof:\
:ct=tcp:\
:mc#20:\
:mx#0:\
:pl#66:\
:pw#80:\
:sd=/var/spool/lpd0:
```

Please note that the foregoing example shows only a small subset of the many possible fields in /etc/printcap. See the printcap(4) reference page for information on all of the available options.

If the printer log files don't yield any clues, make sure the printer daemon is running. Use the following command to check for lpd processes on the system:

```
# ps aux | grep lpd | grep -v grep
```

One or more lines of output indicate that the daemon is running. Multiple lines are not a problem; lpd forks a copy of itself for each print job, so there will be one additional lpd process for every print job "stuck" in a print queue. However, if the above command doesn't indicate any running lpd processes, the daemon needs to be restarted. This can be done with either of the following commands:

```
# /usr/lbin/lpd [-l]
# /sbin/init.d/lpd start
```

Even if lpd is already running, it may be worthwhile to restart it in case the daemon or one of its child processes is hung. To restart lpd:

```
# /sbin/init.d/lpd stop
# /sbin/init.d/lpd start
```

Troubleshooting Tip

Starting the printer daemon (/usr/lbin/lpd) with the -l switch causes it to log all printer requests over the network. This can be useful when troubleshooting problems with remote printers.

If lpd is running, use the lpc utility to check the status of a particular printer and its print queue:

```
# lpc status lp0
lp0:
        printer is on device '/dev/tty00' speed 9600
```

```
queuing is enabled
printing is enabled
no entries
no daemon present
```

Both queuing and printing should have a status of "enabled." If not, you can enable them with the lpc "enable" and "start" options, respectively. There are numerous other useful options for controlling printers; see the lpc(8) reference page for more information.

Troubleshooting Tip

When using lpc, keep in mind that remote printers have queues on both the local and remote hosts, but lpc affects only the local queues. To manage the remote queue (i.e., the local queue on the system that actually hosts the printer), you'll need access to the remote system.

Problems can also arise if the printer spool directories or log files are missing or don't have the proper ownership or permissions. The lpd daemon runs as user "daemon," so the spool directories and log files must be writable by that user. The spool directories, which are generally located under /var/spool, should have owner "daemon," group "daemon," and permission bits equal to 775. For example:

```
# ls -ld /var/spool/lpd0
drwxr-xr-x    2 daemon    daemon       8192 Aug 21 13:29
 /var/spool/lpd0
```

The printer log files must also be writable by user "daemon." For example:

```
# ls -l /var/adm/lp0err
-rw-r–r–    1 daemon    daemon          0 Aug 21 13:27
 /var/adm/lp0err
```

Another thing to be aware of is that /var/spool/lpd is a Context-Dependent Symbolic Link (CDSL) in Tru64 UNIX version 5. If the CDSL is replaced with a regular directory, it will cause problems in a TruCluster configuration. (It's harmless on a standalone system.)

One final issue in the printing subsystem affects only local printers connected to the parallel interface port, /dev/lp0. The presence of the "rw" field in a printcap entry indicates that the printer is a read/write device. However, /dev/lp0 is a write-only device, so it's not possible for lpd to open the device in read/write mode. Because lpd fails to open the device, it can't send any output to the printer. This problem was more frequent with old versions of Tru64 UNIX (prior to V4.0), when the printer setup utility didn't always set up parallel printers correctly. If it should occur on your system, simply edit /etc/printcap and remove the "rw" field from the printer entry.

If the UNIX printing subsystem looks good and the printer is working, the problem must be in the connection between the UNIX system and the printer. The troubleshooting methods for each connection type have significant differences, so we'll discuss each of them separately.

11.2.2 Local Printers

A local printer is connected to a parallel or serial interface port on the local system. The parallel port is always /dev/lp0. Alpha systems generally have one or two serial ports; the first is /dev/tty00 and the second is /dev/tty01. If additional serial ports are available (e.g., from a multiplexer device), their device names will also start with "/dev/tty."

To test a parallel interface connection, try to "cat" a small ASCII file to the printer port, as shown in section 11.2.1. If the file prints correctly, the connection is fine; any remaining problems are part of the UNIX printing subsystem. If the file doesn't print—and you've verified the printer operation with a self-test—then it's time to start troubleshooting the connection.

The first thing to check is that the printer configuration on the UNIX system matches the actual printer configuration. For example, if the printer has multiple connection methods, is it set to accept print jobs from the correct port? For serial printers, is the baud rate correct? If the baud rates on each end don't match, the printer will print garbage or nothing, but activity lights on the printer may flash while the job is being received.

The next thing to check is the cable between the printer and the Tru64 UNIX host. If a spare cable is available, try swapping it for the existing cable. If things start working, you've isolated the problem to a bad cable. Cable length can also be an issue, particularly for serial interfaces at high baud rates. It may be worthwhile to try a lower baud rate or a shorter cable.

In addition, verify that the cable is a "null modem" cable. Finally, if the host system has more than one serial port, verify that the printer cable is connected to the right port. (This may seem obvious, but it's often a source of confusion.)

One further technique may be helpful in troubleshooting serial printer connections. If a serial terminal, such as a DEC VT220, is available, try hooking it up in place of the printer. Make sure the baud rate is correct, and then try sending a file to the printer with cat(1). If the correct output appears on the terminal, the connection isn't the problem.

11.2.3 Remote Printers

A remote printer is attached directly to another system on the network. Print jobs are first sent to the remote host, which receives the job and spools it for transmission across its local interface to the printer. Remote printers are indicated by the presence of the "rm" and "rp" fields in a printcap entry. The "rm" field defines the remote host name, while "rp" defines the remote printer name—that is, the local printer name on the remote host. For example, in the following printcap entry, the printer known locally as "lp1" is a remote printer hosted by system "labserv," which is a valid host name in the local network address space. The printer is known as "lp3" on its host, labserv.

```
lp1|1|labprinter:\
        :lf=/var/adm/lp1err:\
        :lp=:\
        :rm=labserv:\
        :rp=lp3:\
        :sd=/var/spool/lpd1:
```

When troubleshooting remote printers, try to verify that the printer is operating normally as a local printer on the remote host. If it isn't, the problem needs to be worked at the remote host. If the printer works locally, but not from your host, try isolating the problem by attempting to print from a third system. If this succeeds, the problem is isolated to your local system; if not, the problem is most likely on the remote host.

The next step is to verify basic network connectivity between the local and remote hosts. Can you ping the remote system successfully? If not, there's a network problem between the two hosts. See Chapter 7 for information on troubleshooting network problems.

If the ping succeeds, try connecting via telnet to port 515 on the remote system. Port 515 is used by lpd (or the equivalent on other operating systems) to listen for remote print requests. There are three possible outcomes to the telnet attempt: it succeeds, it hangs, or it fails with a "connection refused" message. A successful telnet attempt will look similar to the following:

```
# telnet labserv 515
Trying 10.1.0.17...
Connected to 10.1.0.17.
Escape character is '^]'.
```

This verifies that the remote printer daemon is listening for connections. Enter "Control-]" to terminate the connection. In this case, the most likely cause of the problem is a difference in configuration between the local and remote hosts. For example, the remote printer name defined in /etc/printcap might not match the local printer name on the remote host.

If the telnet attempt hangs, a network problem exists and further troubleshooting should focus on the network. On the other hand, if the connection is refused, it means that the printer daemon isn't listening on port 515. On the remote system, check the port using the commands shown below. (This assumes that the remote system is a UNIX system; if it's not, use the equivalent command for its operating system).

```
# netstat -Aa | grep printer
1ddaf00 tcp        0      0  *.printer       *.*
LISTEN
```

If this doesn't generate any output, check for port 515 as follows:

```
# netstat -Aan | grep 515
1ddaf00 tcp        0      0  *.515           *.*
LISTEN
```

If there is no output from either netstat command, nothing is listening on port 515; verify that the printer daemon is running on the remote system. If you get output from "515" but not from "printer," something other than the daemon is listening on port 515. This could be something like a spooler application, which is not a problem; however, it could also indicate that some other program has inappropriately grabbed port 515, preventing the printer daemon from listening for incoming print requests.

11.2.4 Network Printers

Network printers contain a network interface card that allows them to connect directly to the local network. Print jobs are sent directly from host systems to the printer without requiring an intervening host. Network printers are characterized by an "lp" field in /etc/printcap of the form @nodename/servicename. In this field, nodename is the printer's network host name or IP address, while servicename is the name of a network service defining the printer's TCP port in the /etc/services file. The port number is specific to the type of printer; for example, most HP printers use port 9100, whereas DEC printers frequently use port 2501 or 10001.

The example /etc/printcap entry earlier in this chapter is for a network printer. That entry contains the following line:

```
:lp=@unln17a/tcpprt:\
```

This indicates that the printer host name is unln17a, which is defined in the local network's DNS database. The service name "tcpprt" is defined in the local /etc/services file:

```
tcpprt      2501/tcp
```

The name "tcpprt" is a locally chosen mnemonic; it could be any arbitrary name not used elsewhere in /etc/services. The service is defined as a TCP service on port 2501, which is used by DEC LN17 printers.

Network connectivity is obviously critical to the successful operation of a network printer, so the first step is to verify connectivity. Try to ping the printer; if it doesn't respond, make sure the printer is operational. If the printer is working, try pinging or printing from another system to see if that works.

If you can ping the printer, try connecting to it with telnet. Some devices, such as an HP JetDirect card, enter a configuration session if you connect to them on the default telnet port (23). For example:

```
# telnet hpjet
Trying 10.12.40.167
Connected to hpjet.
Escape character is '^]'.

Please type [Return] two times, to initialize telnet
configuration
For HELP type "?"
>
```

You can also try telnetting to the printer's listener port. For example:

```
# telnet hpjet 9100
Trying 10.12.40.167
Connected to hpjet.
Escape character is '^]'.
```

Before you call support

Before calling technical support for a printing problem, check the following:

- Check the lpr.log file and the printer's individual error log (e.g., /var/adm/lp0err).
- Make sure that the printer is turned on, is on-line, and has the right size paper available.
- Try to print a test page using the printer's self-test capability.
- Verify that the printer daemon (lpd) is running.
- Use "lpc status" to verify that printing and queuing are enabled for the printer.
- For local printers, copy a small file directly to the parallel or serial port.
- For remote or network printers, check for network connectivity issues. Also try printing from a different host on the network.

If the printer accepts ASCII input (as opposed to PostScript only), anything you type at this point should be printed. This is a great way to verify that the printer is—or isn't—accepting connections and working properly. If it is, but you're still unable to print from Tru64 UNIX, make sure that you've got the correct listener port defined in /etc/services and the correct service name in /etc/printcap.

11.3 The cron Facility

The system clock daemon, cron(8), is used to execute recurring jobs at regularly scheduled times. Users can run the crontab(1) utility to create crontab files, which contain lists of commands to be run and the days and times at which to run them. For nonrecurring jobs, a couple of close relatives to cron—the at(1) and batch(1) commands—can be used to schedule a job for one-time execution by cron.

There isn't a whole lot that can go wrong with cron and its associated commands. However, there are a few problems that crop up occasionally. These can be divided into the following categories:

- Scheduled jobs don't run at all.
- Scheduled jobs run at the wrong time or more often than necessary, or other odd scheduling behavior is observed.
- A job works properly when executed from the command line, but not from cron.
- Users can't schedule new jobs.

11.3.1 Jobs Not Running

If no cron jobs are being executed, it usually means that the cron daemon is not running. Check for a cron process on your system:

```
# ps -ef | grep cron | grep -v grep
root       915    1  0.0   Aug 12 ??       0:00.22
 /usr/sbin/cron
```

There should be one (and only one) cron process running on the system. If cron isn't running, restart it with the following command:

```
# /sbin/init.d/cron start
```

11.3.2 Jobs Running at the Wrong Time

If there are multiple cron daemons running on the same system, jobs can run multiple times or exhibit other strange behavior. In recent versions of Tru64 UNIX, cron is smart enough to check for the existence of a running cron daemon and not start a second copy. However, this was not the case in older versions. Occasionally, the root user would attempt to edit the root crontab file and accidentally type "cron" instead of "crontab," causing a second daemon to start. If you encounter this situation, the best remedy is to kill all of the current cron processes and start a fresh one. The easiest way to do this is with the following command:

```
# /sbin/init.d/cron restart
```

On some versions of Tru64 UNIX, cron jobs can run at the wrong times, or as the wrong user, if either of the following conditions are true:

1. An empty crontab file exists.
2. A crontab file exists for a user whose account has been removed.

To check for these possibilities, enter the following command:

```
# ls -l /var/spool/cron/crontabs
```

If any files have a length of zero, remove them. Also, check the file names against your user database (/etc/passwd and/or the NIS password file). If any crontab files have names that aren't in the user database, remove them.

Another problematic situation can occur in TruCluster version 5 configurations. In Tru64 UNIX version 5, /var/spool/cron and /var/adm/cron are CDSLs. If either of them is changed to a regular directory, strange behavior can result. If this happens, recreate the CDSL with the mkcdsl(8) command.

Depending on the operating system version, cron jobs could run at the wrong times on the day that daylight saving time begins or ends. This was only a problem in older versions of Tru64 UNIX. In version 4.0F and higher (and in older versions with recent patch kits), cron handles the time change correctly.

11.3.3 Job Works from Command Line but Not from Cron

If a cron job fails to execute correctly, but the same job works perfectly when executed from the command line, the cause is invariably a shell environment problem. The cron daemon executes jobs using the Bourne shell and a minimal set of environment variables: HOME, LOGNAME, PATH, and SHELL. If a job requires a different shell or additional environment variables, they must be explicitly specified within the job. As such, it's a good idea to create a shell script that defines all the necessary environment variables before performing the desired commands. This shell script can then be specified in the crontab file as the command to be run.

11.3.4 Users Unable To Create Jobs

If nonroot users are unable to schedule jobs, the problem lies in one of two areas. Either there is a permission problem or the user isn't authorized to schedule jobs. The first problem arises when /usr/bin/crontab or /usr/bin/at has the wrong ownership or permissions. Both files must be setuid root—that is, owned by root, executable by others, and with the setuid bit set. The correct ownership and permissions are illustrated by the following:

```
# ls -l /usr/bin/crontab /usr/bin/at
-rwsr-xr-x    1 root     bin          57840 May 29 04:47
 /usr/bin/at
-rwsr-xr-x    1 root     bin          41472 May 29 04:48
 /usr/bin/crontab
```

If the setuid bit is missing from either file (i.e., the fourth character in the output is not "s"), you can recreate it with a command such as the following:

```
# chmod 4755 /usr/bin/crontab
```

The second problem arises from the ability to restrict the use of cron to specific users. This ability is controlled by two pairs of files in /var/adm/cron. Access to cron (i.e., the ability to run the crontab command) is controlled by the files “cron.allow” and “cron.deny.” Similarly, access to the “at” command is controlled by the files “at.allow” and “at.deny.”

If the “cron.allow” file exists, cron access is restricted to those users listed in the file. If “cron.allow” doesn’t exist, then all users except those listed in “cron.deny” (if it exists) are allowed to use cron. If neither file exists, only the root user can schedule a cron job. Normally, “cron.allow” is absent and “cron.deny” is an empty file, meaning that all users have access to cron. Use of the “at” command is controlled in similar fashion by the “at.allow” and “at.deny” files.

If you intend to restrict access to cron, these files may be doing exactly what you want. However, if a user is unable to schedule a job and it isn’t your intention to restrict that user, check for one or more of the following situations:

- The “cron.allow” file exists and the user is not listed in it.
- The “cron.deny” file exists and the user is listed in it.
- The “cron.deny” file doesn’t exist.

Before you call support

Before calling technical support for a cron problem, check the following:

- Ensure that one (and only one) copy of the cron daemon is running.
- Try restarting cron with `/sbin/init.d/cron restart`.
- Verify that the executable files /usr/bin/crontab and /usr/bin/at are setuid root.
- Check the /var/spool/cron/crontabs directory for empty files or files belonging to a user whose account has been removed.
- Check the “cron.allow,” “cron.deny,” “at.allow,” and “at.deny” files as described above.

12

Display Problems

Experience is that marvelous thing that enables you to recognize a mistake when you make it again.

—Franklin P. Jones

In this final chapter, we discuss problems that arise with graphical displays connected to Tru64 UNIX systems. These problems fall into three general classes:

1. No display
2. Incorrect display appearance
3. Problems with the Common Desktop Environment (CDE)

Each of these problem types is discussed in the following sections. Before beginning, however, there are a few general troubleshooting techniques worth mentioning. These techniques apply to all types of display problems.

12.1 General Troubleshooting Techniques

There are three generic issues that can lead to display problems:

1. Obsolete system firmware
2. Incorrect EISA or ISA configuration
3. Incorrect Open3D version

These can cause a wide variety of problems, so it's a good idea to check for them early in the process of troubleshooting any display problem.

12.1.1 Obsolete System Firmware

Out-of-date system (console) firmware can cause a graphics display to operate incorrectly or not at all. To check the system firmware version, enter the following command at the console prompt:

```
>>> SHOW VERSION
V6.1-1011 Oct 11 2001 13:39:58
```

If your system is already booted, you can still determine the console firmware version without having to shut down the system. The following command will retrieve the firmware version on some—but not all—Alpha systems:

```
# consvar -g version
version = V6.1-1011 Oct 11 2001 13:39:58
```

If the "consvar" command doesn't work on your system, it's possible to find the firmware version in the most recent boot record in the system message file:

```
# grep "vmunix: Firmware" /var/adm/messages | tail -1
Jun 28 03:18:09 hostname vmunix: Firmware revision:
6.1-1011
```

Ensure that the firmware version is compatible with the version of Tru64 UNIX that you're running. If it isn't, upgrade to a compatible version. If you do upgrade the firmware, be sure to run the EISA Configuration Utility (ECU) afterwards.

12.1.2 Incorrect EISA or ISA Configuration

A number of Alpha systems communicate with their graphics adapters via an EISA bus, and a few of the older AlphaStation models use an ISA bus for this purpose. If the EISA or ISA configuration information becomes corrupted, display problems (among others) may occur. In addition, updating the console firmware will clear the EISA/ISA configuration data. Restoring the EISA/ISA configuration may resolve a display problem immediately. Because this is a quick and easy process, it's worth a try in most situations.

If your system contains an ISA bus, you can initialize the ISA configuration by entering the following command at the console prompt:

```
>>> isacfg -init
```

This restores the ISA configuration to a known baseline. Depending on the graphics adapter and operating system version, additional "isacfg" commands may be necessary to configure the adapter for proper operation; check the graphics adapter documentation for details. Also, the necessary console command may be "iconfig" rather than "isacfg" on some systems.

To restore the EISA configuration, run the ECU, which is provided on a floppy diskette with the Tru64 UNIX distribution. Older versions of the ECU came in two versions—one for Tru64 UNIX and OpenVMS systems, the other for Windows NT systems. Be sure to use only the former version, which is labeled "UNIX/VMS" on the diskette. For EISA graphics cards, the ECU automatically configures the correct EISA configuration options. For ISA cards attached to an EISA bus, additional ECU operations may be necessary; check the documentation for your graphics adapter. When finished, choose the "Save and Exit" option. After the ECU exits, reset the system.

12.1.3 Incorrect Open3D Version

In Tru64 UNIX version 4 and earlier, some graphics adapters required the Open3D layered product to operate correctly. (Version 5 systems do not require Open3D.) If the Open3D version isn't compatible with the operating system version, graphics displays may behave strangely or fail to work at all. Check the documentation for your version of Open3D to make sure it supports your version of Tru64 UNIX. If not, switch to an appropriate version of Open3D.

12.2 No Display

If a graphics display fails to work at all, there are a number of possible problems in addition to the general possibilities in the previous section. The following questions will help to verify basic operation and connectivity:

- Is the cable from the graphics adapter to the monitor hooked up correctly? If not, most modern monitors will display a message such as "No Video" or "No Signal."
- Does the graphics card require any jumpers to be set? Check the documentation and verify the jumper settings, if any.
- Does the display work in console mode (i.e., with the system halted)? If so, the hardware is working and there is connectivity for the video signal.

If basic connectivity is verified, the problem may be that the X server isn't running. To check this, log into the system via telnet and determine whether a display manager process (either "dtlogin" or "xdm") is running. This can be accomplished with the following command:

```
# ps -ax | egrep 'dtlogin|xdm' | grep -v grep
```

If the X server is running, the above command should return one line of ps(1) output showing the display manager process. If no output is produced, the X server isn't running. In this case, it's worth a quick try to restart the X server:

```
# /sbin/init.d/xlogin start
```

If the X server isn't running, it's possible that console variable "CONSOLE" is set to "SERIAL" rather than "GRAPHICS." The former setting specifies that the system is using a serial terminal as the system console; in this situation, Tru64 UNIX will not start the X server. To check the setting of this variable with the system halted, enter the "SHOW CONSOLE" command at the console prompt:

```
>>> SHOW CONSOLE
SERIAL
```

On some Alpha platforms, you can use the consvar(8) command to retrieve the console setting while Tru64 UNIX is running:

```
# consvar -g console
console = serial
```

On other platforms, you may need to halt the system to check the variable setting. If the console variable setting is correct, verify that Tru64 UNIX recognizes the presence of a graphics display. To check this, enter the command `sizer -wu`. If this returns a value of zero, Tru64 UNIX does not detect any graphics displays on the system.

Another way to determine whether Tru64 UNIX detects a graphics adapter is with the "sizer -gt" command. If this command doesn't return any output, the operating system doesn't detect a graphics device. On the other hand, if the output is the word "GENERIC," Tru64 UNIX is operating in generic console mode. Generic console mode is a fallback used to operate a graphics display as a console terminal even if no graphics adapter or hardware is detected. (This mode is used only for console terminal support; X windows will not run in generic console mode.)

If the system is in generic console mode, there should be messages on the console and in /var/adm/messages that will help determine the source of the problem. Typical error messages include the following:

```
No graphics console driver configured
Generic console support installed: using firmware callbacks
Generic console support installed: using VGA
```

The presence of any of these messages usually indicates one or more of the following problems:

- The graphics driver for the adapter isn't configured in the kernel. (This is often an Open3D version problem.)
- The graphics device has a hardware problem or incorrect jumper setting.
- The EISA or ISA configuration is corrupt.

If Tru64 UNIX detects a graphics adapter and the graphics console is selected, the X server should at least be trying to start. Try starting the X server manually with the command "/sbin/init.d/xlogin start". If this works, the next step is to determine whether the X server is starting at boot time and then crashing, or failing to start at all. The X server is one of the last things to start as Tru64 UNIX boots to run level 3. The symbolic link /sbin/rc3.d/S95xlogin, which points to /sbin/init.d/xlogin (the actual startup script file), must be present for the X server to start automatically. If this symbolic link is missing (i.e., it was removed or renamed such that its name no longer starts with the letter S), the startup script will not run and the X server will not start.

To verify that the script is running at startup (and if so, to determine whether the X server is starting), edit the startup script file (/sbin/init.d/xlogin) and add " -x" to the end of the first line (i.e., change the line from "#!/sbin/sh" to "#!/sbin/sh -x"). The -x switch causes the shell to echo each line of the script to the console as it executes. Reboot the system and watch the console messages during the boot process. When the commands in the xlogin script are echoed to the screen, you can observe whether the X server starts successfully.

If the X server doesn't start successfully, examine its log file for errors or other messages. The location of the log file is dependent on the particular X display manager that your system is running. For CDE (the default for Tru64 UNIX), the log file is /var/dt/Xerrors. If you're running the older X display manager (xdm), the log file is /var/X11/xdm/xdm-errors. The messages in this log file should help identify the problem.

A common cause of X server startup problems is an error in one of the X server configuration files. These include the general configuration file ("/var/X11/Xserver.conf") and a specific file dependent on which display manager you're running: "/var/dt/Xservers" for CDE or "/var/X11/xdm/Xservers" for xdm. If you have made any changes to the X server configuration, try backing out the changes by reverting to the previous version of the modified configuration file.

Another problem that can prevent the X server from starting is not having the appropriate display fonts installed. In this case, the Xerrors log file will contain messages indicating that a font was not found. There are two different display font subsets to be concerned with. If both subsets are installed (as in the following example from a V5.1 system), there is nothing to worry about:

```
# setld -i | grep dpi
OSFFONT15510     installed  DECwindows 100dpi Fonts
 (Windowing Environment)
OSFFONT510       installed  DECwindows 75dpi Fonts
 (Windowing Environment)
```

However, if only one font subset is installed, it may be the wrong one. Graphics devices with a resolution of at least 1280 x 1024 use the 100dpi fonts, whereas the 75 dpi fonts are used for resolutions of 1024 x 768 and lower. If you have a graphics device whose default resolution is 1024 x 768, it's possible that only the 75 dpi font subset is installed. If you upgrade to a graphics adapter with a resolution of 1280 x 1024 but the 100 dpi fonts weren't installed, the X server will not be able to start. This problem is quickly resolved by loading the missing subset from the Tru64 UNIX installation CD-ROM.

Another no-display problem occurs when trying to run a graphical interface application on a remote system (i.e., with an X display on the local system). This requires that X access control be set up to allow connections from the remote system to the local X server. To enable or disable X access, use the "xhost(1X)" command. If X access is not properly configured, attempting to run a program remotely results in a sequence of error messages similar to the following:

```
Xlib: connection to "martin.alf.cpqcorp.net:0.0" refused
by server
Xlib: Client is not authorized to connect to Server
Error: Can't open display: martin.alf.cpqcorp.net:0
```

In this situation, remote X access from hostname "foo" can be enabled with a command such as the following:

```
# xhost +foo
```

See the xhost reference page for more information.

12.3 Incorrect Display Appearance

If a graphics display works (assuming a reasonably tolerant definition of "works"), but the display appearance is incorrect, there are a number of possibilities:

- Incorrect X server configuration
- Incorrect graphics adapter type
- Incorrect jumper settings on the graphics card

"Incorrect appearance" includes problems such as strange or missing colors, incorrect resolution, text overflowing the surrounding boxes, and similar problems.

An incorrect setting in one of the X server configuration files ("/var/X11/Xserver.conf" and either "/var/dt/Xservers" or "/var/X11/xdm/Xservers") can cause a graphics adapter to generate incorrect display output. This is most frequently a problem with the screen resolution or vertical synchronization rate. These parameters can be configured by defining X server switches in the server configuration file. For example, the following line at the end of the configuration file sets screen 0 (the first or only graphics display) to a resolution of 1280 x 1024 and a vertical sync rate of 70 Hz:

```
:0  Local local@console /usr/bin/X11/X -screen0 1280
 -vsync 70
```

If the display appearance is incorrect after making such changes and restarting the Xserver (with "/sbin/init.d/xlogin restart"), the resolution or vertical sync rate might not be a supported option for your graphics adapter or monitor. Check for error messages in the appropriate log file ("/var/dt/errors" for CDE, "/var/X11/xdm/xdm-errors" for xdm). It's also possible that the resolution is controlled by jumper settings on the graphics card, in which case it may not be adjustable by the X server; check the hardware documentation to see if this is the case.

Caution

Not all monitors support all resolutions or vertical synchronization rates; check your monitor documentation before making adjustments. Older monitors can potentially be damaged when attempting higher resolutions or sync rates.

If Tru64 UNIX doesn't recognize a graphics adapter correctly, it may attempt to use the wrong graphics driver or, more likely, default to either generic console mode (described above) or to standard VGA mode. Standard VGA mode supports a resolution of 640 x 480 and a maximum of 16 colors. Since this is quite limited compared to most graphics devices currently in use, most displays won't look too good. If the "sizer -gt" command returns "VGA," Tru64 UNIX is operating in standard VGA mode. In this case, the problem is usually one of the following:

- The graphics driver for the adapter isn't configured in the kernel (check the Open3D version).
- The graphics device has a hardware problem or incorrect jumper setting.
- The EISA or ISA configuration is corrupt.

12.4 CDE Problems

The Common Desktop Environment (CDE) is the default display manager for Tru64 UNIX systems. It's also possible to use the older X Display Manager (xdm) instead of CDE. The choice of display manager is controlled by environment variable XLOGIN in /etc/rc.config. If XLOGIN is set to "xdm", xdm is selected; if it's set to "cde" or blank, CDE is used. In this section, we'll discuss some common problems that can prevent users from logging into and working with CDE.

Login problems are probably the most common type of CDE problem. The login problems discussed in Chapter 4 can arise when logging in from CDE or any other source; in addition, there are a number of CDE-specific issues that can affect logins. When troubleshooting a CDE login problem, the first step should be attempting to log in from another source, such as a telnet connection or serial terminal. If logins fail regardless of the connection method, use the techniques in Chapter 4 to troubleshoot the problem. On the other hand, if logins fail only through CDE, it's pretty clear that the problem is CDE-related.

When a CDE login problem exists, it's important to try logging in from multiple accounts in order to determine whether the problem affects all users (with the possible exception of root) or just one user. If root is the only user who can log in, the problem is frequently a file permission issue; in this case, the allverify utility described earlier in this book will help to locate the problem. If no users (including root) are able to log in, the cause is usually a misconfigured network setup. Typical problems include the local host name not being consistent between /etc/rc.config and /etc/hosts, incorrect information in /etc/svc.conf, and many others. This type of problem is usually, though not always, indicated by the error message "DT messaging system could not be started" during log in. In this situation, see Chapter 7 for information on troubleshooting the network configuration.

If all users, including root, are unable to login, it might be a little tricky to get access to the system in order to troubleshoot the problem. This is particularly true if the problem is a network configuration problem, because network issues could also prevent access via telnet. In such cases, there is a "failsafe" login option at the system console. From the CDE login screen, pull down the Sessions menu and select "Failsafe Session." This will provide a generic terminal window with no additional CDE features or options. Once logged in, you can start troubleshooting the problem. A good first step is to check the following log files:

```
/var/dt/Xerrors
$HOME/.dt/errorlog
$HOME/.dt/startlog
```

A useful troubleshooting technique in this situation is setting the environment variable DTNONETWORK to "true." This can be done by adding the following two lines to /.dtprofile, which is the root user's CDE login script:

```
DTNONETWORK=true
export DTNONETWORK
```

This variable setting tells CDE to use the "localhost" loopback interface for messaging, rather than a real network interface. After editing /.dtprofile, log out of the failsafe window and try a normal CDE login as root. If the login now succeeds, a network configuration problem almost certainly exists. The reverse is not strictly true: If the CDE login continues to fail with DTNONETWORK set to true, it's still possible (though less likely) that the problem is due to a network misconfiguration.

The preceding technique is also useful when only one user is unable to log in. Add the lines shown above to the user's $HOME/.dtprofile file and try another CDE login. If the login succeeds, it usually indicates some type of corruption in the user's local CDE configuration. In this case, try removing or renaming the following files:

- $HOME/.dt (a directory)
- $HOME/.TTauthority
- $HOME/.Xauthority

CDE automatically creates these files if necessary, so removing them is not harmful. If this cures the problem, then corruption in the user's CDE configuration was the cause; recreating the files resolved the problem.

In addition to logins failing, logins that take a long time to complete (e.g., several minutes) or hang indefinitely are possible problems. These tend to have the same causes as logins failing completely; therefore, the troubleshooting techniques described above apply to these problems as well. A related problem with a different cause is "one-shot" CDE login. In this situation, the first CDE login from the system console works fine; however, after the user logs out, the login box doesn't reappear, which makes it rather difficult to log in again. This problem occurs if the X session manager doesn't terminate properly when the user logs out. To resolve this problem, you can force the session manager to terminate when the session ends by adding the -terminate switch to the X server command line at the bottom of the "/var/dt/Xservers" file. The modified line should look like this:

```
:0  Local local@console /usr/bin/X11/X :0 -terminate
```

A less serious login issue occurs when a user logs in with CDE, but the shell startup script ($HOME/.profile for the Bourne and Korn shells, $HOME/.login for the C shell) is not executed. This is actually the default behavior for CDE logins. At session startup, CDE executes the commands in $HOME/.dtprofile. (These commands can use either Bourne or Korn shell syntax.) The last line in .dtprofile is the following:

```
# DTSOURCEPROFILE=true
```

If the DTSOURCEPROFILE environment variable has a true value, CDE executes the appropriate shell startup script (.profile or .login) after executing the other commands in .dtprofile. However, the above line is commented out by default, which means that the variable doesn't get set and the shell startup script is not executed. To change this behavior, simply uncomment the line by removing the initial "#" character. On subsequent logins, the variable will be set and the desired startup script will execute.

The problems described in the preceding text are among the most common that arise when using CDE. This is by no means a comprehensive list of possible CDE problems; CDE has a rich set of features and options, and problems might arise with any of them. However, a detailed treatment of

CDE's capabilities is beyond the scope of this book. For further information, we recommend the three CDE manuals in the Tru64 UNIX documentation set:

- *Common Desktop Environment: User's Guide*
- *Common Desktop Environment: Advanced User's and System Administrator's Guide*
- *Common Desktop Environment: Product Glossary*

Before you call support

Before calling technical support with a display problem, perform the following troubleshooting steps:

- Check for basic connectivity; does the display work in console mode?
- Check the jumper settings (if any) on the graphics card.
- Ensure that the system firmware is up-to-date.
- Rerun the ECU to restore the EISA configuration.
- If you have an older AlphaStation with an ISA bus, redo the ISA configuration.
- If your graphics adapter requires Open3D, verify that you have the correct version installed.
- Log in via another method (e.g., telnet) and verify that the X server is running (see section 12.2).
- Check the system message file and the Xerrors log file for error messages.
- Verify that the system recognizes the graphics adapter correctly ("sizer -gt").

Electronic Resources

Even with the best information we can provide in this book, you may still end up with a tricky Tru64 UNIX problem to solve. In this appendix, we list some additional electronic resources (outside of HP technical support) to help you solve the problem as quickly as possible. Some of these resources will prove to be very valuable, but others may be less so. We provide as comprehensive a list as possible because experience shows that it is impossible to tell in advance where the solution to a problem will come from.

A.1 Mailing Lists

There are a couple of mailing lists that are of direct interest to a Tru64 UNIX system administrator. These mailing lists contain a great deal of useful information and can be an invaluable resource. Be aware, though, that mailing lists can easily overwhelm you with their volume. An active mailing list may generate hundreds of e-mails per day. One useful strategy when subscribing to mailing lists is to use an e-mail client with filtering capabilities to transfer incoming mailing list traffic into another folder for later perusal. In addition, many mailing lists provide the ability to receive digests in which you are periodically sent a summary of list activity. Such digests may be sent daily, weekly, or monthly, depending on the list volume. Some mailing lists are also archived, allowing easy keyword searching through months or years of list activity.

Note: Always regard information from a mailing list with caution, especially if the list is unmoderated. While there will always be expert individuals who happily share their experience and knowledge, there are also less experienced folks who, either through error or malice, provide incorrect information to the list. Never blindly believe a single person's contribution. Always substantiate any piece of information if you are unsure of either its source or validity. Remember as well that even experts can make an error. Mailing lists are frequently valuable sources of useful and pertinent information, but you should tread carefully.

A.1.1 Tru64-UNIX-Managers List

The Tru64-UNIX-Managers list is a quick-turnaround troubleshooting aid for people who administer and manage Alpha systems running Tru64 UNIX. Its primary purpose is to provide a Tru64 UNIX system administrator with a quick source of information for system management problems that are of a time-critical nature. This list allows any subscriber to pose a question to the entire list or contribute a possible answer to another individual's question.

To subscribe to the list, send an e-mail to majordomo@ornl.gov containing the command "subscribe tru64-unix-managers." The Tru64-UNIX-Managers list is archived at

```
http://www.ornl.gov/its/archives/mailing-lists
```

Additionally, the following URL provides the ability to keyword search the entire archive of the Tru64-UNIX-Managers list (and its predecessor, the Alpha-OSF-Managers list):

```
http://www-archive.ornl.gov:8000
```

Here are two more archive search engines:

```
http://www.geocrawler.com/lists/3/Miscellaneous/530/0
http://www.xray.mpe.mpg.de/mailing-lists/tru64-unix-managers
```

A.1.2 Tru64 UNIX Patch list

The Tru64 UNIX Patch list is a nondiscussion list provided by HP that announces the latest patches for the Tru64 UNIX operating system and layered software products. These notices cover both public and entitled patches. Whereas the entitled patches are available only to contract customers, the public patches are readily available via anonymous FTP from

```
http://ftp.support.compaq.com/public/unix
```

You can also visit

```
http://www.support.compaq.com/patches
```

To subscribe to the mailing list and receive individual patch notices, click on the "join mailing list" link found on the above page.

A.2 USENET Newsgroups

There are several USENET newsgroups that may be of interest to a Tru64 UNIX system administrator. These newsgroups tend to have an even higher "noise ratio" than mailing lists, and the recommendation is to be cautious with information presented in a newsgroup.

- comp.unix.tru64—the primary Tru64 UNIX discussion group
- comp.unix.osf.misc—miscellaneous Tru64 UNIX discussions
- comp.unix.admin—general UNIX system administration topics
- comp.admin.policy—general UNIX system administration policy issues
- comp.security.unix—UNIX security
- comp.security.misc—miscellaneous system and network security
- comp.unix.questions—a forum for general UNIX user questions
- comp.unix.wizards—advanced UNIX topics

A.3 Web Resources

The World Wide Web (WWW) has grown tremendously since its inception and is now an invaluable resource for Tru64 UNIX administrators. Some Web pages are extremely broad in content, while others are narrowly focused or address single topics. The pages listed below make a good starting point for a Tru64 UNIX system administrator. Many of these pages provide links to other, associated pages. Over time, you will build a personal set of favorite pages.

Note that on-line resources do change, and these addresses may not apply in the future. Readers can always use a Web search engine to identify the new location if an address is not found.

A.3.1 The Tru64 UNIX Home Page

HP has created a comprehensive Tru64 UNIX Web site with many useful and informative links to other Web pages related to Tru64 UNIX. The main page is located at

```
http://www.tru64unix.compaq.com
```

A.3.2 Tru64 UNIX Technical Documentation

HP has created a Web resource containing the entire documentation set for Tru64 UNIX. This includes online versions of the Release Notes, Installation Guide, System Administration Guide, and many other manuals. This online library is an invaluable reference and may be found at

```
http://www.tru64unix.compaq.com/faqs/publications/pub_page/doc_list
```

A.3.3 HP Services On-line

The HP Services Division provides a variety of on-line services, including access directly to the HP Business Critical Services call-logging systems and problem-diagnosis systems, the Tru64 UNIX patch repositories, and miscellaneous product support information. The address is

```
http://www.compaq.com/support
```

A.3.4 Tru64 UNIX Patch Services

The Patch Services page provides easy access to Tru64 UNIX patch kits, including publicly available and contract-only patches. Users are permitted to search for individual patches either through a search and download utility or via traditional FTP access:

```
http://www.support.compaq.com/patches
```

A.3.5 The Alpha Systems Firmware Update Page

The firmware update page provides online access to current and past versions of the Alpha system firmware images. In addition, this Web page is also the place to check for interim firmware versions released between regular firmware CD-ROM distributions:

```
http://gatekeeper.research.compaq.com/pub/DEC/Alpha/firmware
```

A.3.6 Tru64 UNIX Freely Available Software

You can find free and demo software from the following HP sites:

```
http://tru64unix.compaq.com/demos
ftp://gatekeeper.research.compaq.com/gatekeeper.home.html
```

A.3.7 DECevent Home Page

The DECevent utility, an optional product that can be used in place of the uerf(8) program, is a highly recommended addition to a Tru64 UNIX system. See Chapter 3 for a discussion of this tool. The latest version may be downloaded from

```
http://www.support.compaq.com/svctools/decevent
```

A.3.8 WEBES Home Page

The Web-Based Enterprise Services (WEBES) kit includes some useful diagnostic tools that we discussed in Chapter 3, such as Compaq Analyze and the Compaq Crash Analysis Tool. You can find the latest software kit from HP at the following address:

```
http://www.support.compaq.com/svctools/webes/index.html
```

A.3.9 Compaq Best Practices

This site has recommended methods for how to get the most from your Tru64 UNIX system. These best practices are designed to go beyond the mere factual information found in the documentation. They provide real, practical advice from the experts at HP. As of this printing, there are documents at this site to help a system administrator in areas such as the following:

- Performance
- Networking
- Patches

- Clusters
- Security
- Programming

These documents can be found at

```
http://www.tru64unix.compaq.com/faqs/publications/best_practices
```

We recommend that you check this page often, because this is a "living" Web page: HP engineers are constantly updating and adding new best practices to this site.

A.3.10 Tru64.org

This site is an excellent resource for the Tru64 administrator. The site includes such useful items as mailing lists, forums, articles, and FAQs. The site provides a link to a searchable database of the mailing lists and forums so you can find a problem that someone has seen before, along with the summary of answers, if provided. This site, at

```
http://www.tru64.org
```

is run by Tru64 UNIX gurus and aficionados and is not affiliated with HP.

A.3.11 Authorized Training Vendors

Bruden Corporation and the Institute for Software Advancement are two HP-authorized training vendors that provide training, ranging from basic user level up to Tru64 UNIX system internals. See the following Web sites for more information about these vendors:

```
http://bruden.com
http://www.softadv.com
```

A.3.12 User Group

The Encompass HP User Group (formerly DECUS, U.S. Chapter) Web site contains lots of useful links; go to

```
http://www.encompassus.org
```

A.3.13 Test drive

At the following Web site, you can test drive or try out Tru64 UNIX (and other operating systems for that matter):

```
http://www.testdrive.compaq.com/os
```

B

Recommended Reading

Many of the topics discussed in this book are so broad that they require more space to cover them adequately than we could provide in this book. Happily, there already exist a number of excellent books on both Tru64 UNIX and generic UNIX topics. The reader is encouraged to refer to the following titles for further discussion of these topics.

B.1 UNIX System Administration

Cheek, Matthew; Scott Fafrak; Steven Hancock; Martin Moore; and Gregory Yates. *Tru64 UNIX System Administrator's Guide*. Digital Press, 2001.

Nemeth, Evi; Garth Snyder; Scott Seebass; and Trent R. Hein. *UNIX System Administration Handbook*. 3rd ed. Prentice Hall, 2000.

B.2 File Systems and Storage

Hancock, Steven M. *Tru64 UNIX File System Administration Handbook*. Digital Press, 2000.

B.3 Backup and Recovery

Preston, W. Curtis; and Gigi Estabrook. *UNIX Backup and Recovery.* O'Reilly & Associates, 1999.

B.4 TruCluster

Donar, Tim. *Tru64 UNIX–Oracle9i Cluster Quick Reference*. Digital Press, 2002.

Fafrak, Scott; Jim Lola; Brad Nichols; Dennis O'Brien; and Greg Yates. *TruCluster Server Handbook*. Digital Press, 2002.

B.5 Networking

Albitz, Paul; and Cricket Liu. *DNS and BIND*. 4th ed. O'Reilly & Associates, 2001.

Hunt, Craig. *TCP/IP Network Administration*. 3rd ed. O'Reilly & Associates, 2002.

Stern, Hal; Mike Eisler; and Ricardo Labiaga. *Managing NFS and NIS.* 2nd ed. O'Reilly & Associates, 2001.

Tanenbaum, Andrew S. *Computer Networks.* 3rd ed. Prentice Hall, 1996

B.6 Sendmail

Costales, Bryan; and Eric Allman. *Sendmail.* 2nd ed. O'Reilly & Associates, 1997.

Vixie, Paul A.; and Frederick M. Avolio. *Sendmail: Theory and Practice.* 2nd ed. Digital Press, 2001.

B.7 UNIX Internals

McKusick, Marshall Kirk; Keith Bostic; and Michael J. Karels. *The Design and Implementation of the 4.4BSD Operating System*. Addison-Wesley, 1996.

B.8 Security

Garfinkel, Simson; and Gene Spafford. *Practical UNIX and Internet Security.* 2nd ed. O'Reilly & Associates, 1996.

B.9 X Windows

Mui, Linda; and Eric Pearce. *X Window System Administrator's Guide.* O'Reilly & Associates, 1992.

Index

E

F

M